POSTCARDS FROM THE BAJA CALIFORNIA BORDER

POSTCARDS

>— FROM THE —<

BAJA CALIFORNIA BORDER

PORTRAYING TOWNSCAPE AND PLACE
1900s-1950s

DANIEL D. ARREOLA

THE UNIVERSITY OF
ARIZONA PRESS

TUCSON

The University of Arizona Press
www.uapress.arizona.edu

ISBN-13: 978-0-8165-4255-0 (hardcover)

Cover design by Leigh McDonald
Cover art: Old Town, Tijuana, Calle 1 and Avenida Revolución. A white border print postcard published for E. Silvestre of Tijuana by M. Kashower of Los Angeles. M. Kashower, no. 23377, 1920s
Typeset by Sara Thaxton in 10.25/15 Warnock Pro (text) and Golden WF, Bebas Neue, and Helvetica Neue LT Std

Publication of this book is made possible in part by financial support from the School of Geographical Sciences and Urban Planning at Arizona State University, and by the proceeds of a permanent endowment created with the assistance of a Challenge Grant from the National Endowment for the Humanities, a federal agency.

Library of Congress Cataloging-in-Publication Data
Names: Arreola, Daniel D. (Daniel David), 1950– author.
Title: Postcards from the Baja California border : portraying townscape and place, 1900s–1950s / Daniel D. Arreola.
Description: Tucson : University of Arizona Press, 2021. | Includes bibliographical references and index.
Identifiers: LCCN 2021012041 | ISBN 9780816542550 (hardcover)
Subjects: LCSH: Cities and towns—Mexico—Baja California (State)—History—20th century—Pictorial works. | Postcards—Mexico—Baja California (State)—History—20th century—Pictorial works. | Baja California (Mexico : State)—History—20th century—Pictorial works. | Tijuana (Baja California, Mexico)—History—20th century—Pictorial works. | Mexicali (Mexico)—History—20th century—Pictorial works. | Tecate (Mexico)—History—20th century—Pictorial works. | Algodones (Baja California, Mexico)—History—20th century—Pictorial works. | LCGFT: Illustrated works.
Classification: LCC F1246.2 .A54 2021 | DDC 972/.23—dc23
LC record available at https://lccn.loc.gov/2021012041

Printed in the United States of America
♾ This paper meets the requirements of ANSI/NISO Z39.48-1992 (Permanence of Paper).

For
Beatrice Díaz
and
Salvador Arreola

CONTENTS

ILLUSTRATIONS

TABLES

FIGURES

PREFACE AND ACKNOWLEDGMENTS

Postcards have a magical pull. Wherever I travel I look for them, and my study closet is full of storage boxes with postcards from explorations to distant and nearby lands. Even though those wanderings are feverishly documented with thousands of slide transparencies and digital images, the lowly postcard still appeals. The postcard is a capsule representation of place that is unique as an artifact of travel.

Postcards have been part of my life for decades, and apparently they also touched the lives of my ancestors. Years after I began to collect postcards, I learned from family members that some of the oldest snapshots taken of them as children were in fact photographic postcards. That format of domestic photography was well suited to families without cameras, and local photographers visited working-class neighborhoods to snap pictures using specialized postcard cameras and then printed those images on postcard stock. A particular treasure handed down to me shows my maternal grandfather, León Díaz, with his friend in a photo postcard. The two are posed in a car in front of a painted backdrop of San Francisco, California, a studio snapshot made during one of grandfather's early labor sojourns north from Jalisco, Mexico, to the Golden State in 1913.

The postcard collecting habit has been a personal avocation cultivated by an early childhood fascination with maps, stamps, coins, and baseball cards. It gained momentum from my geography mentor, Christopher "Kit" Salter, who sent me postcards from his travels, inspiring an appreciation of the format. I continued that sharing by asking my own PhD students and even other colleagues to send me postcards from their travels. For a time I tallied the number of cards from these postcard allies and circulated a short yearly report about cards sent to me. One student, Kevin Blake, was so diligent in this exchange that every year his postcard correspondence would far exceed the number of cards sent by other contributors, including Kenneth Madsen and Yolonda Youngs. To this day Kevin and I share postcards from our world travels, a communication habit that is both satisfying and challenging because one is always trying to find an unusual card to send.

A Mexican proverb is a poignant reminder of one's course, to wit, *del dicho al hecho hay gran trecho* (from saying to doing is a long way). *Postcards from the Baja California Border* completes a project I launched in 2013 to write four separate books about how Mexican border towns have been shown in picture postcards from the 1900s to the 1950s. Many individuals, from family and friends to professional colleagues, have made this journey possible.

Growing up Mexican American in Santa Monica, California, I benefited from a familial network of shared life experiences. It was León Díaz, my maternal *abuelo* (grandfather), who first turned me toward geography as lifelong learning. Grandpa Díaz, an avid walker, would regularly escort me around the town, pointing out landmarks and relating stories about people and place. Exploration was part of his passion, and storytelling was one of his well-honed talents. I look back with gratitude to those formative times that shaped me in ways I would not recognize until later in life. My paternal grandfather, Juan Santana Arreola, like León Díaz, was a Mexican immigrant. Several summers spent with the Arreola grandparents on a ranch near Escondido, California, exposed me to the backcountry of San Diego and later to urban San Diego when these *abuelos* moved to a trailer park on Mission Bay. My first journeys across the Baja California border to Rosarito Beach, south of Tijuana, were made possible courtesy of Juan Arreola, who never relinquished his Mexican citizenship, owned property in the area, and used to regale family and friends at that now-famous seaside locale. Years later I recall visits to Tijuana with my mother, her sister—my *tía* (aunt) Amelia—and her son—my cousin Rudy—where we ventured to make donations of used clothing to churches. Those encounters sometimes enabled an overnight in a local motel and explorations of Tijuana's infamous tourist street, Avenida Revolución.

Four years of undergraduate and later graduate education at California State University, Hayward, and the University of California, Los Angeles, sealed my future to become an academic geographer. Teaching assignments at Southern California institutions led to appointments at Texas A&M University, the University of Arizona, and Arizona State University, where I spent twenty-six years. My professional path was chartered early from mentors who shared the University of California, Berkeley, tradition of cultural and historical geography, a training that proved foundational to my scholarly evolution. Beyond mentors such as Christopher Salter, Henry Bruman, Gary Dunbar, Herb Eder, and Richard Nostrand, two distant guiding lights and their works have inspired my geography: John Brinckerhoff Jackson's persistent lessons about reading landscapes and Donald W. Meinig's inimitable regional historical geography writings.

It has been said that writing is never finished and the trick is to know at what point to leave it unfinished. As the final installment in a four-part series, I come to a stopping point in the border-postcard odyssey. *Postcards from the Baja California Border* emerged from my passion for the past and a desire to tell the story about a region that has occupied my professional experience for some four decades. Nevertheless, while writing may be a solo task, research engages many others who enable the process. Foremost in this particular project have been postcard dealers who tirelessly gather, organize, and make available the stock of historic vintage postcards that are the foundation of my collection and the basis for this study. Many of these individuals have been recognized and thanked in previous installments, but here again, I tip my hat to their efforts. Without them the collecting of these materials would be considerably more difficult. The others who are essential to the research enterprise are librarians, archivists, and curators who manage documents and materials essential to the writer's purpose. For this particular volume, I want especially to thank the following institutions and their staffs: Sanborn Map Collection, California State University, Northridge; Geography and Map Division, Library of Congress, Washington, DC; Special Collections and Archives, University of California, San Diego; Museo Comunitario de Tecate, Tecate, Baja California; Border Collection, San Diego State University, Imperial Valley Campus, Calexico, California; San Diego State University Library, San Diego, California; Interlibrary Loan and Library Express, University of New Mexico, Albuquerque; Special Collections, San Diego Public Library, Main Branch, San Diego, California; San Diego History Center, Research Library, San Diego, California; and Interlibrary Loan, Arizona State University Library, Tempe.

A special thanks is accorded to the Center for Regional Studies at the University of New Mexico and its former director, Professor Gabriel Meléndez, who generously provided funds for a field visit in early 2020 to the Baja border towns. That research visit enabled contact with important archival repositories in California.

Individuals and friends have been instrumental in assisting me in the research and production of *Postcards from the Baja California Border*. Postcard collector colleague Carol Hann in El Centro, California, has been unstinting in her support of this project. Carol not only allowed me to reproduce postcards from her own amazing collection, she made contacts with others on the Baja border that were able to assist. She provided volumes of online and printed materials about Mexicali and acted as an informed source on so many questions about the region. I owe Carol an enormous debt and will forever be grateful for her friendship. In Tijuana I am thankful to André Williams, the premier collector of Tijuana postcards, for allowing me to reproduce several items from his splendid collection. Over several decades, André has been generous to many authors, allowing them to borrow from his incomparable archive. *Gracias* André for your hospitality during my visit and for your extended friendship.

Academic voices have shared in the larger border-town postcard project. Oscar J. Martínez, the dean of U.S.-Mexico border historians, has through his many writings inspired my work. Oscar generously read and commented on several volumes in this series. John Jakle, distinguished cultural geographer of roadside America, introduced me to the value of applying the historic postcard to geographic study. His many writings on the American scene have been models of scholarship melding informative text to historical imagery. Closer to the work at hand, geography colleagues William Manger, William Crowley, and Lawrence Herzog shared enthusiasm for the Baja border project. Manger, a Mexican-postcard collector, author, and professor at Northwestern State University in Natchitoches, Louisiana, contributed significantly by researching biographical materials on Mexican postcard photographer Rafael Castillo. Crowley—professor emeritus, Sonoma State University—a cultural geographer with expertise in Latin America, read and provided important feedback on several draft chapters. Herzog—professor emeritus, San Diego State University—acclaimed especially for his books and papers about Tijuana, was generous with his time and answered questions, recommended contacts, offered hospitality, and shared his passion for the Baja California urban border. Herzog was instrumental in making improvements to the final chapter of this work.

At Arizona State University, cartographer Barbara Trapido-Lurie has, once again, given her time and talent to drafting original maps from my sketches. I am indebted to Barbara for her years of service to my projects. Elizabeth Wentz, director of The School of Geographical Sciences and Urban Planning, generously arranged for a subvention that contributed to the publication of this book. At the University of Arizona Press, an amazing group of professionals guided this project to its conclusion. Kristen Buckles, editor-in-chief, and Elizabeth Wilder, editorial assistant, were instrumental in shepherding the project in its early and middle stages. Leigh McDonald designed the attractive cover, and Amanda Krause oversaw the production process along with Sara Thaxton, who typeset the manuscript. Abby Mogollón managed marketing and promotion. The incomparable C. Steven LaRue, on his third assignment with my border postcard books, copyedited the Baja California volume.

My spouse and life companion, Susan Katherine Arreola, proofread an early draft of the entire manuscript, a task to which she is especially suited given her experience with the written word gained, in part, from a voracious appetite for reading. She saves me regularly in my various writing episodes, and for *Postcards from the Baja California Border* she was my ultimate counsel about phrase structure, sentence clarity, and word choice.

Finally, *Postcards from the Baja California Border* is dedicated to my parents, Beatrice Díaz and Salvador Arreola, who grew up in Southern California and ventured to Tijuana, Baja California, on Mexican Independence Day—September 16—in 1949 to be wed on the soil of their ancestors.

POSTCARDS FROM THE BAJA CALIFORNIA BORDER

Introduction

In an essay titled "The Places We Go Aren't Passive" in the *New York Times Magazine*, Teju Cole commented on how travelers as well as most others take pictures in a particular way. "The resultant images are . . . the poignant commonality of our eyes. The world individually mesmerizes us toward reiteration. Our coincident gazes overlay the same sites over and over and over again."[1] The point is that repetition in popular photography structures vision where we collectively want to capture a site in a standard frame, the overlook of a scenic landscape or the architectural façade of a small-town main street. Postcard imagery—whether a street scene, building, monument, or natural vista—typically follows a convention that is more common than novel. The history of postcards is one in which views of the same sites are represented over and over and over again. Reiteration of the view can be illuminating when one is trying to understand the evolution of a place or a landscape through time.

Postcards from the Baja California Border is the final installment in a four-part project to reconstruct and assess the postcard representation of Mexican border towns. Previous ventures explored the Río Bravo border, the Sonora border, and the Chihuahua border.[2] In each of these excursions the goal has been the same: to understand how a popular media form, the postcard, is a window into the historical and geographical past of Mexican border communities that were tourist destinations from the 1900s through the 1950s. This form of place study is not meant to substitute for other forms of historical investigation. Rather, it calls attention to how we can see a past through a serial view of places enabled by a popular media form never intended for this type of vision but that, nevertheless, allows for such reconstruction. In this way, a 1950s postcard view of a street can inform a 1920s postcard view of the same street. The visual transformation or persistence of elements in the scene permits geographic and historic insight about change.

The late historian Paul Vanderwood called this manner of storytelling "Writing History with Picture Postcards."[3] Vanderwood, along with colleague Frank Samponaro, pioneered this method in two seminal studies, *Border Fury* and *War Scare on the Rio Grande*.[4] Some geographers have followed in their footsteps. Their specific interests were not always writing history as much as writing historical geography, the study of past geographies.[5] Whereas the historian uses the postcard to illustrate a past event or circumstance, the geographer's principal focus is explaining place. Postcards by their very nature as material fragments of a place's imagery facilitate a historical geography of a past place.

Postcards from the Baja California Border is a historical geography of the Mexican border towns of Tijuana, Mexicali, Tecate, and Algodones from the 1900s through the 1950s. Like many historical geographic studies, the work is thematic and time specific. Its focus is the townscapes or built landscapes of these border communities during the first half of the twentieth century when these places were chiefly founded and emerged as recognized border towns. In this light, the historical geography presented in this work is not a complete picture of a place; instead, it is a series of portraits of that place in time where emphasis highlights the tourist view of place as captured by postcard photographers. Postcards as commercial products typically repeat common views. Multiple views when studied systematically over time enable this serial vision.

ITINERARY

Postcards from the Baja California Border is organized into five parts and thirteen chapters. Part I introduces Baja border towns and postcards in separate chapters. Baja California abuts an international divide yet it is a boundary with environments different from other segments of the U.S.-Mexico border. Here are coastal, mountain, desert, and river delta habitats across less than two hundred miles. Tijuana, Tecate, Mexicali, and Algodones emerged chiefly in the early 1900s, and by midcentury all were established border towns although varied in population size and economic importance. Chapter 1 establishes the sequence of founding for the towns and their demographic profiles, the brief interlude of the Mexican Revolution on the northern Baja border, the relative isolation of these towns from the heartland of Mexico, and the development of a regional transportation network that linked the towns along the boundary zone. Chapter 2 describes the postcard as a pictorial format through the types of postcards published for the Baja border towns. Separate case studies follow about postcard photographers, postcard publishing companies, and the ways in which postcards are used in the content chapters that follow.

Part II comprises six chapters that explain how Tijuana was represented in postcards. The chapter subjects explore the townscape and town plan of Tijuana, greetings from Tijuana, crossing over the boundary, Avenida Revolucíon, cabarets, and landmarks. Chapter 3 lays out the geographic space and principal physical framework of Tijuana, its development from a rancho land grant to an emerging urban concentration by the middle twentieth century. Maps and postcards highlight this evolution, setting the stage to understand later postcard representations. Chapter 4 illustrates how postcards were used to call attention to the international boundary monument as a tourist destination, the town's popular fair that attracted tourists from Southern California, and the famous staged burro cart pictures of visitors and other featured imagery. Chapter 5 describes the changing landscapes of crossing the international boundary by automobile and by railroad as featured in postcards. Chapter 6 explains Tijuana's main street, tracing the historical development of this now infamous streetscape and the built environment of business enterprises—including curio stores—that emerged, disappeared, or persisted along a ten-block stretch over a half century. Chapter 7 highlights the most popular enterprises of Tijuana's tourist legacy: drinking, dining, and entertainment. Finally, chapter 8 comprises selected vignettes of some of Tijuana's most symbolic spaces, from bullrings, racetracks, and resorts to hotels, drinking establishments, and amusements. Many of these landmarks have been erased while others survive into the present; all were captured through the popular postcard.

Part III includes three chapters that explore Mexicali, Baja California's desert oasis. Chapter 9 features the townscape and town plan of Mexicali to establish the historical geographic parameters of the border town from its early twentieth-century founding up to the late 1950s. Chapter 10 examines three linear spaces of Mexicali: the international boundary as a cultural divide; Avenida Obregón, Mexicali's principal residential boulevard between the 1920s and 1950s; and the unusual railroad corridor that emerged as the first industrial alignment of Mexicali. Chapter 11 shifts from linear landscapes to district spaces: the cabaret landscapes of the early twentieth century with a vignette that traces the historical geography of Mexicali's famous Owl Café; an analysis of the Baja border town's distinctive ethnic Chinese quarter, La Chinesca; and an assessment of Mexicali's curio street, Calle Melgar. In all of these, postcards and historic maps enable a visual and spatial revisiting of Mexicali's past.

Part IV consists of a single chapter (12) that visits Baja California's other border towns, Tecate and Algodones. In these smaller and lesser-known towns, postcards once again enable time travel highlighting past townscapes and landmarks that celebrated even these out-of-the-way places as tourist destinations.

Finally, Part V is chapter 13, which reviews the findings gained from the content chapters in Parts II–IV. Postcards are a unique media form that can deepen the study of the past geographies of the Baja border towns.

MINDFULNESS

In any writing there are inherent conditions and qualities that deserve special attention. This work is no different. The Spanish language is, of necessity, part of this book because it engages Mexican places and sources. Mexican Spanish terms such as *aduana* (customs house) are italicized, and commonly accepted terms such as *plaza* are not italicized. When a Spanish-language term or text is used, translation is given in parentheses or in context and for extended passages in notes.

The overwhelming number of figure illustrations that are postcards in this book are derived from the Arreola Collection and not sourced in figure captions. A number of figures including some historic maps are part of the author's collection and are identified as such in captions. If a figure is drawn from another source it is so identified and credited in its caption.

As a work of synthesis, the author's intention is for text and image to be appreciated compatibly. This creates a special demand to move fluidly and persistently between the written word and an image or images that illustrate a theme. Consequently, there is a considerable amount of cross-referencing of figures, both maps and postcards. While this effort might appear repetitious to a reader, it is a means of cross-checking locations and the comparability of illustrations to enhance understanding of the subject content. Given the large numbers of visual materials from historical maps, ephemera, and of course postcards, the reader is strongly advised to keep a magnifying glass close by. Historic maps and postcard imagery in particular can be dense with detail, and the reader's awareness of those details will be significantly improved with a simple aid to the naked eye. Finally, it is hoped that reading *Postcards from the Baja California Border* is an enjoyable experience, one that takes you on a time-travel journey of appreciation for borderland geography and the visual stimulation of the postcard view. *Buen viaje.*

PART I

Towns and Postcards

The emergence of a system of cities in the borderlands region illustrates how this region has moved from a nineteenth-century frontier zone at the margin of national territory to a twentieth-century area of economic dynamism.

—Lawrence A. Herzog[1]

The images may appear random and incidental to the casual observer, but Mexican postcards of yesteryear have much more to offer than simply pleasant, nostalgic reminiscence. Small, inexpensive, ephemeral, these rectangles of paper that came to form an essential part of the vacation ritual reveal unsuspected historical and social dimensions.

—Gloria Fraser Giffords[2]

ONE

Baja California Border Towns

Tijuana, Tecate, Mexicali, and Algodones are, by most measures, typical of Mexican border towns that emerged, flourished, and evolved during the first half of the twentieth century. Nevertheless, two of the towns along the Baja California border are settlements that grew out of nineteenth-century ranchos, and two others have their roots in agricultural colonization schemes. Unlike the Chihuahua border, where two of three towns emerged from colonial beginnings, the Baja border communities generally lack direct Spanish colonial ancestry. Whereas three of five Sonora border towns capitalized on their positions as railroad gateways connecting the American Southwest to northern Mexico, Baja border towns became linked to American rails, which chiefly looped across the boundary before rejoining trunk lines back in the states. Perhaps more so than any other regional group of Mexican border towns, the Baja settlements were historically isolated from the heartland of the republic, and thus their development inspiration came principally from American enterprise and connection. That isolation further distanced the Baja border towns from the central battles of the Mexican Revolution, although a brief episode in 1911 resulted in rebellion in three towns in the region. This chapter introduces the towns of the Baja California border and sketches the critical parameters of the first fifty years of historical geographical development of these places from the 1900s to the 1950s.

Chapter 1 first discusses the environmental characteristics of the Baja California border region, an area that includes coastal, mountain, and desert habitats. The region is also bounded on its eastern edge by an extensive deltaic plain created by the Colorado River, which crosses the international boundary. A brief examination of the geographical circumstances of the border towns in Baja California follows. While each town is proximate to the borderline, local issues of access and environmental impact were unique on the Mexico-U.S. boundary.

Remoteness from central Mexico was a geographical fact of life for the Baja border towns. In this chapter, that theme is explored in light of the early settlement orientation of the towns, their positions in the evolution of railroad and highway transportation systems, and their marginal roles in the Mexican Revolution. On the other hand, and in common with most Mexican border towns, the Baja towns benefited significantly from U.S. Prohibition in the 1920s as well as from the forces of tourist development that followed World War II. The demographic changes brought by these social and economic events are described and discussed in order to understand the differential growth of the Baja border settlements. Two of the towns, Tijuana and Mexicali, emerged as major cities during this era, and two others, Tecate and Algodones, remained smaller places into the mid-twentieth century.

ENVIRONMENTS

Baja California, or Lower California as it is sometimes called, is an elongated, icicle-shaped landmass that is separated from the mainland of Mexico by an equally long Gulf of California, called the Sea of Cortéz in Mexico. The Gulf is a rift or downfaulted block of earth invaded by the sea. Geologically, it is the southern extension of the San Andreas fault system in California. The northern reach of this rift extends into southeastern California as the Imperial Valley (fig. 1.1).

The Baja California border towns are situated in a series of environmental habitats unique in their arrangement along the Mexico-U.S. boundary. Tijuana, on the western edge of the region, is nearest the Pacific Ocean, a coastal littoral where mountains cascade into the sea and marine terraces have emerged from changes in ocean levels over millions of years. As a consequence, Tijuana is nestled behind coastal hills along a riverine habitat—the Tijuana River—that rises in the uplands to the east of the town and crosses the international boundary to empty into the Pacific south of San Diego (fig. 1.2).

The second unique habitat of the Baja California border is the mountainous spine of the peninsula that encompasses the border town of Tecate, approximately forty miles east of Tijuana. This rugged upland is an elongated fault block extending south from California (fig. 1.3). Tecate is positioned on this uplift, which becomes even more elevated south of the boundary as the Sierra Juárez (not labeled on map) and the Sierra San Pedro Mártir (see fig. 1.1). The northern reach of this upland in Baja stretches along the international boundary some one hundred miles and climbs to elevations of about six thousand feet before plunging into desert at an abrupt escarpment of the Sierra Juárez beyond Tecate and west of Mexicali near the northern edge of the Sierra de Cocopah (fig. 1.4; see also fig. 1.3).

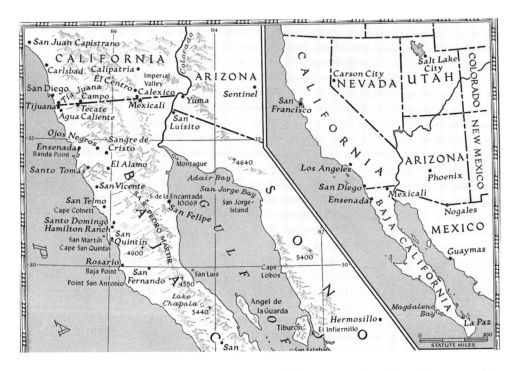

FIGURE 1.1 Map detail with inset illustrating Baja California *norte* (north) and its geographical position. Three of four Baja border towns are shown on this map; not shown is the small town of Algodones on the Colorado River between Mexicali and Yuma, Arizona. *National Geographic Magazine*, August 1942, 258. Author's collection.

The third unique habitat of the Baja border is the delta of the Colorado River created by the waterway's discharge of sediment into the northern Gulf of California. The delta of the Colorado River is a massive depositional landscape that occupies much of the surface of Baja's northeast quadrant as the river meanders nearly fifty miles from near Algodones south toward the Gulf. This environment is largely flat, hot desert with only occasional elevation relief.[1] It would later develop with settlement as an extensive irrigated farming zone on both the Mexican and American sides of the boundary (fig. 1.5). Mexicali and Algodones are the principal Baja border towns of this subarea, often called the Mexicali Valley (see fig. 1.3).

BORDER BEGINNINGS AND EARLY TOWNSCAPES

The Baja California border was defined in the original boundary surveys between 1849 and 1857 conducted by American and Mexican commissions and agreed to by Mexico

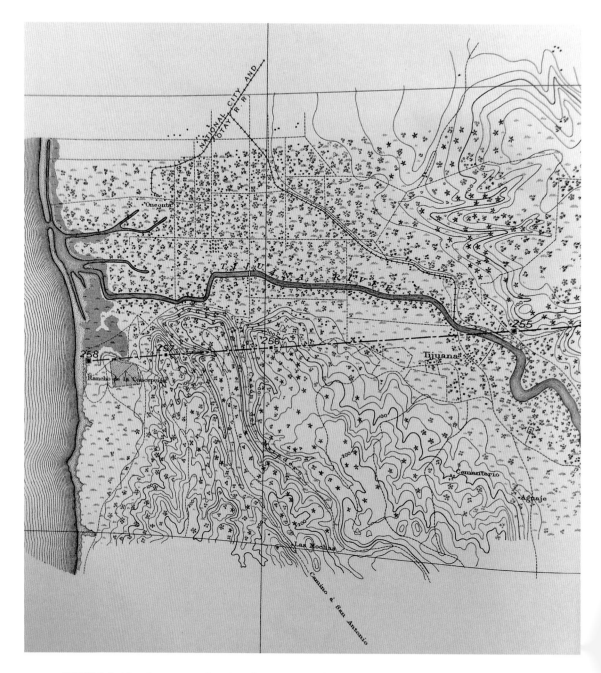

FIGURE 1.2 Map from 1889 showing the position of Tijuana below the international boundary, west of the Tijuana River and flanked by uplands as evidenced by tight contour lines. The border is shown as a broken line with survey monuments at the numbers 255, 256, 257, and 258. International Boundary Commission, *Boundary Between the United States and Mexico*, detail from map no. 1.

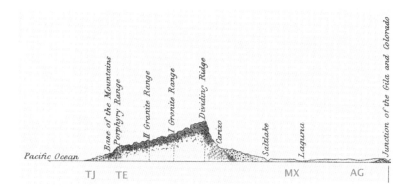

FIGURE 1.3 Terrain profile of a part of the Baja California boundary constructed from surveys under the direction of W. H. Emory, U.S. Commissioner, 1857–1859. Emory, *Report of the United States and Mexican Boundary Survey*, vol. 1, facing p. 52. Tijuana (*TJ*), Tecate (*TE*), Mexicali (*MX*), and Algodones (*AG*) are inserted by the author at approximate locations along this transect. The horizontal scale is forty miles to one inch, and the vertical scale is six thousand feet to one inch.

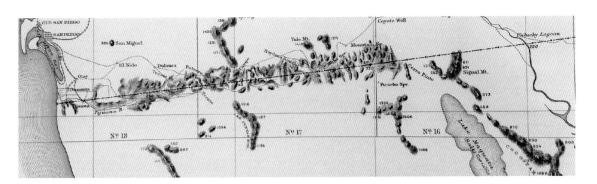

FIGURE 1.4 Map from 1889 showing mountainous transect east of Tijuana including location of Tecate and the edge of the escarpment where the Baja border transitions to a desert habitat near the Lake Maquata (Laguna Salada) and the Sierra de Cocopah. Mexicali was not yet founded when this map was created but would be located proximate to boundary monument 220 east of what became known as New River. International Boundary Commission, *Boundary Between the United States and Mexico*, detail from Index Sheet B.

and the United States following the Mexican War. Chiefly, the boundary was a straight line from the Pacific Ocean edge below San Diego east to the Colorado River with no regard for terrain or territory then largely considered wilderness.[2] The Baja border towns were each founded proximate to the international boundary but at different dates and under different circumstances of the nineteenth and twentieth centuries.

The town named Tijuana was created from a small piece of land-grant ranch property in the northwest corner of Baja California. In 1874 a customs house was established near

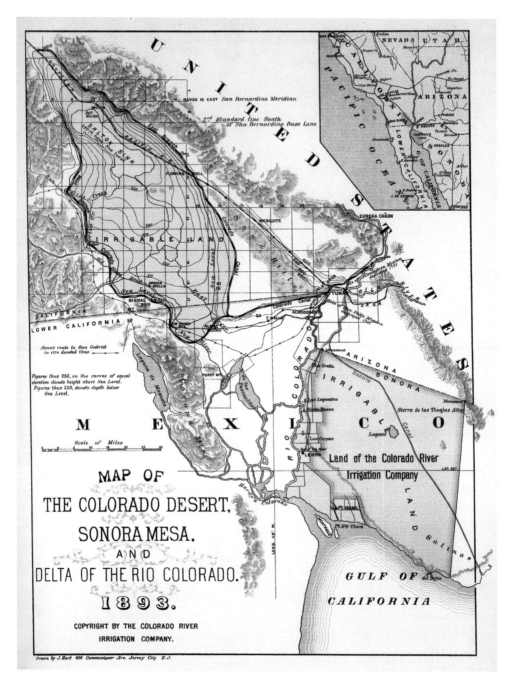

FIGURE 1.5 Delta of the Colorado River. The delta occupies the northeastern quadrant of the Baja Peninsula east of the Sierra de Cocopah, the northwestern edge of Sonora, Mexico, and a small piece of Arizona east of the river. This map, produced in 1893, does not show Mexicali, which would be located immediately east of New River, shown on this map as proximate to the Sierra de Cocopah. Algodones, a rancho that was part of a larger land grant, is shown on the map west of the Colorado River below Yuma, Arizona. Irrigable land was especially developed in the Imperial Valley of California and reached across the boundary into the delta proper once Mexicali was founded in 1903. J. Hart, *Colorado Desert, Sonora Mesa, and Delta of the Rio Colorado, 1893*. Author's collection.

the boundary to control access to ranching and mining claims in the region, and a small cluster of residences emerged at this initial settlement. In 1889 the town of Zaragoza was platted on Tijuana ranch land as an incorporated village, although the settlement was not officially named Tijuana until 1929.[3] The frontier town was less than one thousand residents when a postcard view published in the late 1910s glimpsed the shallow outline of the townscape across the Tijuana River (fig. 1.6).

Figure 1.6 is a real photo postcard made by an unknown photographer who probably positioned himself on the roof of a building at the border crossing in the lower left foreground where a sign points to the Monte Carlo Casino located down the road on the left out of the picture. The view looking southwest captures the dirt road that leads to a wooden bridge over the Tijuana River. The town across the river appears to be a modest assembly of mismatched dwellings and structures with pitched roofs, suggesting how early construction was shaped by architectural norms from the U.S. side of the border, where building materials originated. Scanning left to right across the image one can discern a water tower, the twin domes of the Tijuana Fair built to capitalize on San Diego's Panama-Pacific Exposition of 1915, the steeple of the town church, the Gothic outlines of the Tijuana fort, and the triple-gabled façade of the Tijuana schoolhouse. Behind the town is open land ascending the coastal hills beyond which lies the Pacific Ocean.

Tecate, like Tijuana, emerged from rural beginnings when lands were sparsely settled by Mexican land grantees from San Diego. The local area is an upland valley with a small

FIGURE 1.6 Tijuana, Mexico, looking southwest from near the international boundary. The Tijuana River in Mexico courses immediately in front of the town. Photo postcard, 1910s.

stream that winds through the vicinity. Given the historic presence of grass-covered hills and water in this valley, it is understandable why Tecate was perceived as prime ranch land and part of Southern California's nineteenth-century livestock economy. Several stalled rancho developments following the creation of the international boundary ultimately lead to Mexican government efforts to create agricultural colonies in the Tecate Valley in the 1860s–1870s.[4] The town of Tecate emerged as one of these settlements, and although these developments did not fail, their success was arrested chiefly by lack of access to markets for goods. Significant agglomerated settlement arrived with the construction of the San Diego and Arizona Railroad circa 1914. The municipality of Tecate was declared in 1917.[5]

Figure 1.7 is a real photo postcard from an unidentified photographer illustrating the hamlet of Tecate during the 1920s when the town population hovered around five hundred residents. The view looks west from a hillside above the town. The valley bottom with a narrow stream channel is visible south of the main concentration of the town, and a railroad line is situated just behind the town (although not clearly evident from this image). Except for a few flat-roof buildings on the main drag that are signed bars and cantinas, most structures in this view, like the Tijuana vista above, are pitched-roof constructions, again echoing the American influence in the built townscape. The street running uphill and perpendicular to the principal road leads to the international boundary

FIGURE 1.7 View overlooking Tecate, Baja California. Cars concentrated on the main road through town in front of bars and cantinas testify to the chief attraction of the town during the Prohibition era. Photo postcard, 1920s.

less than a mile north, and across the divide is the even smaller settlement of Tecate, California.

Mexicali, Baja California, has its origins in various land transfers from Mexican to American development interests. At the turn of the century, irrigation systems were put in place to capitalize on the development scheme that had been successful north of the border in the Imperial Valley (fig. 1.5). Mexicali was organized in 1903 as the municipality to serve this regional economy in Mexico. The Baja northern district territorial capital was relocated in 1920 from Ensenada to Mexicali, and in 1952, when Baja California Norte became a federal state, Mexicali became the only Mexican border town that is a state capital.[6]

Within three years of its founding, Mexicali became imperiled by an environmental disaster that is now legendary in the history of the border region. The catastrophe centered on an intake to the Álamo Canal from the nearby Colorado River in 1905, which was breached, and water flowed into the New River. This brought a deluge into the Mexicali Valley and the Imperial Valley, parts of which are below sea level (see fig. 1.5).[7] Water flowed into this lowland trough for more than a year, and the flood nearly drowned the new border town. Figure 1.8 illustrates two early print postcard views of the Mexicali town site before and during the concentration of floodwater. The top view, circa 1905, looks south across the western edge of Mexicali perched on a bluff above New River that flows past the border town on its way north across the boundary. The bottom view, dated June 1906, shows the western edge of Mexicali looking due west toward the Sierra de Cocopah in the background. In this postcard, the New River drainage is completely inundated with floodwater that flowed into the area.

Figure 1.9 is a 1911 panoramic photograph showing the towns of Mexicali, Baja California, and Calexico, California, divided by the international boundary. The view is west toward the Sierra de Cocopah on the far horizon. The townscapes here, like those shown previously for Tijuana (fig. 1.6) and Tecate (fig. 1.7), mirror clusters of dwellings and structures built in an American architectural aesthetic, making the two towns appear as one community separated by the border. On the north side, however, one can just make out a U.S. infantry camp signaling the American response at this time to rebellion that was brewing across the boundary. Whereas the Revolution was largely inconsequential on the Baja California border, this image shows (with magnification) two battle sites on the outskirts of Mexicali labeled in white text, one west of New River and just below the silhouette of the Sierra de Cocopah at the center of the image, and another, also west of New River, on the far left of the panoramic view.

Algodones, Baja California, emerged out of land grants in the Colorado River Delta made to Mexicans in the late nineteenth century. Guillermo Andrade, a Mexican developer and former banker who had worked in San Francisco, consolidated many of these grants and received title to most of the irrigable land in the Colorado River Delta by 1888.

Mexicali B. C. Mexico.   June 1906.

FIGURE 1.8 Mexicali circa 1905 (*top*) and in 1906 (*bottom*), showing the flooding that inundated New River, which courses west of the town. Published by M. Rieder, Los Angeles, California (*top*), and for A. M. Shenk, Calexico, California by M. Rieder, Los Angeles, California (*bottom*).

FIGURE 1.9 Panoramic photograph showing the towns of Mexicali, Baja California (*left*) and Calexico, California (*right*), separated by the international boundary. Photographer Schuyler U. Bunnell of Brawley, California, appears to have positioned himself on a water tower (iron bars visible at lower left) to make the dramatic photograph. S. U. Bunnell, [Bird's-eye view of Mexicali and Calexico]. May 10, 1911, Library of Congress, Prints and Photographs Division, Washington, DC.

Andrade sold some eight hundred thousand acres of land to the Colorado River Land Company controlled by Harrison Otis and Harry Chandler, owners of the *Los Angeles Times*. The territory that gave rise to the border town was a piece of the larger grant lands proximate to the river and officially designated Rancho de Los Algodones (fig. 1.10). While the population had clustered around a settlement identified on maps as Algodones as early as the 1890s, the town was not formally declared as a legal entity until 1918.[8]

Figure 1.11 is a real photo postcard from the 1950s looking north along the Gran Canal del Álamo with part of the town of Algodones shown on the left of the image and west of the artificial waterway. By 1950 the Morelos Dam (seen at the top of the canal in the photo postcard view), a principal diversion project, was installed at the location where the Colorado River intersects the international boundary. Algodones was a small village during this period with a population of about one thousand. In this view the town at left

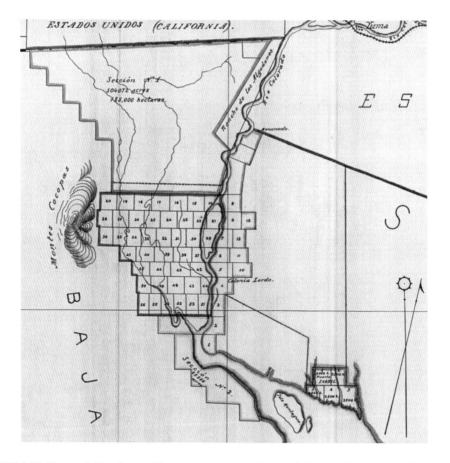

FIGURE 1.10 Town of Algodones. The town was carved out of the Rancho de Los Algodones, which paralleled the Colorado River south of the international boundary. Detail from Serapio Echeverría, *Plano de los Terrenos del S. D. Guillermo Andrade en los Estados de Sonora y Baja California*, Mexico City, 1888. Author's collection.

FIGURE 1.11 Panoramic view of Algodones, Baja California, looking north along the Álamo Canal with the Morelos diversion dam visible at the top of the canal, 1950s. Romero Foto. 11.

is shrouded under a canopy of trees, and a pedestrian bridge crosses the canal. In the left background is a prominent landmark and peak, Pilot Knob, a volcanic plug that rises 876 feet in the Cargo Muchaco Mountains just across the boundary in California.

ISOLATION OF THE BAJA BORDER

Until the post–World War II era, Baja California, especially the border region, was largely isolated from the mainland of Mexico. This reality had two important consequences for the Baja border towns. First, transit by automobile and railroad—the two principal transport forms of the second half of the twentieth century—was chiefly confined to cross-boundary movement so that Baja border towns became interconnected to places in California more so than to locations elsewhere in Mexico. Second, geographic isolation created social and economic distance between the Baja border and the heartland of Mexico. This was especially the case for economic exchange because goods and services generated in the north were largely inaccessible to the south and vice versa. Regional separation further affected the principal social event of the early twentieth century in Mexico, the Mexican Revolution. While there were isolated instances of disturbance and even conflict between insurgent actors and the federal government, by and large these skirmishes were minor compared to those played out on the Sonora, Chihuahua, and Tamaulipas borders.

Railroads

In keeping with the transportation history of the border region, railroads proved the earliest and most significant developments to link towns across northern Baja and Southern California. The initial routing of the Southern Pacific trunk line through the region largely bypassed the Baja border. Figure 1.12 shows the railroad systems of the Compañia del Ferrocarril Inter-California, a subsidiary of the Southern Pacific Railroad. The original Southern Pacific line through this region connected Los Angeles with Yuma, Arizona, before heading east to Tucson; El Paso, Texas; and beyond. A piece of this railroad running east of the Salton Sea, west of the Chocolate Mountains in Southern California, is visible in figure 1.12.

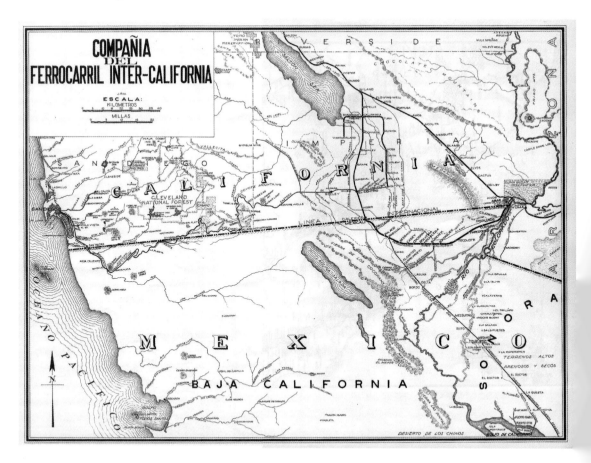

FIGURE 1.12 Inter-California Railroad, Baja California border, 1926. *Compañía del Ferrocarril Inter-California.* Author's collection.

The earliest railroads to serve the Baja border were, as noted by John Kirchner, "step-children of geography."[9] Their appearance was the result of routing decisions made by American railroad designers to avoid less favorable terrain in the United States and to capitalize on potential development interests in Mexico. The purpose of these railroads was to facilitate freight and passenger service in the United States. To enable this, the lines were organized as independent subsidiaries according to Mexican law. The railroads were the Ferrocarril Inter-California and the Ferrocarril Tijuana y Tecate.

The Ferrocarril Inter-California was formed in 1902 by the Southern Pacific to provide railroad service to the agricultural development of the Imperial Valley. Figure 1.13 is a detail from figure 1.12 that shows the reach of the Inter-California line from Niland in the Imperial Valley, where it breaks from the main Southern Pacific railroad south to El Centro, and then to Calexico on the international boundary. The difficulty and expense of extending this line due east from Calexico was the position of the Algodones Dunes, identified as "Medanos Arenosos" (sand hills) on the map. The default route was to build south and loop the line back to the border, thereby circumventing the dunes. The Inter-California Railroad became an international carrier once it crossed the border to Mexicali. In 1904 construction of this segment of the line was initiated with the goal of routing in a semicircle northeast to Algodones where the railroad again crossed the boundary into California to reconnect with the main Southern Pacific line at Araz Junction on the Yuma Indian Reservation.

The Baja segment of the Inter-California was completed and fully operational in August 1909. The railroad chiefly served the interests of growers in the Imperial Valley, who could in 1926 ship produce from Brawley to Yuma via Mexicali in five hours. In that year 12,082 cars of melons and 9,168 cars of lettuce were transported (fig. 1.14). Crossing the boundary two times in one direction created certain operating issues because freight rail cars reaching the border were sealed and manifested by both the United States and Mexican governments, and customs inspections were incurred in each direction (fig. 1.15). By the late 1940s passenger traffic on the Inter-California improved, and Mexicans traveling between Algodones and Mexicali became a small part of the railroad's service.[10]

The post–World War II period brought increased railroad service to the eastern Baja border with the completion in 1948 of the Ferrocarril Sonora-Baja California, which used Inter-California rails to link Mexicali with Puerto Peñasco, Sonora, on the Gulf of California and Benjamin Hill, Sonora, where the railway connected to the main West Coast line of the Mexico rail system, the Ferrocarril Sud-Pacífico de México (see fig. 1.12, where this railroad is identified as the Inter-California del Sur). With this routing in place, the Baja California border became connected to the mainland of Mexico, and the capital of Baja California, Mexicali (1952), witnessed increased passenger and freight service.[11]

The Ferrocarril Tijuana y Tecate is coupled to the story of the more famous San Diego and Arizona Railway, and like the Inter-California it owes its existence to the decision

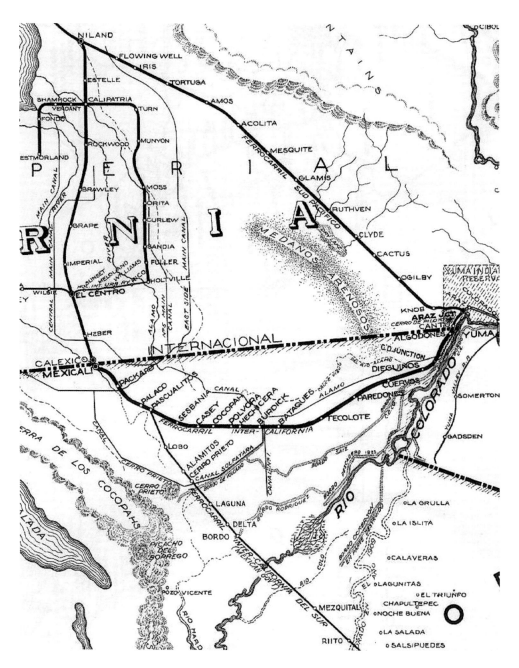

FIGURE 1.13 Map detail showing Inter-California railroad route through the Imperial Valley and the Baja California border, 1926. *Compañia del Ferrocarril Inter-California.* Author's collection.

Propiedad registrada Rafael Castillo. Foto.   Estación del Ferrocarril. Mexicali, B. C.

FIGURE 1.14 Estación del Ferrocarril, Mexicali. The Ferrocarril Inter-California was principally a freight railroad servicing the Imperial Valley and exporting produce via Baja California. This photo postcard shows a steam locomotive pulling boxcars through Mexicali en
route to Algodones, where the line again crossed the international boundary to connect to
the main Southern Pacific line heading east in Arizona. Rafael Castillo Foto., no. 16, 1910s.

American Custom House.
Andrade. U.S.A.

Mexican Custom House.
Algodones, Mex.

FIGURE 1.15 Inter-California freight trains at the Algodones-Andrade international boundary
required customs inspection by the Mexican and American governments. Photoette made
by C. U. Williams, Bloomington, Illinois, 1910s.

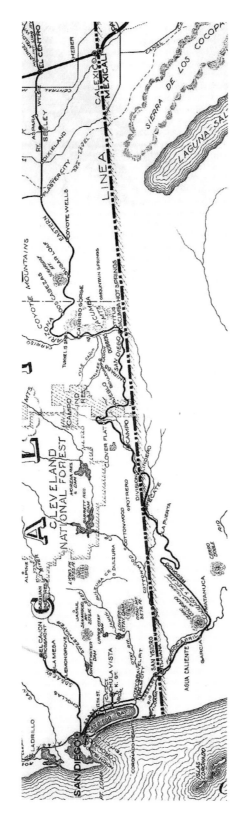

FIGURE 1.16 Map detail showing the Ferrocarril Tijuana y Tecate along the western Baja California border in 1926. This Mexican segment of railroad was an extension of the San Diego and Arizona Railway. It reached Tecate in 1914. *Compañía del Ferrocarril Inter-California*. Author's collection.

by American railroad engineers to construct the rail line along gentler grades in Baja California than directly across the grain of the Peninsular Ranges of California between San Diego and the Imperial Valley. The Tijuana y Tecate, therefore, is a Mexican subsidiary of the American railroad. San Diego had for several generations lost repeatedly in its efforts to connect by rail to the Imperial Valley and points east. The San Diego and Arizona Railway, organized in 1906, was said to be the brainchild of capitalist John D. Spreckels, although the Southern Pacific Railroad, which desired a San Diego routing, was the financial backer to Spreckels.

Spreckels secured the Mexican concession to route the Tijuana y Tecate railway through Baja in 1908. Figure 1.16 is a detail from fig. 1.12 that illustrates the entire route from San Diego south to San Ysidro, where rails crossed the boundary to Tijuana and then headed south and east, climbing to Tecate, beyond which it crossed the border again and encircled the treacherous Jacumba Mountains before dropping over the escarpment into the Imperial Valley to El Centro. The western segment of this railroad was completed and operating by September 1914, extending fifty-two miles from near sea level at San Diego to 1,685 feet at Tecate on the international boundary.[12]

The Tijuana y Tecate railroad was, unlike the Inter-California, of little consequence for the western Baja border because most freight traffic was conducted on the San Diego and Arizona Railway segment in the Imperial Valley. Further, passenger traffic over the entire line from San Diego to El Centro was a six-to-seven-hour journey that quickly became uncompetitive with a five-hour automobile journey over the mountains on the American side of the boundary. Perhaps the most lucrative service on the Mexican segment was the passenger traffic between San Diego and Tijuana, which carried thousands of tourists to the Agua Caliente Casino and racetrack from the late 1920s into the 1930s. At Tecate a handsome depot was constructed in 1915, and trains in both directions made stops in the small Mexican border town (fig. 1.17). The San Diego and Arizona Railway was sold to the Southern Pacific Railroad in 1933 and became the San Diego and Arizona Eastern Railway, a wholly owned subsidiary. Freight and some passenger service continued for the Tijuana y Tecate through the World War II years but declined into the 1950s when bus and automobile transport replaced railroad travel.[13]

Roads and Highways

While railroads were major carriers of freight in parts of the Baja border region during the first two decades of the twentieth century, automobiles quickly replaced the slow demand for rail passenger service. Even over marginal graded roadways, travelers in the border region clearly preferred auto transport to other alternatives. When busses began to ply these routes with greater efficiency in the post–World War II era, travel

S. D. & A. RY.   STATION AT TECATE, CAL.

FIGURE 1.17 Tijuana and Tecate Railroad depot at Tecate, Baja California, 1919, part of the San Diego and Arizona Railway. Photograph attributed to C. M. Kurtz. Postcard published by H. L. Christiance, San Diego, California. Manufactured by the Albertype Co., Brooklyn, New York.

between border towns and connections across the boundary became almost exclusively auto oriented.

Figure 1.18 is a detail from a map showing the road and highway network across the Baja border region in 1928. The bold red lines like the one shown linking Tijuana to Tecate and Mexicali were then considered first-class roads. This road, completed in 1918 and named Camino Nacional, paralleled the Tijuana y Tecate railroad and continued to Mexicali.[14] Parts of this road might have been paved or concrete, but most of the surface was probably graded. The slighter red lines like those stretching across the Colorado River Delta south of Mexicali were then considered secondary roads and labeled "wagon roads."

While first-class roads made it possible for Mexicans in Baja border towns to travel between places, certainly the greatest volume of automobile traffic was north–south across the international boundary. During the Prohibition era, traffic was particularly heavy between San Diego and Tijuana and between Calexico and Mexicali. Sometime in the post–World War II epoch, Tijuana boasted that it was the most visited city in the world. As figure 1.19 suggests, however, a generation or so before that declaration, Tijuana was already being inundated by day-tripping Southern Californians who simply

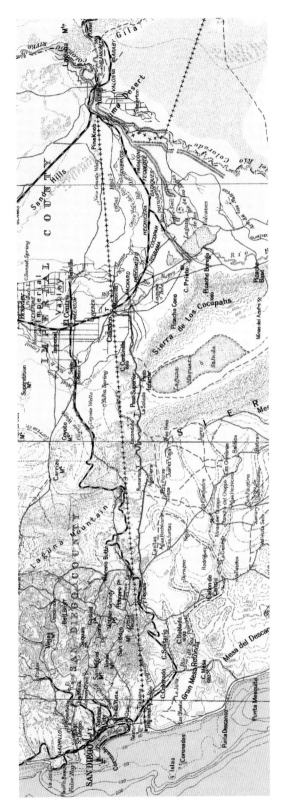

FIGURE 1.18 Detail from a map showing transportation as well as general location and terrain information for the Baja California border region on both sides of the boundary. Red lines are labeled as roads with the heaviest lines, like the one connecting Tijuana–Tecate–Mexicali, then considered first-class roads. *Baja California-Norte*, 1:1,000,000 scale, American Geographical Society of New York, 1928. Author's collection.

FIGURE 1.19 Tijuana bridge. Traffic into and out of Tijuana was especially heavy during the pre-Prohibition era when hordes of Southern Californians crossed the border to imbibe, gamble, and play because California prohibited certain forms of vice that were quite legal in Mexico. Attributed to Roy Warfield Magruder, 1910s.

drove across the border to partake of the eccentricities of the jazz age. The bridge shown here was entirely inside Mexico because the international boundary was crossed a mile or so before negotiating the sometimes water swollen Tijuana River. During the early 1900s, when the population of Tijuana was less than seven hundred, nearly 4,200 visitors crossed into the Baja border town each year.[15] Further, because California prohibited some forms of gambling, such as pari-mutuel betting, and some cities, towns, and counties passed prohibitions on the consumption or sale of alcohol before national Prohibition in 1920, the attractions of casinos, racetracks, and drinking palaces across the boundary in Tijuana were already in place.[16]

Following the Second World War, highway improvements between the Baja border towns enhanced regional transport and trade. Nevertheless, ease of travel across the region would not improve markedly even with paving, guardrails, and safety measures. Perhaps one of the most difficult transit sections along the border highway in Baja was the so-called Rumorosa, a stretch of switchbacks and hairpin turns in the ascent and descent between Tecate and Mexicali. Figure 1.18 shows the location of the town of Rumorosa on the highway some forty miles east of Tecate. East of this town whose name means "the whispers," the red line squiggles to suggest the treacherous roadway as it drops over the northern reach of the Sierra Juárez to the desert below, north of the Laguna Salada.

REVOLUTION ON THE BAJA BORDER

The Mexican Revolution on the Baja California border is commonly known as the Magonista Rebellion of 1911. Organized by the Partido Liberal Mexicano, or PLM, the early uprising was only briefly successful in northern Baja California. The rebellion is named after Ricardo Flores Magón, a Mexican anarchist and one of the leaders of the PLM. Circa 1907, Magón moved to Los Angeles, where the PLM established a regional office to solicit support from sympathizers in the city. The PLM in Los Angeles decided to ignite a campaign in nearby Baja California, hoping it could hold the territory and use it as a recruiting base.[17]

The first strike would be at Mexicali, where the PLM imagined it would soon be operating on Mexican soil. Guns and ammunition secured in Los Angeles were smuggled across the border to Mexicali, a small village of about five hundred people at the time. In late January 1911, a mere handful of PLM leaders and Mexican rebel recruits captured the defenseless border town, although a contingent of Mexican federal troops was quickly dispatched to Mexicali from a garrison in Ensenada, then the territorial capital. PLM fighters entrenched themselves on the outskirts of Mexicali and rebuffed the federal advance on the town in February 1911, forcing the federal troops to return to Ensenada (the battle sites in Mexicali, marked on fig. 1.9, are discussed above). The PLM victory inspired a radical movement in the United States and beyond, and soon men flowed to Mexicali to take up arms for the rebellion. These were mostly Americans and included Wobblies, and veterans of the Spanish-American War, but there were also volunteers from Canada, England, Germany, Australia, South Africa, France, and Austria.

Despite a victory at Mexicali, the *insurrectos*, as they were being referred to in the press, were short of ammunition and unable to secure resupply because American president William Howard Taft sent thousands of U.S. troops to the border to stifle the illegal flow of armaments across the boundary into Mexico (see the infantry camp in Calexico across from Mexicali shown in fig. 1.9). Several skirmishes with federal troops dispatched to protect waterworks facilities east of Mexicali proved indecisive. In April 1911 the insurgents became locked in an internal leadership struggle between Mexican and Euro-Anglo volunteers. The commander, Rhys Pryce, a Scot who fought with British forces in the Boer War, ignored the recommendation of the PLM leadership to stay and defend Mexicali and, instead, marched his army of some two hundred men to Tijuana, then defended by a small garrison of Mexican federals at the Tijuana fort (fig. 1.20).

On May 8, 1911, the rebels arrived at the outskirts of Tijuana, and Pryce, commander of the contingent, demanded the surrender of the federal troops at the fort. The federals refused to surrender, and hostilities commenced that evening. Before the fighting, most of Tijuana's population, including some of the federal troops who were short of ammunition, fled across the border to a village (later known as San Ysidro) on the American side. The federal troops that remained took up positions at the Tijuana bullring and installed

FIGURE 1.20 Mexican fort at Tijuana. The fort was a small garrison of troops in 1911. Attributed to Roy Warfield Magruder, 1910s.

sharpshooters in the tower of the church in town. Pryce ordered the burning of the bull-ring and church to flush out the federal resistance. The battle of Tijuana lasted about sixteen hours and resulted in several dozen dead and wounded. The surviving federal defenders fled to Ensenada.

The insurgents occupied the nearly deserted town for several weeks (fig. 1.21). Pryce closed down the gambling casinos and destroyed stocks of alcohol. Within days curious sightseers began to enter the town. Rebels were said to have stood outside the town's curio shops and allowed American shoppers to remove whatever they could carry for a small sum. But the victory, like the one earlier in Mexicali, soon dissolved through continued dissention among the insurgents. Finally, in June 1911 an army of reorganized federal troops marched from Ensenada and with superior manpower and armaments quickly defeated the ragtag rebel forces, scattering some of the Mexican volunteers and capturing over one hundred American and European survivors who were duly marched across the boundary and surrendered to the U.S. Army in San Diego.

The battle in Tijuana, coincidentally, occurred in the same week as the assault by Francisco Madero's rebel forces against federal troops in Ciudad Juárez, a battle that became the so-called spark that ignited the Mexican Revolution. As a consequence, the American and Mexican press gave front-page coverage to the Chihuahua conflict, thereby relegating the Tijuana incident to the back pages. Unfortunate timing combined with at least one

FIGURE 1.21 Barricaded Mexican customs house following Battle of Tijuana, May 9, 1911. Published by the Photoprint Company, San Diego, California.

other important circumstance to blunt the rebellion in Baja California. The total population of Mexicali, Tecate, Algodones, and Tijuana during the time of the rebellion was not much more than one thousand people. Most showed little sympathy for the Magonista movement, a political exercise that was less about Mexican nationalism and more about an ideological struggle between capitalists and radical socialists. Further, because the rebellion was overwhelmingly fought by mercenary forces, the likelihood of ultimate victory may have been checked from the beginning.

Nevertheless, a significant outcome of the battle of Tijuana may have been the renaming of the main street. First called Avenida Olvera, and then known variously as Avenida A, Avenida Obregón, and Avenida Libertad during the 1920s, the street was finally called Avenida Revolución in 1932, the name that survives, infamously, to this day.

DEMOGRAPHIC CHANGES IN BAJA BORDER TOWNS

Baja border towns were relatively small places with few residents in the first decade of the twentieth century.

Tijuana in 1911 had little economic, political or geographical significance. It was a tiny hamlet of about 100 people, most of them Anglo-American and Mexican merchants catering to tourists from nearby San Diego. Isolated from the other towns in Baja California, its only means of rapid communication with Ensenada was a telegraph line, which ran from San Diego.[18]

Over the next five decades, two of the towns would transform to become some of the largest cities of the border while two others grew gradually, remaining modest towns over the same span. This section reviews the population changes that transpired in Algodones, Tecate, Tijuana, and Mexicali, both the relative absolute numbers by decade, and population change by natural increase versus migration.

Table 1.1 shows the absolute population counts for the Baja border towns from 1900 to 1960 compiled from various sources. At first glance, the populations suggest that the Baja border towns were all less than one thousand each from 1900 to 1910. This means that even Tijuana and Mexicali were then villages on par with Algodones and Tecate. Populations in Mexicali and Tijuana expanded considerably over the next decades, reaching nearly twenty thousand each by 1940, whereas Tecate climbed to more than one thousand and Algodones reached only to about half that many in the same time period. The most recent times, especially the post–World War II era, reveal the greatest episodes of population growth among the Baja border towns.

Human populations grow in only two ways: through natural increase—people reproducing in place—and through migration—people moving from one place to another.

TABLE 1.1 Baja California border-town populations, 1900–1960

Year	Tijuana	Mexicali	Tecate	Algodones
1900	242	220[a]	127	30[b]
1910	733	462	116[c]	52[d]
1920	1,028	6,782	493	189[e]
1930	8,384	14,842	566	528[f]
1940	16,486	18,775	1,635[g]	—
1950	59,950	64,658	3,676[h]	991[i]
1960[j]	152,374	174,540	6,588	1,162

Source: Population counts from various Mexican censuses presented in Arreola and Curtis, *Mexican Border Cities*, table 2.2, p. 24, and Ganster and Lorey, *U. S.-Mexican Border Today*, table 6.2, p. 140.

[a] Censo de 1904, cited in Meade, *Origen de Mexicali*, 71.

[b] 1899 estimate, Hendricks, *Guillermo Andrade y el desarrollo del delta mexicano del Río Colorado*, 147.

[c] *Estados Unidos Mexicanos, division territorial, Territorio de la Baja California, censo de 1910*, 31.

[d] *Estados Unidos Mexicanos, division territorial, Territorio de la Baja California, censo de 1910*, 12.

[e] *Estados Unidos Mexicanos, censo general de habitantes de 1921, Baja California, Distritos Norte y Sur*, 35.

[f] *Estados Unidos Mexicanos, quinto censo de poblacion de 1930, Baja California (Distrito Norte)*, 46–47.

[g] Cruz Piñero and Ybáñez Zepeda, "Demographic Dynamics of Tecate," 23.

[h] *Estados Unidos Mexicanos, septimo censo general de poblacion 1950, Baja California Territorio Norte*, 13.

[i] *Estados Unidos Mexicanos, septimo censo general de poblacion 1950, Baja California Territorio Norte*, 12.

[j] *Estados Unidos Mexicanos, VIII censo general de poblacion 1960, Estado de Baja California*.

The decadal population changes shown in table 1.1 are results from both natural increase and migration, but differentiating these measurements for each Baja border town is not easily accomplished. Birth records and places of origin for Tijuana between 1914 and 1931 establish that overwhelmingly most population growth during this period resulted from natural increase. A compilation of the decadal population numbers for 1910–1930 shows an increase of 7,651 (table 1.1). During the period 1914–1931, at least 2,989 people migrated to Tijuana from other places in Mexico.[19] Most (737) who migrated to Tijuana were from other places in the north of Baja California. Following northern Baja, places in southern Baja were the second largest contributing source region (538) to Tijuana. The remaining source regions were other states, accounting in total for more than half (1,664) of all the migrants who came to Tijuana in the seventeen-year interval. The states enumerated in this count can be ranked highest to lowest (with a minimum of one hundred migrants sent) and included Sonora (362), Jalisco (324), Sinaloa (282), Chihuahua (138), Guanajuato (123), Zacatecas (118), Distrito Federal (Mexico City) (113), and Michoacán (104). With the exception of Jalisco, three of the top four states in this list are in the far north of Mexico and neighbors near to Baja California, illustrating the principle of proximity as a factor in migration.

In the decades between 1940 and 1960, migration exceeded natural increase as the principal means of population growth for all large cities of the Mexican border, including Tijuana and Mexicali in Baja California. Along the border, municipalities grew over 7 percent during the decade of the 1940s compared to less than three percent for Mexico.[20] Population growth by migration to Tijuana and Mexicali between 1940 and 1950 was more than three times natural increase. Migration continued to be the principal accelerant to population growth in these border towns in the decade 1950 to 1960.[21] It may be reasonable to assume that a similar pattern of change at a much lower population threshold was experienced by Tecate and Algodones during this same period.

Beyond the population numbers described above are the social and economic conditions that facilitated population change. In general, two growth phases on the Baja border follow the patterns established and recognized for other parts of the Mexico-U.S. border region. From 1920 through 1933 national Prohibition in the United States stimulated American investors to flee moral reform north of the boundary and join Mexican politicos and businessmen south of the border in the embrace of gambling, cabarets, and associated forms of vice. The consequences brought substantial growth to most Mexican border towns, including Tijuana and Mexicali as well as Tecate and Algodones, although in the latter smaller towns at lower levels. Following the Great Depression, the post–World War II era witnessed a return to explosive growth. As border economies recovered into the 1940s–1950s, two circumstances enhanced the social and economic conditions on the Baja border: proximity to U.S. military installations, and a migrant labor program that brought Mexican agricultural workers to the American Southwest.

United States military personnel stationed in camps and bases near the border have historically contributed importantly to the consumer service economy of nearby Mexican border towns.[22] Tijuana, for example, is near to both the U.S. Naval Station in San Diego and Camp Pendleton Marine Corps Base in Oceanside, north of San Diego. Temporary recreational leave from these bases regularly brought personnel to Tijuana to participate in tourist economies, and that demand created a need for service labor in the Mexican border city that encouraged migrants to travel to the Baja border seeking employment. Further, the wartime economic boom in the United States, especially in California, pulled Mexican migrants north. Many of these migrants were displaced from rural Mexico, where agricultural communities were hard hit during the Depression and failed to recover sufficiently to accommodate a growing population following the period of economic decline. Perhaps the greatest effect of this migration on the Baja border towns resulted from the Bracero Program, a U.S. federally mandated contract labor arrangement that enabled Mexican agricultural workers to enter the country temporarily. Between 1942 and 1947, fully one-half of all Bracero Program workers labored in California. On the heels of this program, other migrants sought economic opportunities in the north, and on the border they often assembled in towns such as Mexicali and Tijuana, which became major cities in the 1940s–1950s (table 1.1). That extraordinary growth elevated Baja California Norte, a former territory in the Mexican Republic, to become the state of Baja California in 1952.[23]

T W O

Postcards

A postcard, or post card, is a rectangular piece of heavy paper intended for writing and mailing without an envelope, usually at a lower cost than a letter. Before postcards, personal messaging by letter and envelope was private. Postcards eliminate privacy, and messaging is unmasked and readable whether on the front or back of the card. The first postcards were developed in Germany and Austria in the middle of the nineteenth century. By the end of the nineteenth century, postcards incorporated pictures and scenes of places on one side of the card. These postcard types were view cards or topographical postcards. In this project the view card popularized between the 1900s and the 1950s is the primary data source analyzed to understand the historical geography of Baja California border towns.

Chapter 2 assesses the history and use of postcards to understand the media form highlighted in this work. Following a discussion of the postcard as a historical artifact, attention is focused on three types of postcards—real photo, print, and chrome. For each type, there is a detailed examination of the postcard format used in the Baja border towns, including descriptions, examples, and discussions of postcard photographers and publishers. Vignettes highlight selected postcard photographers, publishers, and manufacturing companies that best represent the variety of postcards of the Baja border towns. A final section of the chapter presents information about the postcards used and the systems of dating postcards in this project.

A BRIEF HISTORY OF POSTCARDS

The story of the postcard and its evolution has received increased attention in popular writing and scholarly research.[1] In the first year of the twenty-first century, an English writer published *The Postcard Century*, an inventory of two thousand postcards and their messages to celebrate the twentieth-century popularity of the postcard in pictures and words. More recently, American professional geographers, for example, have used historic postcards of the Lincoln Highway in the United States to understand how places featured along the transcontinental route were promoted by 237 separate postcard views.[2]

The earliest private postcard format in the United States was the Private Mailing Card. By an Act of Congress on May 19, 1898, publishers of privately printed postcards, or private mailing cards, were granted permission to sell postcards that could be mailed at the rate of one cent. On the Baja California border several examples of private mailing cards were published by the Detroit Photographic Company. Figures 2.1a and 2.1b illustrate one of these private mailing cards for Tijuana. The front, or recto (fig. 2.1*a*), of the private mailing card shows a lithographic print of the earliest permanent boundary marker in the Baja region between Mexico and the United States and includes a space below the image where a message can be written. The back, or verso (fig. 2.1*b*), of the mailing card was reserved exclusively for the address and includes the title "Private Mailing Card" and the authorization declaration by Congress along with a penny postage stamp and cancel date of January 14, 1900, from Coronado, California. Private mailing cards were the only type of private postcard allowed in the United States between 1898 and 1901.

On December 24, 1901, the U.S. Post Office permitted the use of the word "Post Card" to be printed on the undivided back of a privately published card. The previous authorization inscription was discontinued, but those mailing postcards were still restricted to writing the address only on the back of the card so that any messaging had to be scribed on the front.

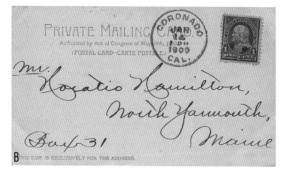

FIGURES 2.1 Private mailing card. The card restricted the message to the front (*a*), and the back (*b*) was exclusively for the mailing address. Boundary monument, Mexico and United States. Detroit Photographic Company, no. 163, 1899.

FIGURE 2.2 Divided-back "Post Card" circa 1915. The verso shows message and address spaces divided by a vertical line, the stamp box with postage costs, and the name of the publisher along with the colophon of the manufacturer. The logo of the Panama-California Exposition is printed in the upper left. Published by Eno and Matteson, no. 3489, San Diego, CA, manufactured by Bamforth and Co., no. 17615, New York.

On March 1, 1907, the U.S. Post Office permitted private postcard publishers to issue divided-back cards. Figure 2.2 is a rearview example of an early divided-back postcard. The space left of center is reserved for the message and to the right of center for the address only. The stamp box in the upper right instructs that domestic mailing including Mexico, Canada, and Cuba requires a one-cent stamp and foreign postage two cents. This postcard, published by Eno and Matteson of San Diego, California, includes in the lower left the colophon for the manufacturer of the postcard, B. and Co. (Bamforth and Company, New York). The postcard also illustrates in the upper left a logo of the Panama-California Exposition staged in 1915 in San Diego to celebrate the completion of the Panama Canal. The front of the typical divided-back postcard was then completely occupied by a view, and there was no space allocated for a message. The early divided-back postcard period was considered by some historians to be the golden era of postcards, when publishers printed millions.

Following World War I, printing costs affected the production of postcards, and manufacturers surrounded the front image of a card with a white border. This period, up to 1930, is referred to as the white border era. Before the war, Germany had been the premier lithographic print postcard manufacturer, and many American postcard publishers had

FIGURE 2.3 "Aztec Brewing Company, Mexicali, Mexico." A white border postcard format popular from 1915 to 1930, this image emphasizes the access to an alcoholic beverage restricted in the United States between 1920 and 1933. MX18: Brewers of the famous A. B. C. Beer published by M. Kashower, Los Angeles, California, and postmarked Calexico, California, November 16, 1933.

relied on German high-quality printing, an industry that never regained prominence after the war. While the quality of many white border postcards was lacking compared to earlier German manufactured print postcards, some American companies became known for better white border cards. Figure 2.3 is a white border postcard published by M. Kashower Company of Los Angeles (1914–1934), which contracted with various printers to manufacture its postcards. This postcard—labeled Aztec Brewing Company, Mexicali, Mexico—is clearly made from a photograph that has been altered and color enhanced through commercial printing. The verso of this postcard remains in the divided-back format and identifies as "Post Card" with a trademark "MK" of the M. Kashower Company printed between the two words; the name and address are printed along the left edge of the postcard.

A postcard type that emerged in the early 1900s and continued to be produced into the 1950s was the real photo. A real photo postcard is not a print; rather, it is a true photograph made from a negative and printed on photo-sensitive paper. Unlike colorful lithographic print postcards, real photos were printed in black and white or sometimes in sepia. In 1906 Eastman Kodak of Rochester, New York, began producing postcard cameras that made a negative the size of a standard postcard. Some cameras had a small door on the back that opened to enable one to scribe a simple caption on the negative with a metal pen. In other instances, postcard photographers who produced real photo post-cards printed captions on cards in studio darkrooms as part of the printing process. Not all real photos, however, are captioned or even attributed to a photographer. Kodak even manufactured small print machines that were not much bigger than the cameras. These devices enabled individual postcard photographers to print from the negative without a studio darkroom. Figure 2.4a is an example of a real photo postcard titled "Business Section, Tijuana, Mex." There is no attribution on the front or back of the postcard, so we cannot know who made or published this card. The verso (fig. 2.4b) of this real photo postcard, however, contains clues to the approximate date of the postcard beyond what can be surmised by the front view, which shows period automobiles, building architec-ture, and male and female dress of the early twentieth century. The style and arrange-ment of words on the back—POST CARD and CORRESPONDENCE ADDRESS—and especially the name on and design of the stamp box—AZO on the border, triangles in the corners and triangles on the bottom pointing down—suggest that the paper used to print the image was manufactured by Eastman Kodak in October 1917.[3] This postcard, therefore, is probably one made in the 1910s, and it reveals a street scene with pedestri-ans in the foreground, a series of storefronts in the background, and early automobiles parked against a boardwalk. The faithful detail rendered in real photo postcards made them especially popular, although they were probably more expensive to purchase than a print postcard. As a consequence, publishers sometimes received permission to convert a photographic postcard to a print version and in other instances simply pirated the real photo to reproduce as a print card (fig. 2.5).

Advances in printing ushered in the linen postcard era between 1930 and 1945. Sev-eral national postcard producers specialized in linen postcards, where color printing techniques created the appearance of linen paper. Linen postcards were brightly colored, unlike any postcards before. The brilliance of this format made for exquisite postcards that featured roadside attractions and business advertising.[4] Small regional printers also produced linen postcards. Figure 2.6 is a large-letter linen postcard titled "Greetings from Tijuana in Old Mexico," manufactured by the Herz Postcard Company in San Diego. The large-letter format was pioneered by the Curt Teich Company of Chicago (discussed below) and featured the name of a location with local landmarks pictured inside the letters. A colorful place name was, in this way, an advertisement for a place, not simply a business.

Chrome postcards are the most recent iteration of the postcard type, and their for-mat mirrors postcards that are still produced today. Chrome is the suffix for photo-chrome, a postcard printing technique started in 1939 by the Union Oil Company of California. Chrome postcards have the appearance of a photograph although, in fact, they are not real photographs; rather, they are print postcards that look like a photo. The

FIGURE 2.4 *a*, "Business Section, Tijuana, Mex.," a real photo postcard circa 1910s. *b*, back of the postcard, illustrating the arrangement of words and stamp box format that enable a dating of the paper used to print the postcard from a photographic negative.

FIGURE 2.5 "Business Section, Tijuana, Mexico," is a white border print postcard made from the real photo postcard—figure 2.4a—above. Print postcard publishers sometimes converted photo postcards to print postcards because the latter were typically less expensive to sell than the average photographic postcard. Published by The Big Curio Store, Lower California Commercial Co., Tijuana, no. 15326. Manufactured by H-H-T Co. (H. H. Tamman Co., Denver, Colorado), 1910s.

technique converts a color photograph to a print format with a glossy exterior. Like its cousin the linen postcard, a chrome postcard could be a powerful advertising medium, although more often it depicted street scenes in towns. Figure 2.7, a chrome postcard of the El Maguey liquor store, one location of the once largest liquor store chain in Baja California, is both a view card and an advertising postcard. The purchase and consumption of alcohol in drinking establishments by American tourists has a long history on the Mexican border dating to Prohibition (1920–1933) and before, and that popularity was reinvigorated for package liquor consumption with post–World War II tourism. The classic neon arrow directing consumers to the store makes for a dazzling nighttime view. On the back of the postcard the caption declares at El Maguey "you will always be greeted by a friend willing to serve you."

The cost to mail a postcard in the United States jumped from one cent to two cents on January 1, 1952, then increased to three cents on August 1, 1958, and climbed to four cents on January 7, 1963. In just over a decade the cost of postage to send a single postcard, what had been commonly called the "penny postcard," quadrupled from what it had been since 1898.

FIGURE 2.6 "Greetings from Tijuana in Old Mexico." Large-letter linen postcard advertising the Baja border town and selected famous landmarks like the Agua Caliente resort and casino and Avenida Revolución, the town's principal tourist strip. Published by Garcia and Gomez, Tijuana, and manufactured by Herz Postcard Company, no. 42433, San Diego California, 1930s.

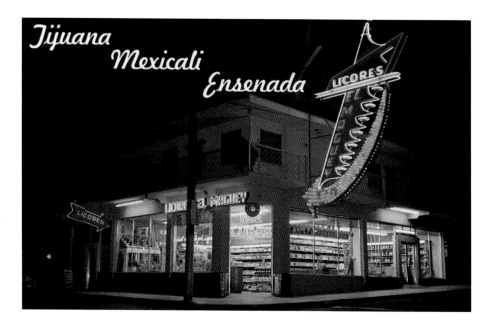

FIGURE 2.7 Licores El Maguey, once the largest chain of liquor stores in Baja California. This is a chrome postcard produced circa 1960s. The caption on the verso is printed in Spanish and English, and the divided-back card has no label designation of "Post Card" or "Postcard." The stamp box is a simple rectangle with the words "Place Stamp Here" inside. By 1963, that stamp cost four times what it cost sixty-five years earlier when the penny postcard was inaugurated.

PHOTO POSTCARDS OF THE BAJA BORDER TOWNS

As discussed above, real photo postcards are actual photographs printed from negatives on photographic paper. The process of making photo postcards has been described in detail in previous works and will not be repeated here.[5] This section discusses the numbers of real photo postcards produced for the Baja border towns, the range of known photographers who created the photo cards, and the publishers and companies who specialized in photographic postcards for Tijuana, Mexicali, Tecate, and Algodones.

Table 2.1 lists postcards held in the Arreola Collection by type of postcard—real photo, print, and chrome—and by Baja border town. For the purposes of the present discussion, it should be noted that real photo postcards were produced for each of the Baja border towns and in total represent 41 percent of all postcards in this collection. In fact, this format of postcard far surpasses in frequency the print postcard type in every Baja border town except Tijuana, although even here, real photo postcards are a significant percentage of all postcards in the collection for this town—nearly one-third. To better assess why real photo postcards were popular in the Baja border towns, we need to know who produced the postcards and where they were printed.

Table 2.2 lists the known Baja photo postcard photographers and publishing companies by border town for the period of study. Both Tijuana and Mexicali count nearly equivalent numbers of photographers and companies, nine and twelve respectively. Tecate shows two and Algodones one. The majority of the photo postcard photographers appear to be individuals rather than large companies because real photo postcard production was typically an individual enterprise.[6]

Individual real photo postcard photographers who operated their own businesses were either studio professionals, in which case photo postcards may have been a supplement to their normal studio portrait photography, or itinerant entrepreneurs, who engaged the opportunity in hopes of maximizing profit from the popularity of photo postcards. In the former instance, studio photographers would often title the photographs and give their names (fig. 2.8). In the latter instance, itinerant photographers might not have bothered to give their names, and sometimes even studio photographers failed to identify the images.

TABLE 2.1 Postcards by type and by town

Type	Tijuana	Mexicali	Tecate	Algodones	Total
Real Photo	270	243	46	9	568
Print	405	86	1	4	496
Chrome	195	100	34	1	330
Total	870	429	81	14	1,394

Source: Arreola Collection.

TABLE 2.2 Baja border-town photo postcard photographers and companies

Photographer/company (location)	Tijuana	Mexicali	Tecate	Algodones
Actual Photo Company (La Jolla and West Germany)	X			
Barrios Fot.		X		
Calexico Chronicle		X		
Casa Carrillo	X			
C. E. Castillo Fot.	X			
Electric Photo Company (San Diego)	X			
Frashers Fotos (Pomona)		X		
GEB	X			
Hippodrome Studio (San Diego)	X			
Hixson Photo (Calexico)		X		
Iris Studio		X		
K. Ogane		X		
La Compañía México Fotográfico (MF) (Mexico City)	X	X	X	
Magruder (San Diego)	X			
Mariano Ma				X
R. Castillo Foto (Calexico)		X		
R./N.		X		
Sholin		X		
Silvestre (Tijuana)	X			
Tito Foto.			X	
Venus Foto. (Mexicali)		X		
Zuckerman Bros. (Calexico)		X		

Source: Arreola Collection.

In addition to conventional real photo postcards as exhibited above, businesses might hire a local photographer to produce a photo postcard. Figure 2.9 is one in a series of photo postcards of Algodones in the Arreola Collection that spotlight Mariano Ma's Oasis Café. In this custom photo postcard, the photograph of the establishment is set within a designed border, which features dancing figures and symbols in the corners to frame the image. Standing on the left of the entrance to the café is the Chinese proprietor, Mariano Ma.

Beyond known or recognized postcard photographers, there were instances when a studio photographer might make photographs in a Baja California border town yet never publish a postcard from the image. Nevertheless, other publishers or postcard companies might acquire or avail themselves of the studio photographers' work and publish their images as photo postcards without attribution. Research conducted in photographic archives in San Diego led to the discovery of at least two established studio photographers whose photographs were used to make photo postcards of Tijuana. Walter Elton Averret operated a studio in San Diego in the 1910s–1920s, and one of his early photographs of a bandstand in the celebration plaza at the Tijuana Fair in 1918 was used to make a photo

FIGURE 2.8 Solar eclipse at Tijuana, September 10, 1923. This real photo postcard was made by photographer C. E. Castillo, who identifies himself in the photograph just to the left of "Beer Hall." The view is looking north, probably from a balcony or rooftop, along Main Street (Avenida Revolución), Tijuana's principal tourist strip during Prohibition. The Beer Hall across the street is the first incarnation of the Mexicali Beer Hall, and north of it is the St. Francis Hotel.

FIGURE 2.9 Mariano Ma, Oasis Café, Algodones, 1940s. This custom-designed photo post-card by an unknown photographer was probably published by the proprietor, Mariano Ma, to advertise his establishment.

postcard (see fig. 3.3). A second set of Averret photographs of the exterior and interior of Tijuana's Moulin Rouge taken in 1929 were the basis for a print multiview postcard of this famous cabaret (see fig. 7.15). Guy Sidney Sensor was another San Diego photographer who operated a studio in the city during the 1920s–1940s and who also made photographs of locations in Tijuana. At least three Sensor photographs appeared as photo postcards without attribution. Circa 1928, he made a photo of Avenida "A" (later Revolución) that became the basis for a popular print postcard featuring the Mexicali Beer Hall, a postcard in the Arreola Collection published by Western Novelty of Los Angeles. A second photograph of the Hotel Comercial on Avenida Revolución made by Sensor in 1935 became the image used by publishers to issue print and photographic postcards of the famous hotel, several of which are also in the Arreola Collection. A third Sensor photograph of the Jai Alai Palace with a "woody" station wagon parked at curbside was used to publish a photo postcard of the scene in the 1950s (see fig. 8.37).[7]

Another instance of a known photographer whose images were used by postcard publishers was that of Kingo Nonaka, a Japanese immigrant to Tijuana in the early 1920s. Nonaka was a prolific photographer of interior and exterior scenes in Tijuana from the 1920s to the 1940s.[8] One of his images, a panorama of Tijuana in 1924, was published as a print postcard by the Big Curio Store (see fig. 3.14).

Roy Warfield Magruder

In the first decades of the twentieth century, when tourists began to flock to Tijuana from Southern California, one enterprising photographer capitalized on the presence of border-town visitors. Roy W. Magruder created the staged real photographic postcard image of tourists dressed in serapes, sombreros, and holding pistols and rifles to mimic rebels, an iconic stereotype that was perpetuated during the period of the Mexican Revolution. A native of West Virginia, Magruder lived in Maryland, Florida, and Colorado before settling in San Diego in 1913.

Magruder formed the Compañía Fotográfica de Tijuana in 1914 to take advantage of the tourist flow into the Mexican border town.[9] His small studio was proximate to the border crossing on the Mexican side of the boundary, and his slogan became "Hacemos Retrates Mientras Ud. Espera" (We Have Costumes While You Wait). A sign on the studio exterior read "Photos Finished While You Wait." Figure 2.10 is a Magruder real photo postcard of tourists dressed in sombreros and holding a banner seated in a Model T Ford in front of his studio on the borderline. Magruder arranged with the vehicle's local owner to utilize the car as a stage prop. Over the course of a decade, Magruder made hundreds of real photo postcards of tourists crossing the border into Tijuana. By 1915 he was so well recognized as a tourist photographer that he became known by the slogan "Magruder Did It" (fig. 2.11).

FIGURE 2.10 Magruder's Compañía Fotográfica de Tijuana, located on the Mexican side of the border crossing from San Diego, became a popular location to have a staged photograph snapped and processed as a postcard while you waited. Roy W. Magruder, 1910s.

FIGURE 2.11 "Auto bridge across the Tijuana River, 1915, Tijuana, Mexico." Magruder produced so many real photo postcards of the tourist crossing that he became known by the slogan, visible in this postcard, "Magruder Did It." Roy W. Magruder, 1915.

FIGURE 2.12 Tourist group sans costumes in front of Magruder's Photo Shop next door to the Big Curio Store in downtown Tijuana. In front of Magruder's are panels holding sale samples of his real photo postcards. On the verso of some of his postcards, Magruder had ink stamped "Duplicates of this Photo can be had by sending 15c and mentioning Negative Number to—ROY W. MAGRUDER, SAN DIEGO, CAL." Roy W. Magruder, 1910s.

The Arreola Collection includes twenty-five real photo postcards signed by or attributed to Roy Magruder. Although he gained fame for his early tourist snapshot postcards, Magruder obtained contracts to photograph Tijuana's horse racetrack and Monte Carlo Casino situated between the border crossing and the Tijuana River. In town, Magruder set up a studio next door to the Big Curio Store, where he again staged tourists and made photo postcards of them while they waited (fig. 2.12). When Antonio Elosúa Farías launched the Tijuana Fair to complement the Panama-California Exposition in San Diego in 1915, Magruder made photo postcards of the Tijuana event to sell to tourists.

Magruder's photographic mainstay, nevertheless, was his staged postcard views of tourist groups at the borderline. Circa 1921, Mexican topographic engineers discovered that the actual international boundary line passed directly through Magruder's studio shack at the border crossing. Because his stage set for photo postcards was now altered by the true boundary line, and because this made it impossible to take photographs with tourists posed in front of the actual border monument, Magruder went so far as to make a life-size replica of the U.S.-Mexico border monument and placed it near his relocated studio so it could act as a backdrop to his tourist photo postcards (fig. 2.13).

FIGURE 2.13 Tourist photo postcard at the borderline of Tijuana showing a group outfitted in serapes, sombreros, and pistols. The monument at the right rear of the photo is the replica border marker Magruder had constructed at his studio when he was forced to shift his building away from the crossing. Roy W. Magruder, 1921.

Although Magruder ceased making photo postcards in the mid-1920s, the borderline location continued to be used by other photo postcard photographers. By the 1930s, as the tourist wave to Tijuana began to ebb with the onset of the Great Depression, Magruder retired from the photographic postcard business and became a chauffeur for a tourist taxi service between San Diego and Tijuana. Roy Magruder died in San Diego in 1948. His legacy to the early photographic history of Tijuana remains substantial. Historian Pablo Guadiana Lozano—who has studied the André Williams Collection, one of the largest private collections of Tijuana postcards—determined that Magruder real photo postcards account for an important percentage of all postcards in the collection.[10]

Rafael Castillo

The explosive growth of Mexicali in the first two decades of the twentieth century created a demand for local photographers to capture images of the emerging border town and the regional agricultural economy it helped support. By the time of Prohibition in 1920, even greater numbers of postcard photographers, both individuals and large publishing companies, flooded into Mexicali to write the town's history with cameras. José Rafael

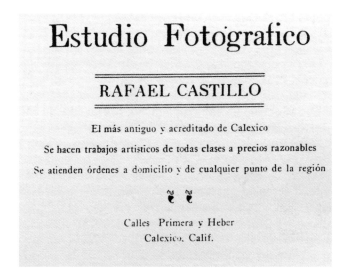

FIGURE 2.14 Rafael Castillo studio. Castillo declared his photography business the oldest accredited studio in Calexico, offering domestic photography (portraiture) and regional views. Author's collection.

Federico Castillo was one of these individual photographers who specialized in real photo postcard views.[11]

Castillo was born in Todos Santos, Baja California Sur, in 1865. He was listed in 1908 as a photographer in La Paz, where he was a prominent businessman and politician. Some of Castillo's photographs of Baja California Sur were published in a 1905 issue of *Sunset* magazine. In 1914 Castillo immigrated to Southern California, leaving La Paz possibly for political reasons stemming from the Mexican Revolution. According to city directories, by 1916 Castillo and his family lived in Los Angeles. Rafael Castillo relocated to Calexico, California, across the border from Mexicali in 1917, where he listed his profession as photographer. That Castillo remained connected to Los Angeles where his family lived and yet operated a business in Calexico was not improbable because of railroad service and automobile accessibility between the coastal city and the desert border town.

In Calexico Castillo established himself as a local photographer who serviced the area through his studio (fig. 2.14). Castillo was hired by the city of Mexicali in 1918 to make photographs of improvements to the municipality. Circa 1920 Castillo's son Rafael Jr. joined his father's photography business. According to stories in the Calexico newspapers, Rafael Sr. regularly visited with family in Los Angeles while maintaining his photography business in Calexico.

The Arreola Collection includes sixteen real photo postcards signed by Rafael Castillo. Views include multiple subjects from street scenes to prominent public and private buildings and landmark spaces such as the city park plaza and train station (see fig. 1.14). With the

FIGURE 2.15 Southern Club, Mexicali, Baja California, a real photo postcard produced by Rafael Castillo, who operated a photographic studio in Calexico, California, and became an early photo postcard photographer of Mexicali views. Rafael Castillo Foto., no. 21, 1920s.

onset of Prohibition, Castillo became known for his exterior and interior views of famous clubs such as the Owl and the Southern Club (fig. 2.15). Castillo was a technically sophisticated photographer who mastered both composition and light to create high-quality photo postcards. Every one of Castillo's photo postcards is identified on the verso in sepia-colored lettering as "Tarjeta Postal" and "Printed in Germany." This was unusual because the German print postcard industry largely collapsed following World War I. However, it is possible that Castillo shipped his negatives to Germany via Mexico to take advantage of the superior photographic print services still available there to non-American customers.

Rafael Castillo practiced another photographer skill by copyrighting his photo postcards. At the lower left of every Castillo postcard is scribed "Propiedad registrada Rafael Castillo, Foto." An inventory number is usually given above the declaration (fig. 2.16). This was not typical of most real photo postcard photographers, although some of the best known on the border, such as Robert Runyon and Walter H. Horne, frequently marked their photo postcards with a copyright trademark.[12] Castillo's practice was, of course, a desire to thwart the photo piracy that was common during the heyday of postcard publishing. Nevertheless, the best intentions were often for naught. Several years after Castillo ceased publishing photo postcards, many, including examples from the Arreola Collection, were copied and reproduced as less expensive print postcards (fig. 2.17).

FIGURE 2.16 The Owl bar, Mexicali. Rafael Castillo copyrighted and numbered his real photo postcards as shown at the lower left of this view. Rafael Castillo, Foto., no. 24, 1920s.

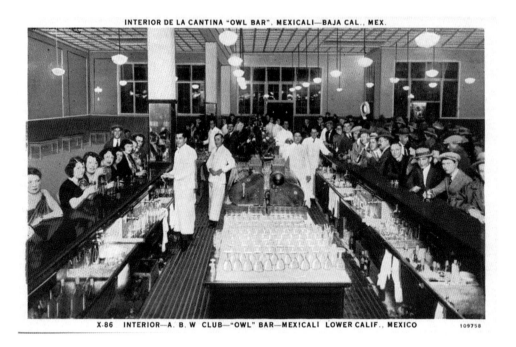

FIGURE 2.17 "Interior de la Cantina 'Owl Bar,' Mexicali, Baja Cal., Mexico," a white border print postcard copy of Rafael Castillo's 1920s real photo postcard shown above as figure 2.16. Piracy and unauthorized borrowing of postcard images was a common practice in the early twentieth century. Western Publishing and Novelty, Co., Los Angeles, CA. Manufactured by Curt Teich Company, no. 109758, Chicago, IL, 1925.

In 1937 Rafael Castillo closed his studio in Calexico, his son Rafael Jr. changed pro-
fessions, and Rafael Sr. moved back to Los Angeles, where he died February 19, 1944. A
critical part of his legacy remains his photographic postcards of Mexicali, at least twenty-
four (if his number system is an accurate accounting) but probably many more. Those
views help tell the story of Mexicali during the 1920s.

La Compañía México Fotográfico

The most prolific producer of real photo postcards for the Baja California border towns
was La Compañía México Fotográfico, founded in 1925 by Demetrio Sánchez Ortega.[13]
México Fotográfico was organized and established as a company in Mexico City to produce and market photographic postcard views of the entire republic. The company's
products are recognized by the distinctive trademark "MF" printed on all of its postcards,
which initially were exclusively real photos.

México Fotográfico became a national enterprise by contracting independent photographers or agents from towns all across the country. The company created business
agreements with regional photographers to send their negatives to México Fotográfico
central offices in the capital, where the images would be selected, printed on postcard
stock, labeled, numbered according to the MF inventory system, and then returned to the
photographer's locale to be sold to various retail outlets. México Fotográfico advertised to
potential photographers using its postcards, and the company assisted in practical training of novice photographers via mailed materials and camera and film sales (fig. 2.18).

México Fotográfico emerged as the most successful vendor of Mexico postcards in the
country between the late 1920s and the 1950s. The Arreola Collection includes 275 MF real
photo postcards for the Baja California border towns of Mexicali (142), Tijuana (117), and
Tecate (16). That total represents 49 percent of all the real photo postcards in the collection
for those towns (table 2.1). Because México Fotográfico depended on local photographers
as agents to provide the company with materials to make into postcards, the photographic
quality sometimes varied, especially in the early years of production. In some towns, such
as Mexicali or Tijuana, there might be more than one photographer agent contracted with
México Fotográfico. As photographers began to excel at their craft and printing techniques improved, the general quality of imagery also advanced (fig. 2.19). During the 1940s
the company began to issue hand-tinted photographic postcards for selected subjects and
locations (fig. 2.20). Another feature of México Fotográfico real photo postcards was the
rounded corner of many of its postcards produced in the 1950s, a distinction unique to the
company among postcard manufacturers and, perhaps, in keeping with the streamlining
that became fashionable in architecture and product design in the post–World War II era
(fig. 2.21). Sometime in the 1960s the company discontinued its production of real photo
postcards as it transitioned to the manufacture of chrome postcards (discussed below).

FIGURE 2.18 Advertising postcard issued by México Fotográfico to advise potential local photographers all across Mexico that the company would assist them in converting their negatives to photographic postcards. The company also sold cameras and film to its photographer clients. México Fotográfico, 1920s.

FIGURE 2.19 Calle Morelos, Mexicali, Baja California. This real photo postcard of a commercial street in Mexicali demonstrates how local photographer agents contracted with México Fotográfico began to improve the quality of their photographic composition. The Mueblería Monterrey, a modern furniture store in streamline architectural style at the center of the image, advertises its many products and advises shoppers that their credit is good. México Fotográfico 103, 1950s.

FIGURE 2.20 New Gambrinus Café, Mexicali, Baja California. An example of the hand-tinted real photo postcards that were produced by México Fotográfico starting in the 1940s. Deckled-edge, the jagged tear suggesting a handcrafted appearance, was popular with some postcard manufacturers from the 1930s to the 1950s. México Fotográfico 23, 1940s.

FIGURE 2.21 Boulevard [Lázaro] Cárdenas, Tecate, Baja California. An example of the rounded-corner real photo postcards that were a hallmark of México Fotográfico during the 1950s. The road in this view leads uphill from the main commercial street to the international border crossing at Tecate, California. Tecate, Mexico, was a tidy and modern small town during this period, evident in the neatly landscaped median, paved street and side-walks, and modern street lighting. México Fotográfico 25, 1950s.

PRINT POSTCARDS OF THE BAJA BORDER TOWNS

Print postcards as compared to real photo postcards are not actual photographs. Instead, they are mechanical conversions from original photographs. The process of making print postcards has been described in detail in a previous volume and will not be repeated here.[14] This section discusses the numbers of print postcards produced for the Baja border towns and the range of known publishers and companies who created the postcards chiefly for Tijuana and Mexicali.

Table 2.1 shows that print postcards in the Arreola Collection exist for every Baja border town (although very few for Tecate and Algodones) and in total represent thirty-six percent of all the postcards in the Baja California border collection. Nevertheless, the table also points out how print postcard production was much more common for Tijuana, where it accounts for eight of every ten Baja border town print postcards in the collection. Tijuana, as will be discussed below, was popular in a way that may have been unique on the Mexican border. That circumstance made print postcard production for the town extraordinary for publishing and print companies in California that capitalized on the visitor experience to Tijuana.

Table 2.3 lists print publishers and manufacturers of Baja border-town postcards in the Arreola Collection. Thirty-three of the forty-six publishers-manufacturers were companies located in California or Mexico, with the greatest numbers in the cities of Los Angeles and Tijuana. A publisher (company) might be an individual retailer such as a curio store or a drug store proprietor who has a photograph taken and then contracts with a printer-manufacturer to produce the print postcard. The finished product is then returned to the retailer, who is responsible for sales. On some print postcards the verso of the card might identify both the publisher—the retail business or company—as well as the manufacturer—the printer (see fig. 2.2). In other cases, the back might only show the name of the publisher without specific reference to the printer-manufacturer. In still other instances, a publishing company might be both the publisher and the printer-manufacturer, or simply the publisher who also contracts with an unidentified printer-manufacturer to produce the postcard. These various combinations of publishing and production are illustrated in the examples below.

SELECTED PRINT POSTCARD
PUBLISHERS-PRINTERS-MANUFACTURERS

Biographical details about individual postcard publishers or companies are scarce. Whereas several postcard clubs have useful websites that contain information about many well-known postcard producers, with few exceptions little is known about Mexican

TABLE 2.3 Baja border-town print postcard publishers and manufacturers

Company (location)	Tijuana	Mexicali	Tecate	Algodones
Adolph Selige (St. Louis, Leipzig, Halberstadt)	X			
Agua Caliente Co. (Tijuana)	X			
Albertype Co. (Brooklyn)	X	X	X	
Auburn Post Card Co. (Auburn, IN)		X		
Benham Co. (Los Angeles)		X		
Big Curio Store (Tijuana)	X			
B. and Co. (Bamforth & Co.) (New York)	X			
Cavalcade News (Calexico)		X		
Curt Teich (Chicago)	X	X		
Detroit Publishing Co. (Chicago)	X			
E. C. Kropp (Milwaukee)	X			
Edward H. Mitchell (San Francisco)	X			
Elmo M. Sellers (Los Angeles)	X			
Eno (San Diego)	X			
Eno & Matteson (San Diego)	X			
Enrique Martínez (Tijuana)	X			
E. Silvestre (Barcelona Comercial) (Tijuana)	X			
Exportador e Importadora, S. A. (Mexico)	X			
Fischgrund (Mexico City)	X			
Garcia and Gomez (Tijuana)	X			
Garita Alemon (Tijuana)	X			
Herz Post Cards (San Diego)	X			
Hester, Frye & Smith (San Diego)	X			
H-H-T Co. (H. H. Tammen Co.) (Denver)	X			
H. L. Christiance (San Diego)	X			
Hopkins News Agency (San Diego)	X			
Imprenta Nacional (Mexicali)		X		
J. C. Packard (San Diego)	X			
Lower California Commercial Co. (Tijuana)	X	X		
MCM Baja California (Tijuana)	X	X		
Metropolitan (Everett, MA)	X			
Mexican Curio Store (Tijuana)	X			
México Fotográfico (Mexico City)	X			
M. Kashower (Los Angeles)	X	X		
M. Rieder (Los Angeles)	X	X		
Nationwide Post Card Co. (Arlington, TX)		X		
Neuner Corporation (Los Angeles)	X			
Newman Post Card Co. (Los Angeles)	X			
Pacific Novelty (Los Angeles & San Francisco)	X	X		
Photo SUB-POST Card Co. (Los Angeles)	X			
Seabury & Co. (Los Angeles)	X			
Spaulding's Indian Craft Store (Yuma, AZ)				X
Talleres Graficos de Tijuana (Tijuana)	X			
Western Publishing & Novelty (Los Angeles)	X	X		
White Cross Drug Store (Calexico)		X		
Woods (Unknown)		X		

Source: Arreola Collection.

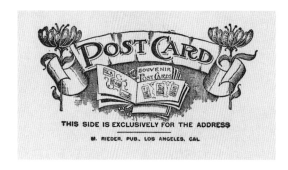

FIGURE 2.22 M. Rieder, decorative colophon. A print postcard publisher of Mexicali and Tijuana border-town views, Rieder sometimes used this decorative colophon on the verso of his undivided-back postcards in the early 1900s.

postcard publishers, particularly those who produced postcards of Baja California border towns.[15]

One of the earliest publisher-printers of Baja border-town print postcards was Michael Rieder of Los Angeles. Born in Philadelphia in 1868 of German immigrant parents, in 1890 Rieder moved to Los Angeles, where his occupation was listed in city directories as salesman. In 1896 Rieder owned a wholesale stationery business in the city, and in the 1910 census he is listed as a publisher in the specialties industry. From 1901 to 1915, Rieder published postcards under the name "M. Rieder" (fig. 2.22).

Rieder published view postcards of the western United States, Native Americans, and Mexico, and all postcards were printed in Germany. An example of a Rieder print postcard is reproduced previously in figure 1.8. After 1915, Rieder stopped publishing postcards. In 1920 he listed his occupation as investments and by 1940 as a real estate insurance agent. Rieder died in Los Angeles, June 24, 1949.[16]

Figure 2.23 is an example of a print postcard published for Enrique Silvestre, a proprietor of a curio store in Tijuana that was operated by his company Barcelona Comercial. This postcard is a white border card from the 1920s printed by M. Kashower of Los Angeles, a manufacturer of some eighty Tijuana print postcards in the Arreola Collection (some contracted with individual publishers like Silvestre, others published exclusively by the Kashower Company). Figure 2.24 is the photographic proof possibly taken by Silvestre and used by M. Kashower to make the print postcard that is figure 2.23. Comparison of the two images illustrates how print postcard manufacturers modified the original black-and-white photograph to convert it to a colorized print postcard. In this instance, Kashower graphic artists expanded the view on the left side and shortened the view on the right side of the original photograph. Further, pedestrians and some autos have been added to the postcard that were not part of the original photo; the light standard in the street, telephone poles in the right background, and details along the roofline in the middle ground have been generalized or eliminated.

In some cases, a postcard publisher might contract with a printer-manufacturer and request that the name of the latter be eliminated from the back of the postcard. Figure 2.25 is a linen postcard published for the Big Curio Store in Tijuana. On the verso of this multiview postcard is the information about the publisher and the declaration "Tarjeta Postal," yet in the stamp box it states "Made in U. S. A." The clue to the printer-manufacturer is on the front lower right where the code "5A-H1120" signals that, in fact, the card was printed by Curt Teich of Chicago. The number and letter code is noted on

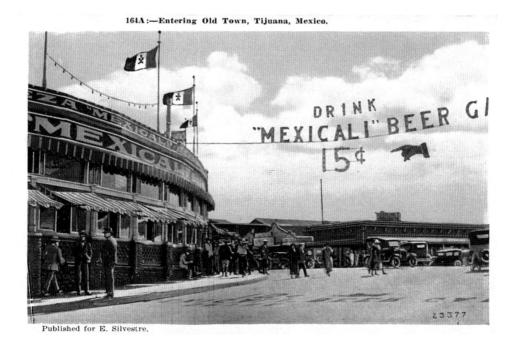

Published for E. Silvestre.

FIGURE 2.23 Old Town, Tijuana, Calle 1 and Avenida Revolución. A white border print postcard published for E. Silvestre of Tijuana by M. Kashower of Los Angeles. M. Kashower, no. 23377, 1920s.

FIGURE 2.24 Photo proof print (not a postcard) "Entrance to Tia Juana, Mexico," 1920s. The photograph was used to manufacture figure 2.23. The photograph, possibly taken by Enrique Silvestre, includes features eliminated by the graphic artists who converted it to a color print postcard. Author's collection.

FIGURE 2.25 "'La Internacional' Tijuana Mexico." A multiview linen postcard published for the Big Curio Store, Lower California Commercial Co., Inc. Tijuana, Lower California, Mexico. This postcard was manufactured by Curt Teich Company, 5A-H1120, Chicago, IL, 1935.

Curt Teich production sheets for Tijuana and records that this postcard, "La Internacional," was part of Teich's Art-Colortone series. Twelve thousand, five hundred copies were ordered by a Mexican publisher on June 7, 1935.[17]

Not all print postcards were colorized from a black-and-white photograph; some publisher-printers preferred black-and-white print. Figure 2.26 is a print postcard of a commercial street in Mexicali published by Pacific Novelty Company, whose trademark emblem was a bear (symbolic of California) on rays of sun highlighted by a banner with the letters P. N. C. Pacific Novelty operated out of San Francisco and Los Angeles between 1908 and the 1960s. The postcard subjects were typically California views and often, as presented here, were printed in halftone, a process where the print based on a photograph simulates a continuous surface through the use of dots and spaces. Many early postcards published by Pacific Novelty were printed in Germany.[18]

Curt Teich Company

Curt Teich worked as a lithographer in Lobenstein, Germany, a spa town in Thuringia near the present-day Czech border. Not coincidentally, Lobenstein means "praise the stone," a fitting connection to a man whose profession, lithography, means to write or draw on stone. Lithography, invented by Alois Senefelder in Bavaria in 1796, is a process

FIGURE 2.26 Halftone print postcard. A busy commercial street in Mexicali during the 1920s is shown. Published by Pacific Novelty Company, no. 4751, San Francisco and Los Angeles, CA, 1920s.

using an oil- or wax-based medium and water to create a repelling effect on paper pressed between two stones. Advances in this method in the nineteenth century led to multicolor printing called chromolithography.

In 1895 Curt Teich immigrated to Chicago and started a printing business for newspapers and magazines. Although he was an early publisher of postcards, according to Alan Petrulis of the Metropolitan Postcard Club, Teich did not start printing postcards until 1908. Many early cards were labeled "C. T. Photochrom." "In response to a loss of business" brought on by the Great Depression, says Jeffrey Meikle in his book about Curt Teich and postcards in America, "he personally traveled across the United States and on a junket to Mexico, Panama, Cuba, and the Caribbean to solicit orders." Between 1931 and 1950, the Curt Teich Company produced some forty-five thousand unique postcard views in multiple colors on card stock that had the appearance of linen.[19] Curt Teich's most well-known innovation was a printing process that manufactured high intensity, quality color postcards trademarked as "C. T. Art-Colortone." This development, which Teich applied to many types of printing, propelled the Curt Teich Post Card Company to commercial success because it created an economically feasible means of quality color reproduction ahead of color photography.

The Curt Teich Company was a prodigious publisher of Baja California border-town postcards. Between 1913 and 1950, Curt Teich published 206 postcards of Tijuana and 11 postcards of Mexicali. Figure 2.27 is an example of an early Curt Teich white border

INTERNATIONAL LINE, LOOKING TOWARDS MEXICALI, MEXICO, FROM CALEXICO, CALIFORNIA. 104978

FIGURE 2.27 "International line, looking towards Mexicali, Mexico, from Calexico, California." This nighttime postcard view was probably made from a daytime photograph and converted to a moody night scene by commercial artists. Published by Woolworth, manufactured and printed by Curt Teich Company, C. T. American Art, 104978, Chicago, IL, 1925.

FIGURE 2.28 Curt Teich production page. One of nine for Tijuana, this shows the title (subject) of a postcard, the number of postcards ordered, the coded identification number for the postcard, the company or publisher who placed the order, the style of the postcard, and the date the order was placed. Curt Teich Company Geographic Index (website).

postcard showing the international boundary at night looking toward Mexicali from Calexico. Print postcards of the night were typically printed from a daytime photograph in which commercial artists create the mood of night with a moon in the sky and automobile lights accentuated. The original photograph for this postcard was probably a daytime scene because the American flag in particular could not be flown at night unless it was spotlight illuminated; this technicality was often missed by graphic artists who converted photographs to a print postcards.[20]

The Newberry Library in Chicago is the principal repository of the Curt Teich Postcard Archives. The core collection consists of 360,000 images produced by the company from 1898 to 1978 and includes 110,000 production files documenting the manufacture of Teich postcards and additional company records.[21] Within this archive is the company's Geographic Index, a digital inventory of Curt Teich postcard production that lists towns and production numbers for postcards. Through this inventory, one can determine the total universe of postcards produced for a single place by the Curt Teich Company. Figure 2.28 is an example of an inventory page for Tijuana postcard production (there are nine such pages in the Tijuana index). In the left column in handwritten script are the "Name of Subject," or postcard titles along with order size for each item. Curt Teich typically sold postcards in lots of 6,000, 12,500, and 25,000. The next column to the right on the production sheet is the identification "Number" assigned to a postcard. The letter and number system is a code sequence that enables one to key the year the postcard was printed. Next is a column titled "Ordered By," with the company or publisher who ordered the postcard followed by another column that indicates the postcard "Style," such as Art-Colortone. Finally, the last column on the right shows the "Date" of each postcard order. To take a single example, look at the title of the postcard third from the bottom of this inventory, "The Spa Hotel Agua Caliente." The notation next to the title is 12.5 meaning 12,500 of this postcard were ordered. Next is the identification number 5A-H1112, which designates that this card was printed in 1935.[22] The next three columns tell that the postcard was ordered by Western Publishing and Novelty Co., a Los Angeles publisher of print postcards (see table 2.3), in Art-Colortone (full-color linen) style on June 7, 1935. Figure 2.29 is this very same postcard.

CHROME POSTCARDS OF THE BAJA BORDER TOWNS

Chrome postcards, like print postcards, are not actual photographs but are conversions from original photographs. A chrome postcard, although it looks like a photograph, is actually a print and not a true photo.[23] Chrome postcards became popular in the United States during the late 1930s when the Union Oil Company of California initiated a line

THE SPA, HOTEL AGUA CALIENTE, TIJUANA, MEXICO

FIGURE 2.29 "The Spa, Hotel Agua Caliente, Tijuana, Mexico." A Curt Teich linen postcard ordered by Western Publishing and Novelty Co., Los Angeles. Printed by Curt Teich Company, C. T. Art-Colortone, 5A-H1112, Chicago, IL, 1935.

of this type of print postcard. The format continued to be produced in the 1940s through the 1950s, and today chromes are the dominant style of modern postcards. Because they were as popular for the Baja border as they were all across Mexico and the United States into the 1960s, they will be used to illustrate aspects of the Baja border towns. This section discusses the numbers of chrome postcards produced for the Baja border towns and the range of known publishers and companies who created the postcards for Tijuana, Mexicali, and Tecate.

Table 2.1 shows that chrome postcards in the Arreola Collection exist for every Baja border town and in total represent 24 percent of all the postcards in the Baja California border collection. Nevertheless, the table also points out how chrome postcard production was minimal for Algodones, moderate for Tijuana and Mexicali, yet much more popular for Tecate, where it accounts for 42 percent of all the postcards for this town in the Arreola Collection.

Table 2.4 lists chrome photographers and publishers of Baja border-town postcards in the Arreola Collection. Twenty photographers-publishers are identified from the chrome postcards in the collection. A nearly equal number of these individuals-companies were located in Mexico as in California, with only a few outside of the region. Most of the Mexico and California producers of chrome postcards for the Baja border towns were small,

TABLE 2.4 Baja border-town chrome postcard photographers and publishers

Photographer*/Publisher (location)	Tijuana	Mexicali	Tecate	Algodones
A. A. de Martinez (Tijuana)	X			
A. M. Bernal (Tijuana)	X			
Ames Color (Escondido, CA)	X		X	
Ammex Asociados, S. A. (México, D.F.)	X			
Arte y Publicidad (Ensenada)	X	X	X	X
Asin Importer (Tijuana and Ensenada)	X			
Colourpicture (Boston)	X	X		
Columbia Wholesale Supply (Hollywood, CA)		X		
Crisban* (Tijuana)	X			
Curt Teich Color (Chicago)	X			
Enrique A. De Frias* (San Ysidro, CA)	X			
Enrique Asín* (Tijuana)	X			
Enrique Martinez (Tijuana)	X			
Hermilo Pérez* (Ensenada)	X	X		X
H. S. Crocker Co. (San Francisco)	X	X		
Kipi & Mark Turok* (Ensenada)	X			
Larry Holland (El Centro, CA)		X		
Louis & Virginia Kay* (North Hollywood, CA)		X		
Marconi Service (Framingham, MA)		X		
Max Mahan* (Hollywood, CA)		X		
México Fotográfico Fotocolor (México, D.F.)	X	X	X	
Mike Roberts* (Berkeley, CA)	X			
Papalera Internacional (Mexicali)		X		
Road Runner Card Co. (San Diego)	X			
R. W. Ames* (Escondido, CA)	X			
Thompson Photo Service (San Diego)	X			
V. Raul Corral (Mexicali)		X		
Western Publishing & Novelty Co. (Los Angeles)	X			

Source: Arreola Collection.

independent operators (fig. 2.30). This section explores two chrome postcard photographers and publishers for which historical information exists: Mike Roberts of Berkeley, California, and Mexfotocolor, the chrome production format for postcards published by México Fotográfico of Mexico City.

Mike Roberts

There were more than a handful of chrome postcard photographers who worked in the Baja border towns (table 2.4), but none was more important to chrome postcard photography than Mike Roberts. Roberts is said to have been the first printer-publisher of photochrome postcards utilizing the new Kodachrome color film introduced by the Eastman

FIGURE 2.30 Chrome postcard showing Avenida Revolución—where nightclubs and curio stores abound—published by independent postcard photographer Mark Turok, who pioneered *"la tarjeta postal en color"* (the color postcard) in Mexico. Foto. Mark Turok, 1956. Turok, "Mark Turok y la postal de los 50."

Kodak Company in 1936. A self-taught pioneer in the development of color photography and printing, Mike Roberts was known as "America's Postcard King."[24]

Mike Roberts was born Charles Elmore Roberts on a farm near Gallatin, Missouri, in 1905. According to his son Bob Roberts, who published his story, Mike Roberts left home in 1921 at age sixteen with thirty-five dollars and a box camera and headed west on his Harley-Davidson motorcycle. In San Bernardino, California, Roberts worked in a local photo studio from 1922 to 1925 before traveling the country to do freelance photography and then opening his own business, Roberts Photo Shop, in 1928, which did not survive the Great Depression. In 1930 he married and changed his name to Mike Roberts. He moved to Oakland, California, in 1933 and became a photographer who traveled the country making pictures for *Caterpillar Magazine*. With his brother Roberts opened Camera Corner in downtown Oakland in 1936 modeled after his Roberts Photo Shop. Roberts shot photographs of the 1939 World's Fair in San Francisco for the *Saturday Evening Post, Fortune*, and *Collier's* magazines. Into the 1940s Roberts, along with Ansel Adams, worked photographing roadside attractions on the "See Your West" promotion for Standard Oil Company. The company printed and distributed scenic photographs to its customers who purchased automobile gasoline at its Standard Oil service stations. The idea was for a customer to accumulate photographs in an album and then become motivated to visit the places in the family car, thereby purchasing more Standard Oil gasoline. Roberts made about eighteen photographs for the oil company but then decided to make postcards of the many others not purchased by Standard Oil.[25]

In the 1950s Mike Roberts started producing chrome postcards using Kodachrome color film, and that association was part of the logo he stamped on the back of his postcards.[26] Roberts's first Baja border-town postcards, published under the company Color Card, included his trademark, a stylized outline figure pointing a camera that resembled an R for Roberts (fig. 2.31*a*). Postcards of this early era were identified as Mike Roberts Color Productions, Berkeley, California. The Color Card logo evolved to become the R in Mike Roberts when he began to publish the postcards with his own name in the script of the trademark (fig. 2.31*b*). In this period Roberts used several different distribution companies for his Baja border postcards, including Asin Importer, Ensenada, and Sparkletone Photo Services in San Diego. Several postcard photographers such as Enrique A. De Frias of San Ysidro, California, freely borrowed Robert's logo and adapted it to their own postcard products of Tijuana (fig. 2.31*c*).

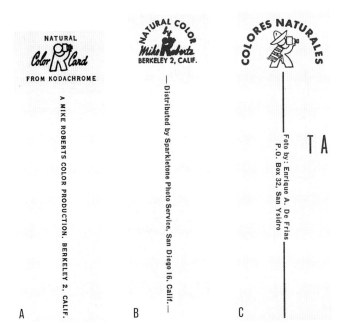

FIGURE 2.31 *a*, Verso detail El Sombrero, Tijuana, Mexico. Mike Roberts (Color Production), Berkeley, California, C4482, 1950s. Distributed by Asin Importer, Ensenada, Mexico. *b*, Verso detail of The Fronton Palace, Tijuana, Mexico. Mike Roberts, Berkeley, California, C4483, 1950s. Distributed by Sparkletone Photo Studio Services, San Diego, California. *c*, Verso detail of Swed's, Tijuana, Mexico. Enrique A. De Frias, Foto., SC4741, San Ysidro, California, 1950s.

FIGURE 2.32 "El Sombrero, Tijuana, Mexico." A Natural Color Card from Kodachrome by photographer Mike Roberts. Mike Roberts, Color Production, C4482, Berkeley, California, 1950s.

The Arreola Collection includes only a handful of Mike Roberts's postcards for the Baja border towns, all Tijuana scenes. Figure 2.32 is an example of a Roberts chrome postcard, El Sombrero curio store on Avenida Revolución. This landmark curio crafts store was identified from afar by the gigantic sombrero on its roof. The caption on the back relates, "One of Tijuana's colorful shops. Cars from five states attest its appeal."

Mike Roberts died in 1989. According to Bob Roberts, Mike Roberts's postcards, especially his Hawaii and western United States views, were widely distributed around the world through many different companies. Bob estimates that Mike Roberts published 150 million postcards a year, 3.5 to 4 billion postcards in all. His legacy as America's Postcard King is borne out by the massive inventory of his productions, in the neighborhood of thirty-seven thousand separate postcards, including a few of the Baja border towns.[27]

Mexfotocolor

La Compañía México Fotográfico, the Mexico City–based company that inaugurated the mass production of real photo postcards of Mexico in the late 1920s, began to diversify its production of postcards in the 1940s when it published a line of color-tinted real photo postcards. In the 1960s La Compañía entered the world of chrome postcards as

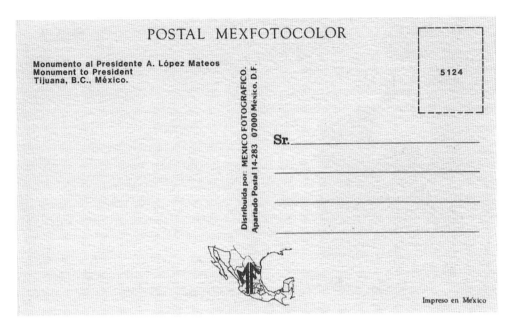

POSTAL MEXFOTOCOLOR

Monumento al Presidente A. López Mateos
Monument to President
Tijuana, B.C., México.

Distribuida por: MEXICO FOTOGRAFICO.
Apartado Postal 14-283 07000 México, D.F.

5124

Sr._____

_____

_____

_____

Impreso en México

FIGURE 2.33 Postal Mexfotocolor by México Fotográfico showing the divided back of a chrome postcard. The distinctive MF logo is set with a map outline of Mexico, and the distribution address for the company is given as México, D. F. México Fotográfico 5124, 1960s.

a new format to replace its real photo postcards, which ceased to be manufactured in the same decade. México Fotográfico named its new line of chrome postcards Mexfotocolor.[28] Similar to its previous production and distribution of real photo postcards, México Fotográfico's Mexfotocolor view cards were intended to capture scenes of towns and cities all across the republic as well as in major tourist destinations, although some scenes may have been earlier 1950s views. Local photography agents in towns and cities were contracted to photograph scenes and mail color film negatives of views to México Fotográfico in the capital, where chrome postcard production was centered. The finished postcards made from the prints, initially called "Postales Mexfotocolor," were returned to regional locations for local sales (fig. 2.33).

The Arreola Collection includes ninety-three Mexfotocolor chrome postcards for the Baja border towns: forty-three for Mexicali, twenty-six for Tecate, and twenty-four for Tijuana. The subjects are typically scenes of commercial streets, monuments, and tourist locations. Figure 2.34 shows businesses in Tecate along a street one block below the main highway through town and near the town plaza. Building façades are modern, and most parked cars appear to be 1950s models. Given the crowds seen at the upper right of the image and the bicycle riders on the street, the scene may have been a cycle race. The photographer was probably positioned on a rooftop to snap the view of sidewalk pedestrians watching the cyclists.

FIGURE 2.34 Casas comerciales, Tecate, B. C., Mexico. A Mexfotocolor chrome postcard typical of those published by México Fotográfico with rounded corners similar to its 1950s real photo postcards. México Fotográfico 866, 1960s.

POSTCARD SELECTION AND INTERPRETATION

The Baja California border-town postcard project is primarily concerned with the built landscape of the border towns as visualized through postcard imagery. Scholars, notably geographers and landscape historians, have relied on this form of visual inquiry to understand places and their built environments, although not necessarily using postcards to interpret the landscape of a town. In this project, as in previous border-postcard projects, particular views were selected to illustrate how spaces in and around the border towns were represented.[29] Three subject types of postcard views are shown. Street scenes are the most common type and the richest form of postcard view for this story. Streets capture the nature and pulse of a place, and these types of views reveal a host of elements critical to the project's purpose, from activity levels to building types. Street-level views were made for many parts of the Baja border towns—from the gates and crossings to the main streets of a city. Panorama postcard views are a subtype of street view from above, and this perspective will be noted for selected locations. Landmarks, typically buildings and activity spaces both public and private, are a second type of postcard view. Buildings could be a business such as a bar, eatery, or curio store; a residence; or a public structure such as a customs house, railroad depot, or municipal palace. Buildings and their architectural features telegraphed sophistication to visitors, creating a sense of urban modernity. Activity spaces might be a plaza or park, or an entertainment venue such as a casino, bullring, or racetrack. Local residents and tourist visitors were drawn to these spaces and so, too, were postcard photographers. A third type of view captured local residents in pose or at work. People make place, and human representation is an important compositional element for photographers. In the border towns, postcard views that highlight people enable visitors and consumers of postcard images to glimpse the natives of a city who through their presence reinforce the authenticity of place. Examples in the chapters to follow illustrate these selective view types.

A final word about dates assigned to postcards used in this project. Although collectors have established protocols for dating postcards as discussed above, this project uses decadal dating rather than interval or precise dating. This system records a date for a postcard by the decade identified according to the elements of the image on the front of the card as well as the printing codes on the back of the postcard. For example, if automobiles and other clues suggest a 1920s view, and the back matter of a real photo postcard suggested by the developing paper assigns a date of 1926, the image will still be identified as 1920s. This follows even if the postcard is posted and the stamp date can be read, or the sender dates the message on the card. This system sacrifices some precision but it generalizes the ambiguity that can occur from differences in paper dating as well as disconnection between when a postcard image was made and when the card was mailed. The exceptions to this rule are as follows. First, some postcard photographers put actual dates for the image in the title of the postcard (see fig. 2.8 above). This is rare but it does happen, and it gives unequivocal precision to an assigned date for the image. A second exception is when an exact production date is provided for a postcard image, for example as given above for figure 2.29, which has been dated by the archival records of the Curt Teich Geographic Index. In most cases, this is rare because even where photographers and publishers might have made records of their postcards by some numbering and dating system, the records themselves that might substantiate such a claim have not been preserved.

PART II

Tijuana

No one in town is able to fix for me the derivation of the name of the place. Some think it is an Indian word. Others think the town was named for a woman who lived in a shack in the late nineteenth century, a Mexican Ma Kettle known in the region as Tia Juana. Mexico City tried to get rid of the name in 1925. By an act of Mexico's congress, Tijuana was proclaimed to be Ciudad Zaragoza. A good name. A monumental name. A patriot's name. The resolution languished in a statute book on a shelf in Mexico City.

—Richard Rodriquez[1]

THREE

Tijuana Town Plan and Townscape

The study of place names, or toponymy, associates place naming with several different categories or classifications. The most common are descriptive (according to characteristics of the site), commemorative (celebrating someone or some event), and transported (attaching a previously known name). In the borderlands of Mexico and the United States, colonial Spanish settlers encountered Native Americans who, quite naturally, had their own names for places. Sometimes the Spanish colonists simply corrupted a Native place name into a Spanish-language equivalent and thereby attached a new name to a place based loosely on the Indigenous name. Rancho Tía Juana, an 1829 land grant in Baja California, is an example of this naming process because Tía Juana is said to derive from a Native American word, Tihuan, which may have several meanings. Sources refer to the place as Tía Juana, Tía Juan, Tijuan, and Tehuan, but all these names have been replaced by Tijuana, the name for the town where Richard Rodriguez (part 2 epigraph) was unable to fix from the memories of local informants the precise origin of the place name. In the 1920s the Western Publishing and Novelty Company of Los Angeles could not arrive at an exact name for its souvenir postcard folder of the town. It called the place Tijuana de Zaragoza, in keeping with the 1925 dictate by Mexico City that the border town be known for a Mexican patriot, a commemorative naming.[1] But Tijuana de Zaragoza never caught fire, and for most all of its modern history, the Baja border town has been called simply Tijuana, although some Americans in their idiosyncratic obsession with brevity still call it TJ.

This chapter introduces Tijuana as a border place on the Baja California boundary. Two questions structure the chapter: First, how did the location evolve from land-grant rancho to incipient town by the end of the nineteenth century? Second, how did the town expand in the first half of the twentieth century to become a major border city? These transformations are charted geographically through the use of historic maps to define boundaries of the border town and are supplemented by postcard views to establish a developmental sequence of townscape evolution. The goal is to visualize the changing physical landscape of Tijuana from circa 1900 to 1960. Setting the spatial and townscape parameters of Tijuana will enable a better understanding of the locational settings and historical geographic circumstances explored and discussed in chapters 4–8.

FROM RANCHO TO TOWN, 1820S-1920S

Before the founding of the town of San Diego, Spanish colonial lands in the area of Southern California and northern Baja California were under the authority of the Mission San Diego de Alcalá and the Presidio, institutions that controlled large tracts for ranching cattle. As missions became secularized and presidios faltered in Mexican California, soldiers, in keeping with traditions of reward for service, sought land grants. Between 1822 and 1846, 670 grants were made, and one of these grants, Rancho Tía Juana, was awarded to Santiago Argüello in 1829. Rancho Tía Juana was defined in 1846 as being a total area equivalent to 26,020 acres. A *diseño*, or land-grant map of this area, shows a district stretching from north of the present international boundary above the Tijuana River to include present Mesa de Otay and extending on the south of the present city of Tijuana. The east–west boundaries of the ranch are impossible to account for with any precision because the place names given are no longer recognized names in the local geography.[2]

Santiago Argüello was forced into various legal confrontations following the creation of the international boundary resulting from the Mexican War. Ranch lands on the United States side of the border were lost because of inadequate legal documents substantiating property boundaries, and on the Mexican side of the border, Argüello defended his property through challenges brought by central government proclamations to repossess his lands. In 1862 Santiago Argüello died without a will, and for the next twenty-seven years, his fifteen children and his grandchildren squabbled over family inheritance tied to the Rancho Tía Juana. This became exacerbated by the volatile land speculations gripping Southern California during the 1880s. Two factions of the Argüello family finally agreed in 1889 to divide the Rancho Tía Juana property into two sections and consented to retain engineer Ricardo Orozco to oversee the property division (fig. 3.1).

Ricardo Orozco was a government-appointed inspector in the region charged with reviewing foreign development schemes in Baja California during the Porfirio Díaz regime. Orozco was an architectural engineer who graduated from the Academia de San Carlos in Mexico City and journeyed to Ensenada in 1887 to work for the International Company of Mexico, an American development firm operating in Baja California. Rancho Tía Juana had two geographical advantages that Orozco felt would benefit future development: proximity to the international boundary and the sulfur springs at Agua Caliente. His solu-

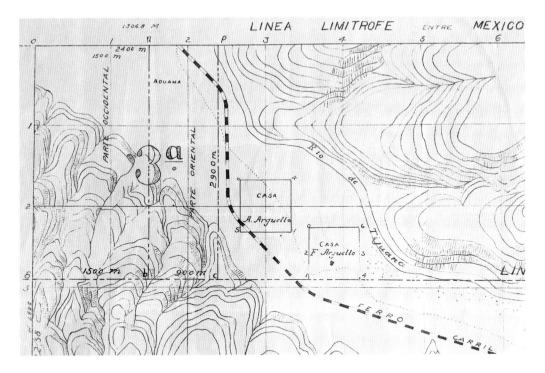

FIGURE 3.1 Map detail showing a piece of the Rancho Tía Juana divided among the descendants of the Argüello family. The property is limited on the north by the international boundary and is centered on land lying west of the Río de Tijuana between two uplands shown by contour lines on the map. A railroad alignment (no railroad at this time) extends through the valley, and the *aduana* (customs house) location is indicated near the borderline and west of the railroad right of way. The faint dotted line that crosses the boundary near the *aduana* and twines the railroad alignment was a stage line. Two Argüello house properties are also shown. Ricardo Orozco, *Plano topográfico de Tijuana con la division del predio en porciones de igual valor*, 1889. Author's collection.

tion in the property division was to award each side of the Argüello clan a share of these perceived territorial benefits. Subsequently, a section of land was set aside to develop a town site, again to be equally divided among the contentious family members.

Orozco's role in dividing Rancho Tía Juana was critical because it was his inspiration to focus on a town plan that would designate properties among the Argüellos. Historian Antonio Padilla Corona suggests that Orozco might have been influenced by the suburban speculation boom transpiring in Southern California and, therefore, decided on a revolutionary urban plan. Pueblo Zaragoza—named for Mexican political hero Ignacio Zaragoza—was the pivot point of the Argüello property division.

Orozco's Pueblo Zaragoza plan was a hybrid design of a conventional grid of intersecting streets meshed with sweeping diagonals and gallerias or circle intersections that were to be plazas (fig. 3.2). The plan set fast to the international boundary on its northern edge,

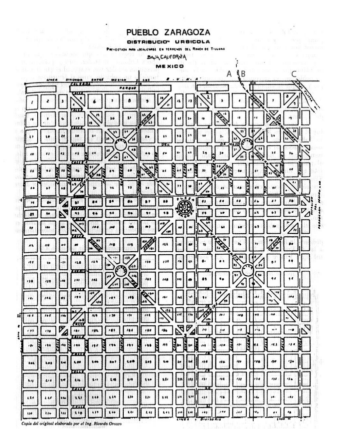

FIGURE 3.2 Pueblo Zaragoza, Ricardo Orozco's unconventional design for the first town plan of Tijuana in 1889. The plan combined a traditional Spanish grid of streets and avenues intersected by diagonal avenues that were connected at circles and identified as plazas. Plaza Zaragoza was a central feature of the plan, although it never served as a traditional plaza flanked by a church and municipal palace. *A*, location of first *aduana*. *B*, location of initial boundary crossing and alignment. *C*, Tijuana River. After copy in Archivo del Centro de Investigaciones Históricas UNAM-UABC.

where the Tijuana River cuts sharply across the northeast corner of the grid. Geographer Lawrence Herzog explains that Orozco combined Spanish urban design—the grid—with European town design—the Baroque diagonal—made popular by Baron Haussmann's plan of Paris and L'Enfant's plan for Washington, DC.[3]

Plaza Zaragoza, located near the center in Orozco's plan, never fulfilled its conventional function as the locus of religious and political authority in keeping with traditional Spanish-Mexican town planning. Orozco's plan included four smaller circular "plazas" flanking Plaza Zaragoza at the intersection of diagonal avenues. These plazas starting in the northeast corner of the grid and rotating clockwise were named Refugio, Lila, Dolores, and María. Refugio, the northeastern most circular space, was near the center

FIGURE 3.3 Tijuana's first plaza. The plaza included the traditional *kiosco*, and it was a celebration space inside the Tijuana Fair enclosed compound. The space was temporary, and Tijuana would not create a formal town plaza for the town until the 1920s. Photo postcard, 1910s. Attributed to Walter Elton Averret.

of early commercial construction because it was proximate to Avenida Olvera, the town's main commercial strip. Nevertheless, there is no evidence that a formal plaza was ever plotted in early Tijuana. When the Tijuana Fair was organized in 1915, a plaza space complete with traditional *kiosco* (bandstand) appears to have been created inside the compound of the enclosed fairgrounds (fig. 3.3).

Beyond the absence of a traditional central plaza, Tijuana had none of the religious exuberance of conventional Mexican cities, where the cathedral was a flamboyant architectural expression mirroring the wealth of the Catholic Church and, traditionally, facing a town's main plaza. Instead, Tijuana's first church was a modest adobe structure (fig. 3.4). This church was never a fixture on any of the designed plaza spaces of Tijuana; rather, it was tucked away in a residential block of the town. The adobe church was completely destroyed by the flood of 1891. When a second church was built in 1902, it was located at a new site, constructed entirely of wood, and named Nuestra Señora de Guadalupe. This church was burned down during the 1911 battle in Tijuana and rebuilt (see fig. 3.17 below). The same rebuilt wooden church was then remodeled with a stucco exterior in the 1930s (see fig. 3.20 below).[4]

The earliest governmental authority at the settlement had been the original customs house erected in 1874 on the international boundary where an old stage line crossed from

FIGURE 3.4 Tijuana's first church. A simple adobe structure, the church was atypical of the extravagance found in the cathedrals of many Mexican towns and cities, and it was not situated on any plaza. M. Rieder Publisher, no. 7137, Los Angeles, CA, 1900s.

San Diego into Rancho Tía Juana (see fig. 3.1 above). This customs house was abandoned following the 1891 flood of the Tijuana River (fig. 3.5), and a new *aduana* was established in town. A formal governmental palace would not be built in Tijuana until 1921.

In the first two decades of the twentieth century, Tijuana's population grew from about two hundred to about one thousand (table 1.1). A bird's-eye view postcard from the 1910s suggests how small the town was then when it was clustered near the banks of the Tijuana River (fig. 3.6). Residents were concentrated almost exclusively in the northeast quadrant of the town proximate to the historical international border crossing. This district of the town was situated on a small, elevated terrace above the river favored for protection against inundation from local flooding. Because the original plan was chiefly a grid of rectangular blocks, Orozco assigned particular sections to the various descendants from the Argüello line as well as to other prominent families.[5] The grid-and-block arrangement enabled easy speculation on lots as properties were sold and changed hands over the first decades of settlement.

Proximity to the international boundary and crossing was an important reason why Tijuana developed where it did (fig. 3.1). The original customs house was located where Avenida Internacional crosses the boundary in Orozco's plan until it was abandoned and Avenida Argüello became the principal diagonal that connected the new bridge across

FIGURE 3.5 Original adobe customs house. Constructed in 1874 on the Mexican side of the boundary, it was abandoned following an 1891 flood of the Tijuana River. Published by Newman Post Card Co., no. 62198, Los Angeles, CA, 1900s.

FIGURE 3.6 Bird's-eye view of Tijuana looking north from south of town. The bullring to the right of center was built in the 1910s on the southern outskirts of town. The ridgeline on the horizon is Mesa de Otay. Published by Eno & Matteson, no. 4284, San Diego, CA. Printed by C. T. (Curt Teich) Photochrom, Chicago, IL, 1910s.

the Tijuana River to the center of town circa 1916 (see fig. 3.2). Avenida Olvera, a north–south street that intersected Argüello at Plaza Refugio on Orozco's plan, was Tijuana's principal commercial street. Storefronts along Olvera were retail establishments chiefly to service tourists who visited from across the border (fig. 3.7).

Several additional locations were significant to Tijuana in this period, lending both an exotic flair to the early town as well as signatures of domesticity. The Tijuana Fair, built in 1915 to complement the Panama-California Exposition then being staged in San Diego, was located near the original crossing and prompted the installation of a short mule car line close to the border crossing to transport tourists to the site.[6] A year later, with American capital, Tijuana built its first racetrack and casino only a few hundred yards from the international boundary and immediately northeast of the Tijuana River.[7] The hippodrome and adjoining casino, the Monte Carlo, unleashed a torrent of seasonal visitors to the town on the eve of Prohibition (fig. 3.8). Tijuana's first bullring, a common entertainment venue in many border towns, was erected on a lot near the intersection of Avenida Olvera and Calle 10. The Escuela Nacional or School House, a prominent wood building with signature dormer windows and roofline, was built one block west from Avenida Olvera on Calle 7 (fig. 3.9).

In the course of almost a century between the founding of Rancho Tía Juana and the development of Tijuana, the town transformed itself several times to achieve a threshold

FIGURE 3.7 Tijuana's main street, Avenida Olvera, looking north. Avenida Olvera was chiefly a tourist drag in the early years. Storefronts were businesses servicing visitors from San Diego who flocked to drinking and curio establishments in the small border town. Photo postcard, 1900s.

FIGURE 3.8 Tijuana's first racetrack and casino. Built in 1916 only yards from the international boundary and across the Tijuana River from the town, the construction of these facilities led to the completion of the first bridge across the Tijuana River, making the border town accessible to automobile traffic (see fig. 1.19). Photo postcard, 1910s.

FIGURE 3.9 Escuela Nacional, a modern schoolhouse building serving early Tijuana. Prominent dormer windows and pitched roofline made the structure visible from across the Tijuana River (see fig. 1.6). Published by I. L., Eno, no. 4785, San Diego, CA, 1910s.

of urban presence on the boundary. The next three decades would accelerate those and other changes in Tijuana, creating a city that would rub shoulders with San Diego across the border only to arrive at even greater notoriety.

FROM SMALL TOWN TO BIG CITY, 1920S–1950S

In the 1920s Tijuana expanded from a small town of about a thousand to an emerging city of greater than eight thousand on the Baja California border (table 1.1). Growth was largely west and south of the original settlement of the town. A Sanborn Fire Insurance Map of Tijuana from 1924 hints at the changes to Orozco's Pueblo Zaragoza plan (fig. 3.10). Significantly, block rearrangement eliminated or truncated earlier diagonals such as Avenida Argüello, which was now called Refugio Argüello Avenue. Former Avenida Olvera was now Avenue A in keeping with a simplification of north–south street names to letters. East–west streets retained the previous numbering with Avenue A being the central divide for numbered streets west or east. This realignment of the grid and elimination of Mexican street names to a generalized arrangement of letters and numbers was yet another example of the American influence in the shaping of Tijuana's townscape.

Figure 3.11, a 1925 plan of Tijuana, illustrates lot divisions within blocks and suggests a greater density of residences than previous maps from the Pueblo Zaragoza era. Tijuana by 1925 was just eight numbered streets north to south and seven lettered streets east to west. The only diagonal street remaining from Orozoco's original plan was the interrupted and renamed Refugio Argüello Avenue. On the southwest perimeter of town was a short diagonal, Calle Septima (7th Street), which may have been a fragment of the former diagonal Avenida Independencia (compare figures 3.2, 3.10, and 3.11). Most of what existed some thirty-six years after Orozco conceived of Pueblo Zaragoza, however, was a functional grid of streets intersecting at ninety-degree angles.

The 1925 map can be paired with figure 3.12, a 1924 aerial view of Tijuana, which shows chiefly the same area as the map but looks north to south across the grid. The aerial reveals part of the rebuilt 1920s bridge crossing the Tijuana River, the two-block stretch of Avenue A (formerly Avenida Olvera) where storefront commercial land use is concentrated, the shortened diagonal of Refugio Argüello just beyond Avenue A, and the Tijuana bullring (rebuilt and relocated after the original burned down in 1911) positioned several blocks south along Avenue B. Building density drops off rapidly only a few blocks into the grid, and the east and north edges of the town are surrounded by cultivated land. South and west are terraced uplands leading to the coastal hills that in 1924 divided Tijuana from the Pacific Ocean. This terrace proved to be a postcard photographer's favorite perch from which to snap images of the growing border town.

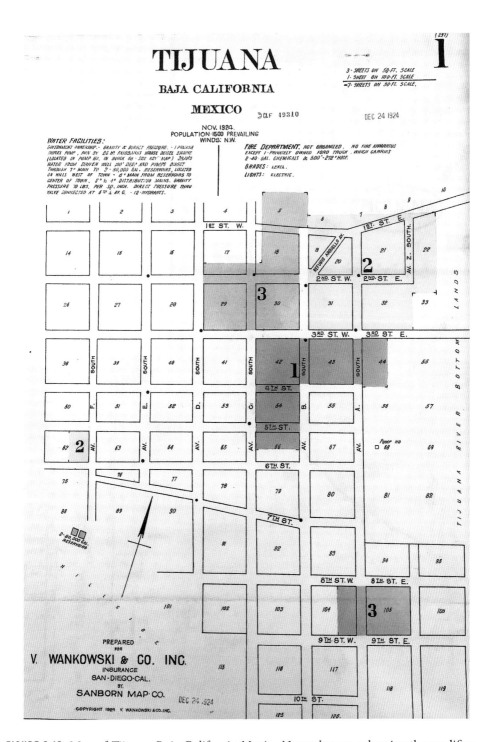

FIGURE 3.10 Map of *Tijuana Baja California Mexico November 1924* showing the modifications to the 1889 Orozco town plan where diagonals and plaza circles have been eliminated or shortened. Prepared for V. Wankowski Insurance in San Diego by Sanborn Map Company. Library of Congress.

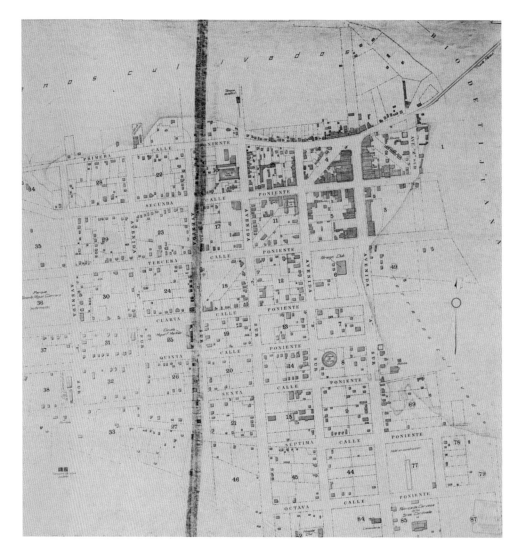

FIGURE 3.11 *Plano de la población de Tijuana, 1925*, detail showing the compact nature of the Baja border town, just eight numbered streets north to south and seven lettered streets east to west. Special Collections and Archives Library, University of California, San Diego.

A ground-level perspective of the Tijuana periphery during this period can be seen in figure 3.13, a 1920 real photo postcard view from the southern outskirts of town. The street in the center of this image is Avenue B with the Tijuana bullring visible just right of center. The street to the right of the bullring is Avenue A, and distant beyond clear definition is the main center of commercial land use for Tijuana at this time. The faint ridgeline in the right background is Mesa de Otay. This image emphasizes how Tijuana's dispersed population was a periphery of scattered small properties.

A complementary postcard view also from the 1920s is figure 3.14. This perspective, like figure 3.13 looking north, is similarly taken from the terrace along the south side of

FIGURE 3.12 Tijuana, June 20, 1924. Aerial view looking south. The bridge across the Tijuana River is at lower left. Avenue A is the first long street one block beyond the bridge, and the Tijuana bullring is visible in the distance along Avenue B. National Archives 18-AA-176–31.

FIGURE 3.13 Panorama of Tijuana looking north along Avenue B. The Tijuana bullring is visible on Avenue B, but the center of town along Avenue A on the far right is not distinguishable. Attributed to Roy W. Magruder, June 7, 1920.

FIGURE 3.14 Tijuana bird's-eye view looking north from the southern outskirts of town near Avenues C and D. Print postcard published by the Big Curio Store, Lower California Commercial Co., Tijuana. Photograph by Kingo Nonaka, 1924.

Tijuana between Avenues C and D. This image is a print postcard view of a photograph made by Kingo Nonaka dated 1924. Comparison of this image with the view in figure 3.13 shows how Tijuana properties were being developed in a short couple of years.

Inside the town and beyond the tourist allure of commercial activities along Avenue A was the residential townscape of Tijuana. Figure 3.15 is a postcard view looking west on Second Street. On one side of the street is the Royal Beer Garden, and on the other side is a *panadería*, or bakery. Elevated sidewalks above a graded street lined by a mix of single-family homes and storefronts, landscaped ornamental vegetation, and automobiles parked at curbside all reveal a domestic scene as modern then as any small town in America. In 1918 Tijuana installed its first electrical generation, and service was extended to the town's main street (Avenida Olvera) and Second Street.[8]

In 1921 Tijuana finally established a seat of governmental authority with the construction of a federal palace on Avenue B near the intersection with Calle Segunda (Second Street) and next door to the Teatro Zaragoza (fig. 3.16). Tijuana was part of the Distrito de Baja California Norte, and while the capital of the territory was first Ensenada then Mexicali, the West Coast border town was considered an important place within the federal district.

Tijuana was chiefly a town of workers and small shopkeepers during the 1920s. Figure 3.17 is a street view one block west of Avenue A showing the transition from storefronts to residences along the street near the corner where a new church had been built.

FIGURE 3.15 Postcard view looking west on Second Street in Tijuana, 1920s. On the right is the Royal Beer Garden, and on the left is a *panadería*, or bakery. Published by Lower California Commercial Co., Tijuana-Mexicali-Ensenada-Tecate.

FIGURE 3.16 Municipal palace. This seat of governmental authority was finally built in Tijuana in 1921 on Avenue B. The location was next door to the Teatro Zaragoza. Photo postcard, 1920s.

FIGURE 3.17 Street scene in Tijuana showing the transition from storefronts to residences only a block from Avenue A, then the border town's main street. Photo postcard, 1921.

The crenelated wall with circular towers in the middle ground of the image is the Tijuana Fort (see fig. 1.20).

Following the Great Depression, Tijuana's rapid growth from the previous generation slowed somewhat, but population still doubled from eight thousand in 1930 to over sixteen thousand by 1940 (table 1.1). Growth created a suburban periphery of separate *colonias*, or subdivisions, surrounding the center city, or Zona Central (fig. 3.18). There were districts north and south of the town center west of the Tijuana River and colonias east of the river and proximate to the border. Southeast and lying immediately west of the Tijuana River on the city outskirts was the Agua Caliente resort complex served by the Tijuana y Tecate railroad and an airport.

Despite the geographic spread of Tijuana during this era, postcard photographers rarely ventured into peripheral colonias, in large part because tourists stayed away from these neighborhoods (the exception was Agua Caliente). Consequently, postcards from this period and into the 1940s chiefly showed locations and scenes in the Zona Central. Figure 3.19 is a typical scene of a commercial street during the 1940s showing an automobile parts store, a hotel, and a clinic on one side of the street and a Texaco gasoline station on the other side of the street.

Postcard photographers most often concentrated on recognizable landmarks in the townscape. Local churches, schools, and parks were common views during the 1940s (figs. 3.20, 3.21). The Parque Teniente Guerrero was originally private land donated to

FIGURE 3.18 Aerial view of Tijuana in 1948 looking south. The new Puente México (bridge) over the Tijuana River is visible northwest of the old oval of the Monte Carlo Racetrack at lower left and leading into the Zona Central. In the decade following the Great Depression, suburban development extended west and south of the historic center. Detail, Tijuana Aerial S-2025, Research Library, San Diego History Center.

FIGURE 3.19 Street scene, Calle 4 in Tijuana, showing neighborhood services in the Zona Central during the 1940s. México Fotográfico, 123.

FIGURE 3.20 Local church and school captured in a 1940s photo postcard view. This church is shown in figure 3.17 two decades before this image was made. México Fotográfico.

FIGURE 3.21 Parque Teniente Guerrero. The Parque Teniente Guerrero was a hybrid park plaza of Tijuana by the 1930s. The space is shown on map figure 3.22 during the 1950s. This photo postcard was published in the 1940s and highlights the *kiosco*, or bandstand, donated by the local Chinese community.

the city in 1924 and named for a military hero who defended Tijuana from insurgents in 1911. The local Chinese community donated the *kiosco* for the space, and the park plaza remains popular in Tijuana to the present.[9]

Tijuana's population more than tripled between 1940 and 1950, approaching sixty thousand residents (table 1.1). Largely, population growth resulted in greater density within the existing frame rather than spatial expansion. On the southeast edge of the city, Agua Caliente disappeared, having been closed down in the late 1930s and the grounds converted to a technical school, although the racetrack and golf course remained. The airport, previously proximate to Agua Caliente, was relocated father east, and several improved highways connected Tijuana to Tecate and Mexicali as well as to Ensenada. In the Zona Central, Avenida Revolución became identified as Tijuana's major commercial strip, and its extension out of town appeared as Agua Caliente Boulevard (fig. 3.22).

Panoramic postcard views of Tijuana during the 1950s show the increased density of the built environment. Postcard photographers, as previously suggested, typically

FIGURE 3.22 Map showing Tijuana circa 1950 when its population was just shy of sixty thousand residents. Detail, *Map of Mexico and Baja California*, H. M. Gousha, 1961. Author's collection.

FIGURE 3.23 Panoramic view looking east across Tijuana along Calle 3 from the far western edge of the city in the 1950s. Casa Carrillo, Tijuana.

FIGURE 3.24 Panoramic view looking east from the terrace upland known as Colonia Altamira at the western edge of Tijuana. On the far right in the background is the Jai Alai Palace, and on the far left in the background are the streets of Colonia Libertad etched onto the south face of Mesa de Otay. The white building with a slanted roof in the center of the image is the Tijuana Coliseo. México Fotográfico 104, 1950s.

positioned their cameras on the edge of the terrace uplands to the west and south of the city to capture views across the city. Figure 3.23 is a vista looking due east toward Mesa de Otay, with high peaks of the Peninsular Ranges in Southern California silhouetted on the far horizon. Figure 3.24 is a similar perspective looking south and east that shows the Jai Alai Palace on Avenida Revolución to the right of center in the image.

Tijuana continued to expand in the decade of the 1950s, reaching a total population of 152,374 in 1960. This period of explosive growth pushed the boundaries of the border city far beyond its original nineteenth- and early twentieth-century core.[10] That more than twofold expansion of population in one decade would set the tone for the sprawl that became part of the border town's identity in the second half of the twentieth century.

F O U R

Greetings from Tijuana

I n 1920 Frederick Simpich, writing in the *National Geographic Magazine* about the Mexican border, barely mentioned Tijuana, which he called Tia Juana. In a follow-up article, Simpich published a story in the magazine about Baja California in 1942, and again, he gave only passing reference to Tijuana.[1] Simpich's casual mention of Tijuana in his stories—he had more to say about other border towns—is a curious neglect because in Southern California, Tijuana was well known and established in the first half of the twentieth century.[2] Mexican historians David Piñera and Gabriel Rivera write, "At the beginning of the twentieth century . . . Tijuana's profile as a tourist destination was well defined. Visitors came, mostly from California, to the horse races and boxing matches, to buy souvenirs, bathe in the hot springs and to gamble and drink in the bars."[3]

This chapter assesses how Tijuana was presented to tourists as a visitor destination through postcards that helped chronicle the place for outsiders. The annual number of tourists visiting Tijuana at the beginning of the twentieth century was near 4,200, and that number climbed to greater than five million by the first years of the 1930s.[4] Early on, visitors were excursionists, chiefly day-trippers, but in time some tourists chose to stay as accommodations improved in the border town. Guides became a standard service and were employed to inform and direct visitors to the sights of Tijuana. Chief among those destinations in the first decades of the twentieth century were a boundary monument placed on the borderline in the nineteenth century and the Tijuana Fair launched in 1915 to draw tourists from San Diego, where they collected to visit that city's Panama-California Exposition. A legendary memento of tourist visits to Tijuana was the souvenir photograph. Three different photographic types were most popular: the border group shot, typically taken at the crossing but also on the street in town; the burro cart snapshot, captured by a host of street photographers who owned decorated carts pulled by painted burros; and the café folder photograph, usually picturing a couple or a group in a burro cart in front of a dining spot in town.

VISITOR EXPERIENCE

Tourists were attracted to the Tijuana area before there was a town in 1889. Hot springs three miles east were promoted in San Diego circa 1885 as a cure for rheumatism, dyspepsia, and associated ailments. This attraction was rather like a camping experience, with a series of primitive tents and mud baths enclosed in simple shacks, and in nearby hills tourists were encouraged to hunt wild game.[5] In a separate instance following the rancho Tia Juana property settlement in 1889, the descendants of Santiago Argüello in collaboration with a San Diego physician formed a small property of bathhouses on ranch land southeast of Pueblo Zaragoza (Tijuana) called Agua Caliente Sulfur Hot Springs.[6]

Nearly simultaneous with the founding of Pueblo Zaragoza, local merchants in the new settlement erected false-front wooden buildings and established businesses to attract tourists. San Diegans boarded horse-drawn wagons and early automobiles to cross the Tijuana River, where attractions on Avenida Olvera beckoned (fig. 4.1). During the 1890s, José Padilla built the first lodging for excursionists, the Hotel Nacional.

Tourism in Mexican border cities has historically included guide services for visitors. In Ciudad Juárez, bilingual tour guides were widely available.[7] In Tijuana, one guide became famous as a local celebrity and was even included in postcards (fig. 4.2). "Reuben,

FIGURE 4.1 "Tourists departing from Tia Juana, Mexico for San Diego, Cal." Tourists visited Tijuana from San Diego in horse-drawn wagons and early automobiles. The first-generation tourist landscape of Tijuana was a series of wooden buildings fronting Avenida Olvera that offered souvenirs, dining, and lodging. Published by Newman Post Card Co., no. L.109, Los Angeles, CA, 1900s.

FIGURE 4.2 Multiview "Greetings from Tia Juana, Mexico" postcard featuring Reuben, the guide, and local tourist landmarks. M. Rieder, Publisher, no. 531, Los Angeles, CA, 1900s.

the guide," as he was known, was Reuben Williams, a Kansas City–born African American who arrived in Southern California in the 1880s. Williams was employed by the local National City and Otay Railroad to provide guide services to San Diegans who visited Tijuana.[8] Recognized by his sombrero and star badge, he offered a wealth of information to tourists about the sights of Tijuana, including the adobe church, the border monument, and the customs house shown in figure 4.2, a multiview "Greetings from Tia Juana, Mexico" undivided-back print postcard.

In the 1900s Tijuana launched an organized effort to capitalize on tourism, and by the end of the first decade of the twentieth century, American capital interests were being combined with Mexican partnerships to form tourist ventures. Miguel González became Tijuana's customs agent, and together with Tijuana businessman Jorge Ibs, a German immigrant, they created the Compañía Comercial de Baja California to promote tourism in the border town. Not only did they publish postcards of Tijuana but they also founded *El Fronterizo*, Tijuana's first newspaper. During the same decade, American investors established a greyhound racetrack (*galgódromo*) on the outskirts of Tijuana that included a restaurant and bar. They were also permitted to organize the Hipódromo de Tijuana, the border town's first thoroughbred horse racetrack.[9]

Tour guiding grew beyond the single individual, and various touring companies used large automotive busses to ferry visitors to the attractions of the booming border town

FIGURE 4.3 Tourist busses at the Mission Inn, Tijuana. Between the 1910s and 1920s, tour guiding in Tijuana was chiefly run by companies that used busses to ferry tourists to the various sites of the border town. The Mission Inn was strategically positioned at the northwest corner of Calle 1 and Main Street (later Avenida Revolución) so tourists could arrange for guided tours. Photo postcard, 1920s.

(fig. 4.3). In the Arreola Collection are several real photo postcards illustrating competing tour companies, including White Star, Green Line, and GS Auto Tours. In addition, taxi services run by Mexican chauffeurs were an alternative means of transport in and around Tijuana.[10] The crush of tourists that entered Tijuana created a demand for overnight lodging. In 1906 the St. Francis Hotel, a two-story building with a French-Italian restaurant, was built on the corner of Calle Segunda and Main Street, and in 1928 the Hotel Comercial, a handsome brick and stone edifice, went up on Avenue A (later known as Revolución) (figs. 4.4, 4.5).

A short interruption to the Tijuana tourist boom followed the 1911 occupation by insurgents (see chap. 1), the decision in 1917 to require passports to enter the city, and irregular hours of operation at the port of entry. Nevertheless, momentum resumed in 1920 when Prohibition came to the United States and Californians crossed the international boundary to indulge in the availability of alcoholic beverages and attendant entertainments in the Baja border town. On July 4th, 1920, when the town population hovered around one thousand, an estimated sixty-five thousand people and 12,650 automobiles flooded in, supporting the image of Tijuana as a wide-open town.[11] The 1920s were the so-called Golden Age of Tourism for the border town, and postcard production

FIGURE 4.4 St. Francis Hotel. Perhaps Tijuana's first full-service modern lodging, the St. Francis Hotel was built in 1906 on the northeast corner of Calle 2 and Main Street. This 1920 photo postcard also shows other businesses located on the street one block north. Attributed to Roy W. Magruder, August 24, 1920.

FIGURE 4.5 Hotel Comercial. A tourism boom in Tijuana brought new lodging like the Hotel Comercial built in 1928 to provide visitors with overnight accommodations. This print post-card view shows Tijuana streets improved with lighting and pedestrian sidewalks during this era. Published by M. Kashower Co., no. 32206, Los Angeles, CA, 1920s.

FIGURE 4.6 "Greetings from Tijuana, Mexico." This postcard was published for The Big Curio Store, Lower California Commercial Co., Inc., Tijuana, Mexico by Western Publishing and Novelty Co., no. 123366, Los Angeles, CA, 1920s. The Big Curio Store published additional versions of this postcard printed by Curt Teich, Chicago, IL, in 1935 (5A-H1106) and in 1950 (OC-H961).

popularizing the place soared. One of Tijuana's established visitor destinations was Miguel González's Big Curio Store, which claimed to be the town's "Tourist Headquarters since 1887" (fig. 4.6). The sombrero and serape became the tourist icons of the era, and "Greetings from Tijuana, Mexico" was now the modern expression of the historic *gruss aus* (greetings from) postcards of art nouveau tradition.

The Great Depression slowed tourism to Tijuana, and the censure of casino gambling by the Mexican government and subsequent closure of the Agua Caliente resort (see chap. 8) dealt a significant blown to the visitor experience. In 1931, the first year the U.S. Customs Service counted crossers at San Ysidro returning from Tijuana, the total was 5,426,034—90 percent of them U.S. citizens. That number declined in the following decade and was not surpassed until 1946.[12]

By the late 1930s and especially with the post–World War II boom and ensuing prosperity in Baja California, tourists again flocked to Tijuana. Newspapers in Southern California began to trumpet the tourist resurgence with headlines such as "Sleepy Tijuana Awakens, Finds Streets Thronged" and "Tijuana Is Wide Open Town."[13] Writing about the effect of tourism on Tijuana in the post–World War II period, one historian points out "the images linked to tourism, which characterized Tijuana, played a significant role in the development of a historical 'advertisement' for the city. . . . Tourism became the most important component of its heritage, place personality, and image."[14] Postcards participated in Tijuana's image formation. During the 1950s one of the most common postcard types was the large-letter linen (fig. 4.7). An iteration of the earlier "greetings from" postcard style, this card used the letters of a town name to advertise images of tourist landmarks. For Tijuana, the name was stretched across the brim of a Mexican sombrero and included views of Avenida Revolución, the Agua Caliente bell tower, the Revolution monument, the city's bullring, a curio store, the Jai Alai Palace, and the Agua Caliente Racetrack.

FIGURE 4.7 "Greetings from Tijuana in Old Mexico." A large-letter linen postcard with tourist landmarks pictured inside the letters of the town name stretched across an iconic symbol of Mexico, the sombrero. Published for Compañía Comercial de la Baja California, Tijuana, Mexico by Curt Teich, OC-H966, Chicago, IL, 1950.

SIGHTSEEING

Tourists in Tijuana were drawn to a variety of experiences. Two locations in particular were especially noteworthy in the early decades of the twentieth century: the boundary monument and the Tijuana Fair. International boundary monuments were more than legal markers; they became stage sets for early tourist poses. The Tijuana Fair was a celebratory space that capitalized on tourists who visited San Diego to attend the Panama-California Exposition in 1915, and the fair continued to draw visitors until 1920. Because postcard photographers and publishers were savvy to these attractions and their tourist appeal, images of the monument and the fair were popular. The Arreola Collection includes multiple postcards in photographic and print formats, and several examples are presented here to illustrate the locations.

Boundary Monument

The official boundary survey to divide territory following the U.S.-Mexico War and the Treaty of Guadalupe Hidalgo commenced in 1849. Subsequently, the placement of the first border monument was designated as Monument No. 1, west of Tijuana on a bluff overlooking the Pacific Ocean. The joint U.S. and Mexican boundary commission officials specified a white marble monument having a three-foot square base with an obelisk set on top of the base approximately nine feet in height. The eight-ton marker was finally ceremonially installed in 1851 (see fig. 2.1*a*).[15] Another marker in the vicinity of Tijuana was placed along the boundary line near the Tijuana River, but it was nothing like Monument No. 1 and was probably a simple stone marker typical of so many early border monuments.

An 1889 resurvey of the boundary renumbered the monuments that then totaled 258 from the original fifty-two, and as a consequence Monument No. 1, west of Tijuana, became number 258, and the other monument, on the Tijuana River, was renumbered 255. These monument locations and numbers are evident in figure 1.2. A new boundary commission was formed in 1892 to locate and rebuild old monuments and add additional ones as necessary along the land border between El Paso and San Diego.[16] The monument east of Tijuana on the river was buried by the 1891 flood and was, consequently, replaced with a new monument relocated 1,200 feet to the east on higher ground.[17] This monument, number 255, would become a popular tourist attraction in the first two decades of the twentieth century (fig. 4.8). Monument 255, a granite obelisk, was positioned at its new location by the 1892 resurvey and enclosed by an iron fence to protect it from defacement or removal.

The proximity of monument 255 to Tijuana ensured its popularity with tourists to the border town who were attracted by its symbolic representation of the boundary. The original placement proximate to the Tijuana River was strategic because it was fixed

FIGURE 4.8 Boundary monument 255. The monument was positioned east of the Tijuana River by the 1892 resurvey of the land border between El Paso and the Pacific Ocean. This monument became a popular tourist attraction in the early decades of the twentieth century. A "Phostint Card" by the Detroit Publishing Co., no. 5163, 1900s.

at the intersection of an early road that crossed the boundary, and this made it accessible to early visitors to Tijuana (see fig. 1.2). Figure 4.9 is a print postcard view of tourists en route to Tijuana in an early automobile as they approach the monument. With the construction of the San Diego and Arizona Railway that followed the alignment of the old road crossing, monument 255 was again perfectly positioned proximate to the railroad station for tourists to encounter the landmark (fig. 4.10).

Eighteen print and photographic postcards in the Arreola Collection show tourists at the boundary monument. Generations of Tijuana visitors would pose in front of the monument, its identity meshed with the tourist crossing experience. Postcard photographers such as Roy W. Magruder provided costumes for visitors to stand in front of the monument to have a photograph snapped. That image was then printed as a postcard, a nearly instantaneous reproduction that proved a lasting memento of the Tijuana sightseeing adventure (fig. 4.11).

Tijuana Fair

The 1915 Panama-California Exposition in San Diego did much to boom the California town. While in San Diego many of the visitors took time out to cross the border to see a bit of "Old Mexico."[18] The Mexico encountered by visitors to Tijuana in 1915 was Antonio Elosúa's "Typical Mexican Fair." The fair was a major installation for the border town. Built on the corner of Second and B Streets, it occupied the equivalent of a city block close to the border crossing. The arched entrance, flanked by two large towers, enclosed a casino, a nightclub, a restaurant, and a bullring (fig. 4.12). Activities included musical performances, cockfights, boxing matches (recently banned as gambling activities in

FIGURE 4.9 Excursionists at Tijuana boundary monument 255. The monument was accessible to tourists because it was positioned east of the Tijuana River at the intersection of a road that crossed the border. Print postcard published by Edward H. Mitchell, no. 787, San Francisco, CA, 1910s.

FIGURE 4.10 Monument 255 and San Diego and Arizona Railway station. When the San Diego and Arizona Railway crossed the border, its station was located proximate to boundary monument 255, reinforcing with Tijuana tourists the importance of the landmark. Photo postcard, 1910s.

FIGURE 4.11 Tijuana tourists posed in costume in front of the boundary monument. Roy W. Magruder, no. 17, July 14, 1918.

California and several other states) and a circus with a "posing woman." According to one source, it was also the site of Californians' first exposure to tequila as a distilled spirit.[19]

Antonio Elosúa Farías was an administrator for the Cervecería Cuauhtémoc in Monterrey, Nuevo León, in 1910. Circa 1915, while in transit to El Paso, Texas, Elosúa learned about the Panama-California Exposition in San Diego through Esteban Cantú, then governor of Baja California and a friend of the Elosúa family. Through his contact with Cantú, Elosúa devised an arrangement to secure a gambling and liquor license for a proposed fair in Tijuana. In San Diego, Elosúa contracted local financing to fund and architects to design the buildings for the fair. Elosúa promoted the Tijuana Fair in local newspapers and with colorful print advertising brochures to entice California visitors (fig. 4.13). A 1917 newspaper adver-

FIGURE 4.12 Tijuana Fair. Organized and promoted by Antonio Elosúa in 1915, the fair proved a major attraction for sightseeing tourists from San Diego, many who were in town to attend the Panama-California Exposition. Roy W. Magruder, 1916.

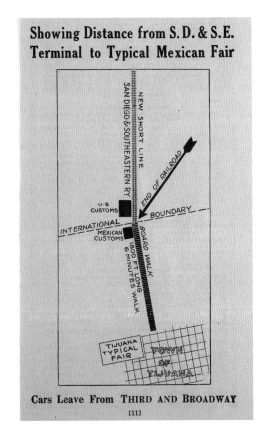

FIGURE 4.13 Brochure promoting the Tijuana Fair. As part of its activities, the Tijuana Fair promoted bullfights and the circus with the so-called posing woman. Brochure issued by Elite Printing Co., San Diego, 1915. Author's collection.

FIGURE 4.14 Page from *San Diego Official Time Tables Interurban Steamship Railroad*, 1915. The San Diego and Southeastern Railway short line to the border and board-walk access to the Tijuana Fair. Author's collection.

tisement advised "Your Visit to the Southland Will Not Be Complete Without Seeing the Regional Fair at Tijuana." Some seven thousand visitors crowded into the Tijuana Fair on opening day, July 1, 1915. Upon entering the grounds, one of the first encounters tourists faced was a kiosk of postcards that illustrated the fair and Tijuana.[20]

The San Diego and Southeastern Railway, completed to the international boundary in the same year the fair opened, advertised its short line to the border and the board-walk connection—a six minute walk—to the town (fig. 4.14). Two other transport links enabled access to the Tijuana Fair: Sutherland's stages, an American taxi service from San Diego (see advertisement on right of figure 4.12), and a *tranvia*, or mule car, that brought passengers in town to the entrance of the fair.[21] The Tijuana Fair proved a spectacular success in its promotion of Tijuana as a visitor destination. When the fair closed in 1920, the grounds were converted to Tijuana's first municipal building, a federal facility that opened in 1921.

SOUVENIR PHOTO

From the Latin *subvenire*, to come to mind, the word souvenir in English is an object through which something is remembered. "For as long as people have traveled to distant lands, they have brought home objects to certify the journey. More than mere merchandise, these travel souvenirs take on a personal and cultural meaning that goes beyond the object itself."[22] Rolf Pott's introduction to his book *Souvenir* captures the essence of why the postcard, as much as any other material object, was so prized by tourist visitors to Tijuana. Like the selfie snapshot of today, the picture postcard that included the tourist was especially prized as proof that one was there. This postcard type was not unique to Tijuana because it was known in other Mexican border towns such as Nogales and Ciudad Juárez. Nevertheless, Tijuana institutionalized the object as a necessary product of the tourist visit. Three versions of this photographic experience were popular in Tijuana. Earliest was the group photo, posed at the boundary or in the street before a recognizable tourist storefront. Next came the burro cart photograph, perhaps the most famous of all Tijuana tourist postcard options. The burro cart snapshot from the early twentieth century survives to this day on the streets of Tijuana. The third souvenir photo that became popular in the border town was the nightclub or dining establishment snapshot. This was

FIGURE 4.15 Postcard depicting tourists lined up for a group photograph in 1912 next to what would become Roy Magruder's Tijuana studio. Published by M. Kashower Co., no. 23388, Los Angeles, CA, 1920s.

often a burro cart photo that was presented in an advertising folder of the business or sometimes as a postcard that could be mailed home.

The group photo postcard was probably one of the earliest formats for a souvenir image that included the tourist visitor. As discussed in chapter 2, Roy W. Magruder was a pioneer in this type of postcard with his border studio and photo postcards made while one waited. Figure 4.15 is a print postcard that may have immortalized Magruder because it shows a photographer staging a group photograph next to a curio store. We know from figure 2.12 that the building next door to the curio store was Magruder's in-town studio in the 1910s.

The Arreola Collection includes some twenty separate photographic postcards of tourist groups staged in this manner. Frequently the group was outfitted in Mexican serapes and sombreros and held souvenir pennants signaling Tijuana (fig. 4.16). Sometimes the group included a burro positioned among the tourists. Other times the group crowded around an automobile. Occasionally a tour-bus driver might be included in the snapshot, and in still other instances with very large groups, the patrons donned only sombreros or no accouterments at all.

The most popular souvenir photo postcard associated with Tijuana is the tourist and burro cart image. While several early photo postcards of this ilk included a burro in the picture

FIGURE 4.16 Typical tourist group photo postcard of the first decades of the twentieth century. A staged snapshot with people wearing serape and sombrero costumes, holding Tijuana pennants, and posing in front of a bar or curio store. Photo postcard, 1910s.

FIGURE 4.17 Photo postcard of tourists with burro. Tourist photographs with burros were an early tradition in Tijuana. This photo postcard with the bullfight backdrop was part of a series of images made in the first decades of the twentieth century. The Arreola Collection includes four separate but similar images to this photo card. Electric Photo Co., San Diego, CA, 1910s.

(fig. 4.17), the overwhelming majority of these tourist souvenir cards included visitors seated in a cart pulled by a burro. The Agua Caliente Jockey Club produced its own versions of burro cart souvenir photos that were set in a cardboard frame and titled "Just to Say Hello." Nevertheless, most burro cart photo postcards were snapped on the street. The Arreola Collection includes thirty-six such postcards; twenty-three are photo postcards, ten are chrome postcards, and three are print postcards. There were thousands of these postcards made in the 1940s–1950s, as any simple search for Tijuana postcards via online auction sites will attest.

In Mexico, street photographers are generally referred to as *fotográfos ambulantes.* The tradition of this form of tourist photography is said to be as old as the camera. In Tijuana street photography became regulated by the 1930s because street peddlers, including photographers, were required to secure licenses to operate.[23] By the decade of the 1940s, photo postcards showing tourists in burro carts became popular. Whereas the technology that would enable street photography clearly predates this era, the 1940s was a time when Tijuana was emerging from the economic depression of the 1930s, and entrepreneurs in the border town may very well have seen this novel idea as a potentially profitable business. The burro cart photographers were chiefly located on Avenida Revolución, Tijuana's premier tourist drag (fig. 4.18). It was not unusual for burro cart photographers to advertise that pictures could be made in five minutes.

While carts could be privately owned by a photographer, burros were regularly rented from the Lorenzo Franco family, who housed and cared for the animals in a corral on Callejón Z, an alley only a short distance from Revolución. The Franco family was responsible for painting burros to resemble zebras, a convention that became popular as a tourist gag.[24] Burro cart decoration was as personal as the artist-photographer. Galindo Gaetán, said to be one of the earliest burro cart photographers and one who made photos at night, created an elaborate Aztec calendar backdrop to his handcrafted cart that was flanked by a cutout of the Agua Caliente bell tower, a popular Tijuana landmark (fig. 4.19). By the 1950s burro cart photographers began to decorate the sombreros to be worn by

FIGURE 4.18 Burro cart photographer posed at a tourist market in Tijuana. The photographer shoulders a serape and is surrounded by assistants who manage the cart, the burro, and other costume items such as the all-important sombreros. México Fotográfico 16, 1940s.

FIGURE 4.19 Burro cart photo with Aztec calendar backdrop. Galindo Gaetán, a burro cart photographer of the 1940s, perfected the nighttime snapshot capturing tourists in serape and sombrero costume posed against his dramatic Aztec calendar backdrop. This photo postcard is dated 1942 and includes an appropriate wartime slogan, "Keep 'em Flying Victorious."

FIGURE 4.20 Honeymoon couple posed in a Tijuana burro cart, 1951. So-called *burros pintados de cebra* (burros painted to look like zebras) became all the rage by the 1950s. The burros were rented to photographers by the Lorenzo Franco family, who maintained the animals in a corral on Callejón Z, an alley off Avenida Revolución.

tourists with simple sayings such as "Honeymoon Trip" or "Kiss Me" (fig. 4.20). With advances in color photography in the same decade, the burro cart and its accouterments popped with visual appeal such that the image became a postcard souvenir for sale in retail shops, not simply for the tourists in the picture[25] (fig. 4.21 and fig. 4.22).

The staged photos called *tipos mexicanos* showing street peddlers began as an early form of photography in Mexico City. Contrived interior snapshots were a specialty type of souvenir photo postcard popular for Tijuana. The Hippodrome and Soldi Studios in Los Angeles operated the enterprise, which included prearranged sets for the "Tia Juana Bar," "Tia Juana Jail," and a passenger train that announced "All Aboard for Tia Juana." The Hippodrome and Soldi ink stamps on the backs of the cards noted "Duplicates Furnished" "Sittings—Day & Night." It is likely that these orchestrated scenes were not produced in Tijuana but rather at amusement locations such as ocean pier parks in Southern California.[26]

More common than staged studio photo postcards were café folders that included a photo of tourist customers, often seated in a burro cart outside of the establishment. Bars, nightclubs, and restaurants offered this service as a form of advertising on the folder cover with the snapshot inside the folder taken by a street photographer contracted to

Typical Streetscene

Actual Photo

FIGURE 4.21 "Typical Streetscene." The burro cart itself became a tourist attraction as advances in color-tinted photography made the postcard image visually appealing. Actual Photo Co., La Jolla, CA (finished in West Germany), 1950s.

FIGURE 4.22 Tijuana burro cart waiting for tourists, 1955. This chrome postcard testifies to the popularity of the burro cart as pop art. Published by Thompson Photo Service, no. P10652, San Diego, CA, and printed as a Plastichrome postcard by Colourpicture Publishers, Boston, MA.

FIGURE 4.23 *a*, Cover of a 1940s café folder advertising the Aloha Café in Tijuana. The iconography is romantic Mexico with stereotypical personality and landscape scenes. Author's collection. *b*, Aloha Café folder with snapshot inside showing sailors on a burro cart photographed by street photographer Gaetán, Tijuana, 1946. Author's collection.

the business. Figure 4.23a is a folder cover for the famous Aloha Café, and figure 4.23b is the inside photo postcard image showing four U.S. Navy sailors on a burro cart with a text on the margin declaring "Pictures by Gaetán Are Second to None."

By the 1950s weekly advertising brochures were freely available to Tijuana visitors, and these pamphlets would often include a map of the downtown showing the locations of services like clubs and restaurants (fig. 4.24). Some of these establishments were the places where tourists might encounter the opportunity to purchase a café folder with a snapshot.

One of the most popular dining establishments in post–World War II Tijuana was the Serena Café located on Fourth Street near Avenida Revolución. The Serena advertised itself as follows on the reverse of one of its postcards.

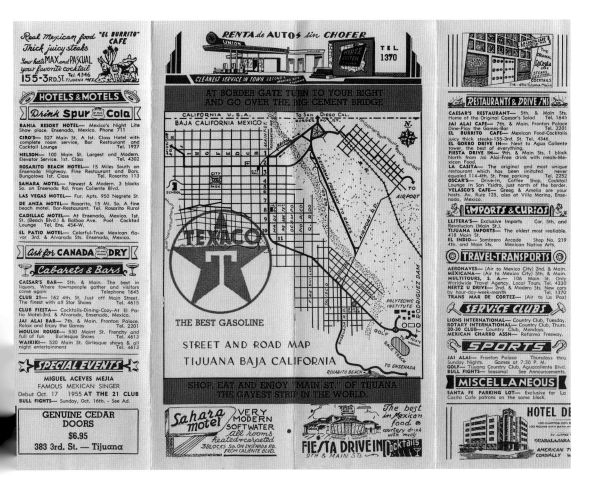

FIGURE 4.24 "Tijuana Mexico The Week Oct. 15–21, 1955." Advertising brochures like this one were free and distributed to visitors. Several of the cabaret, bar, and restaurant establishments featured here might offer café folder tourist souvenir photographs. Author's collection.

FIGURE 4.25 *a*, Serena Café folder cover, Tijuana, 1950s. Typically, iconography on café folder covers emphasized romantic Mexico, in this instance the famous *Jarabe Tapatío*, or Mexican hat dance. Author's collection. *b*, Serena Café folder with snapshot of family posed in a Tijuana burro cart, 1953. Cafés cooperated with street photographers positioned outside of an establishment to provide the photo insert for the folder. Author's collection.

Luxuriously spacious, it seats about three hundred guests and is often chosen for banquets by civic and fraternal organizations and has been host to many visiting celebrities and dignitaries. The dining room has 2500 feet of gleaming dance floor and is lavishly but tastefully decorated in the style of Old Mexico. Your visit to Tijuana is not completed until you have wined and dined in Tijuana's most beautiful restaurant.

In keeping with the popularity of café folder souvenir photos, the Serena Café sold a folder cover that advertised the establishment (fig. 4.25*a*). The cover itself with the photo inside could then be mailed as a postcard package (fig. 4.25*b*).

Café folder souvenir photos were popular with many businesses in Tijuana because they were a form of advertising. The Arreola Collection includes a folder with two retail sponsors on the cover, El Charro Curios and the Continental Shop. More common, however, were clubs and cafés like 21 Club, Tropical Club, California Café, and Arizona's La Prueba Bar. The California Café on Avenida Revolución contracted with photographer T. Villa to take postcard snapshots of visitors on burro carts, and Arizona's La Prueba Bar, also on Revolución, produced a folder that included a popular phrase printed on the inside, to wit, "If You Don't Like This Picture, Blame the ASS."

FIVE

Crossing Over

Borders by their very nature lead to crossing. Visitors to Prohibition-era Tijuana, as noted below, fought lines to come into the wide-open town and oftentimes even longer lines to leave.

> If you have a liking for the sort of life that once made the Bowery famous, you may linger in Tia Juana until 10 p.m. until repassing the gates of respectability on the north side of the river. . . . But long about five in the evening there is usually a rush for the line before dark, as that crazy bridge must be negotiated, and one by one the cars are halted at United States Customs for search. As frequently from 500 to 1,000 — oh, sometimes more — automobiles from the United States are parked like a mass of black beetles at Tia Juana, your chances of getting back to San Diego are slim.[1]

The U.S.-Mexico boundary, like hundreds of borders across the globe, is an artificial line intended to define territorial limits. Crossing the line entails protocols, control, and enforcement on each side. Who crosses the border, how crossing occurs, what physical barriers are erected to control access, and how those crossing landscapes change are a set of features all their own. The landscapes of the border-crossing zone between Tijuana and the United States in the first half of the twentieth century are the subject of this chapter. First, the changing gateways at the international boundary between Southern California and Tijuana are described using maps, postcards, and aerial imagery to understand the ports of entry that have existed at this geographic intersection from the 1900s through the 1950s. Next, postcard images are used to construct a vignette of the 1920s and 1950s border-crossing landscapes, especially gates and bridges and their associated landmarks. In this way one comes to see crossing as more than a simple step over the boundary. It encompasses a landscape of locations, artifacts, and institutions that were part of the to and fro of life into and out of Tijuana.

CHANGING GATEWAYS

Following the initial survey of the international boundary separating California from Baja California, the principal crossing at the border was the Camino de San Diego a la Baja California, shown prominently on José Salazar Ylarregui's 1850 map.[2] This cart road cut across the border approximately one mile west of the location where the Tijuana River crosses the boundary. The route extended south and east of the river to the Rancho Tía Juana (see fig. 3.1). In 1874, prompted by mining activity in Baja California, the Mexican government established an *aduana* (customs house) at this road crossing to control access into and out of the district. This crossroads soon attracted a small cluster of merchants proximate to the customs house creating a physical port of entry (fig. 5.1).

Facing the crossing on the American side of the boundary was the City of Tia Juana, an 1887 speculative development initiated as part of the real estate boom of Southern California. Just fifteen miles south of San Diego, Tia Juana City was seen as a suburban ideal perfectly situated proximate to potentially productive agricultural areas in foothill valleys to the east. In 1888, the first rails to the border, the National City and Otay Railroad, commenced operation with a goal (although not immediately achieved) of service south across the boundary linking San Diego and Ensenada in Baja California. American promoters imagined a pivot point on the international boundary at Tia Juana City where the National City and Otay rail line might connect to a railroad extending to Yuma, Arizona, along the international boundary. That development would afford access to the mining economy taking hold in Baja California south of the border. A consequence of the American development of Tia Juana City was the proposal in 1888 by Luis E. Torres, political chief and military commander of the northern district of Baja California, who suggested that a Mexican Tijuana be built opposite the American town to offer bullfights, cockfights, and other activities on the Mexican side of the border that might draw tourists from San Diego.[3] Some enterprises did locate at the crossing on the Mexican side of the boundary, including bars and a restaurant.[4] When Orozco's Plano de Zaragoza became the official founding of Tijuana in 1889, the nucleus of buildings at the old border crossing west of the Tijuana River survived for two years until the 1891 flood destroyed the crossing and the adobe customs house (see fig. 3.5).[5] A new border crossing was created circa 1895 east of the Tijuana River on a terrace elevated above the river flood plain.

Mexican Custom House, Tia Jauna   Photo SUB-POST Card Co.,L.A.
                                                              Trade Mark

FIGURE 5.1 "Mexican Custom House, Tia Jauna." Tijuana's original customs house was built
west of the Tijuana River in 1874. The *aduana* became a locus for proximate enterprises
to take advantage of visitors crossing the boundary from San Diego. An 1891 flood of the
Tijuana River destroyed the building, and the site was abandoned. This print postcard is
made from a late nineteenth-century photograph and published by Sub-Post Card Co., Los
Angeles, CA, 1900s.

A small wooden shack on the immediate south side of the border crossing was
manned by the Mexican immigration service. The north side of the boundary featured
a larger wooden building staffed by the U.S. Customs Service (fig. 5.2). The crossing was
open varied hours but generally closed about midnight. Thus, American revelers visiting
Tijuana were forced to time their exit sufficiently early to negotiate the line that inevitably
formed, especially on weekends. As one sign posted beyond the crossing on the U.S. side
reminded visitors, "Why Leave? You'll Bc Back." At times when special events might be
held in Tijuana, such as a prized horse race at the track or a bullfight in town, the line
into Tijuana could be equally challenging (see fig. 1.19).

Those who managed the border crossings were sometimes captured as if they were
tourists. Figure 5.3 is a photo postcard showing Mexican immigration officers flanking
a man out of uniform in front of Roy Magruder's Border Studio. On wooden benches to
the right of center are serapes and sombreros piled up and waiting for tourist customers
who might don the apparel as part of Magruder's staged photographic postcards of the
crossing (see chap. 2).

FIGURE 5.2 Cars lined up to enter Tijuana. The international boundary was close to the midpoint between the six cars in line. To the right are the buildings of the U.S. Customs Service, and on the left are the more modest offices of the Mexican Immigration Service. Photo postcard, 1920s.

FIGURE 5.3 Mexican immigration officers in uniform only feet from the boundary and in front of Roy Magruder's Border Studio, 1910s. Attributed to Roy W. Magruder.

FIGURE 5.4 View looking northeast from Tijuana across the improved bridge over the Tijuana River. Across the river and immediately right of the water tower is the Monte Carlo Casino, which was proximate to the international boundary and the border crossing. To the right of the casino is the grandstand of the racetrack. C. Castillo Fot., 1920s.

Circa the late 1910s, the San Diego and Arizona Railway bridged the Tijuana River and extended rail service into the Baja border town. That feat surpassed the previous rail service to the border, which forced passengers to disembark at the international boundary and walk or take carriages into town (see fig. 4.14). In 1916 a *tranvía*, or automobile-powered vehicle attached to rails, was initiated from the border train station on the Mexican side of the boundary to downtown Tijuana via the auto bridge across the river, a distance of less than one mile.[6] This interurban service connected the railroad border crossing to a point near the intersection of Argüello and Second Streets in town. It continued until 1918, when severe flooding on the Tijuana River interrupted the line. Further, the *tranvía* became less and less popular once greater numbers of visitors began crossing in private automobiles.

The first automobile bridge across the Tijuana River was constructed in 1915–1916. It was a wooden structure, and because of its rickety nature, as autos passed across it, Mexicans called it "La Marimba," a reference to its appearance and vibrating similarity to the famous musical instrument. In the early 1920s, this structure, which had suffered from river flooding, was rebuilt as a new wooden bridge extending across the span.[7] The

FIGURE 5.5 Aerial view looking north at the international crossing, 1926. On the left is the paved road that leads to the auto crossing with arched gateway (partly visible), signaling the borderline, United States north and Mexico south. To the right of the paved roadway, cutting along the foothill slope, is the San Diego and Arizona Railway line that intersects the boundary at a railroad depot on the U.S. side. Across the boundary is a covered path that connects to the Monte Carlo Casino and Racetrack (not shown) on the Mexican side. Author's collection.

bridge connected the new border crossing at the international boundary near the Monte Carlo Casino and Racetrack with downtown Tijuana (fig. 5.4).

By the mid- to late 1920s, the crossing had become a fixed landscape feature for anyone visiting Tijuana. Whether arriving at the international border by rail or auto, the crossing landmarks were the same as those in figure 5.5. A paved roadway snaking between a cluster of buildings that included institutional structures for the United States and Mexican authorities, a scattering of commercial businesses, and a metal arch at the boundary line with letters spelling out Mexico facing south and United States facing north. Nearby was a railroad line extending to a depot at the international boundary, where a smaller group of buildings surrounded the border line and the iron-enclosed monument no. 255. Reaching into Mexico from this crossing was a covered path that lead to the Monte Carlo Casino and Racetrack.

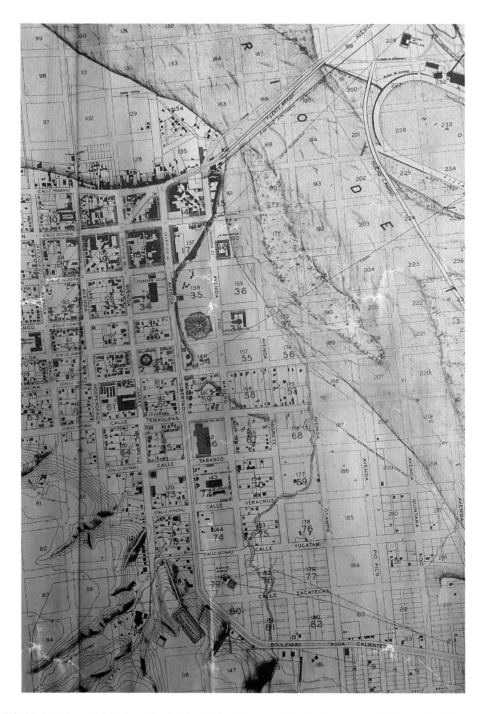

FIGURE 5.6 Puente México. The bridge linked the crossing to downtown Tijuana. In this view, the crossing is off the map at the upper right. The bridge crosses the Tijuana River on the Mexican side of the boundary. The main street of Tijuana at this time was named Avenida Libertad, later known as Avenida Revolución. Detail, *Plano catastral de la población de Tijuana*, 1929. Author's collection.

The crossing to town was negotiated by driving over the Puente México, the new bridge erected in 1923, which linked the crossing to Avenida Libertad (Avenue A, later Revolución), the main street of Tijuana (fig. 5.6).

BORDER CROSSING VIGNETTES

These vignettes assemble three sets of postcard images of the border crossing at Tijuana during the 1920s–1950s. Sets are grouped to illustrate the same view of a crossing landscape from different visual perspectives over time. Seeing the same features of the border crossing from multiple temporal viewpoints enriches the vision of the Tijuana border-crossing experience in different periods of the twentieth century.

BRIDGE
TIJUANA
MEXICO

ENTRADA A TIJUANA B.C. MEX.
TIJUANA'S ENTRANCE

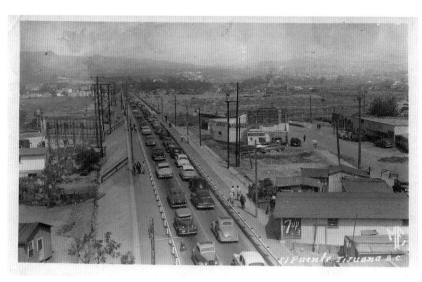

El puente Tijuana B.C.

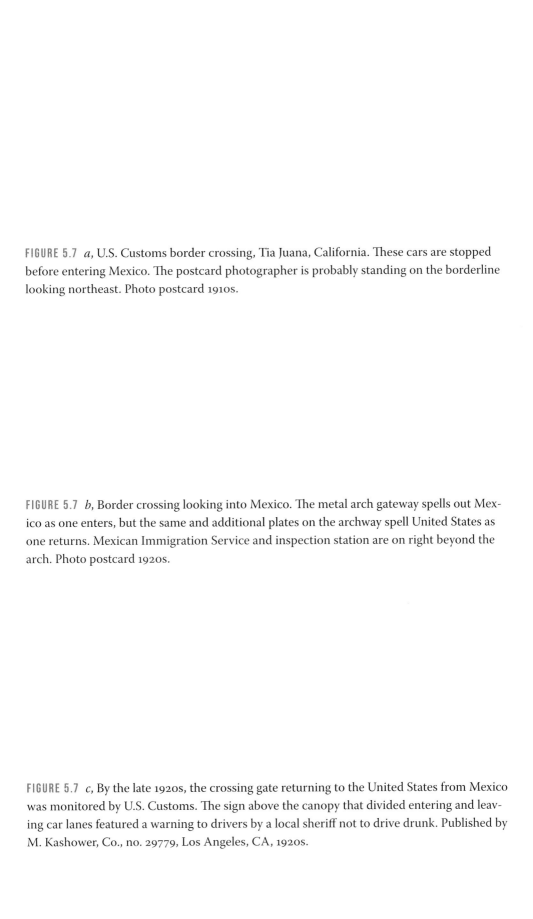

FIGURE 5.7 *a*, U.S. Customs border crossing, Tia Juana, California. These cars are stopped before entering Mexico. The postcard photographer is probably standing on the borderline looking northeast. Photo postcard 1910s.

FIGURE 5.7 *b*, Border crossing looking into Mexico. The metal arch gateway spells out Mexico as one enters, but the same and additional plates on the archway spell United States as one returns. Mexican Immigration Service and inspection station are on right beyond the arch. Photo postcard 1920s.

FIGURE 5.7 *c*, By the late 1920s, the crossing gate returning to the United States from Mexico was monitored by U.S. Customs. The sign above the canopy that divided entering and leaving car lanes featured a warning to drivers by a local sheriff not to drive drunk. Published by M. Kashower, Co., no. 29779, Los Angeles, CA, 1920s.

BRIDGE
TIJUANA
MEXICO

ENTRADA A TIJUANA B.C. MEX.
JUANA'S ENTRANCE

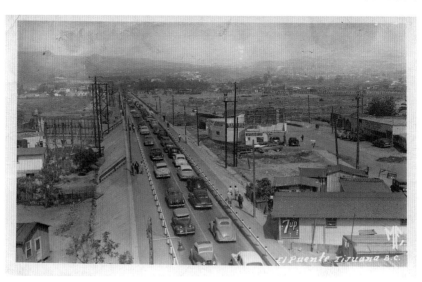

El Puente Tijuana B.C.

FIGURE 5.8 *a*, First automobile bridge across the Tijuana River. The bridge was known as "La Marimba" because of the rattle and chorus of sounds made when cars traversed the crossing. The view is looking northeast toward the international boundary. To the right is the new improved bridge under construction. During this period, tire tracks between the bridges suggest that autos may have crossed the dry riverbed to access Tijuana. Attributed to Roy W. Magruder, 1910s.

FIGURE 5.8 *b*, Bridge over the Tijuana River looking southwest from the border crossing. The buildings at right are the Mexican immigration offices, and the monument at left is known by various names, including the Monument to the Revolution built in 1931. The Tijuana River and Tijuana are visible in the background. This perspective can be imagined on figures 5.5 and 5.6, where the crossing transitions to the bridge. México Fotográfico 72, 1930s.

FIGURE 5.8 *c*, Puente México looking east toward the crossing. The bridge was rebuilt in the 1940s to improve traffic flow into Tijuana; autos are entering and departing Tijuana. The Tijuana River is visible beneath the crossing corridor in the background. The postcard photographer was probably positioned on the roof of a building near the corner of Calle Primera (1st Street) and Avenida Revolución. México Fotográfico 1, 1950s.

LINEA INTERNACIONAL
TIJUANA, B.C. MEX.

INTERNATIONAL BORDER - MEXICO AND U.S.A. - SAN YSIDRO, CALIF.

International Border

FIGURE 5.9 *a*, Mexico immigration and crossing gate Tijuana. A high metal mesh sliding gate on the boundary line divides the border and suggests the crossing is probably closed at certain hours. Vehicles, including taxicabs, scurry about the zone with entering cars nearest the building and exiting vehicles on the far right out of picture, where a patrol officer tries to direct traffic. México Fotográfico 119, 1940s.

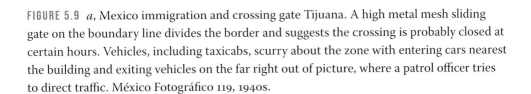

FIGURE 5.9 *b*, Close-up view looking south from the San Ysidro, California, border crossing into Tijuana, Mexico. The Mexico immigration building seen in figure 5.9a is viewed here with twin entry portals, where vehicles must stop for inspection before entering. Warning signs abound. On the U.S. side at right, crossers are advised that fruits and plants entering Mexico may not be returned to the United States, whereas Mexican officials warn visitors at left they must possess valid visas and should consult American officials before crossing. Photo postcard, 1950s.

FIGURE 5.9 *c*, Late 1950s chrome postcard view of the international border crossing at Tijuana–San Ysidro looking north into California. The metal crossing gate seen previously in figure 5.9a appears to have been removed, which suggests the border is now open twenty-four hours. The international boundary exists near the small checkpoint in front of the modern glass building just beyond the centermost pedestrian crosswalk. Autos move freely through a no-man's-land between Mexico and the United States. On the far right is the stone base of the Monument to the Revolution in Mexico seen previously in figure 5.8b. In the background right is the U. S. Customs House from the 1930s with extended canopy, where vehicles returning to United States must pass inspection.

SIX

Avenida Revolución

"Tijuana is several million lifetimes posing as one street, a metropolis crouched behind a hootchy-kootch curtain. Most Americans head for the tourist street called Avenida Revolución."[1] Main Street, Calle Principal, and La Revu are some of the names for the street that has defined Tijuana since the 1940s. Without question Avenida Revolución is the most popular street in what has been called the most visited city in the world. Yet try to find a single book about the history of this street and chances are you will come up empty. Most histories of Tijuana mention Revolución but few devote more than passing mention to its commercial personality. Mexican historians point out its early name, Avenida Olvera, or its simplified transformation to A Street in the early twentieth century, but none seem to linger on the legacy of the street or dwell on the name change to Revolución. Consult any number of volumes that reflect literary writings about Mexico, including the border and Tijuana, the sixth largest city in the country; none share anything about Avenida Revolución, as if recognizing the street would somehow inflate its stereotyped identity. In light of the fact that Tijuana claims to be the most visited place in the world and since visiting Tijuana has long meant visiting its main street, Avenida Revolución, it is perhaps, as the expression goes, stranger than fiction that La Revu is so frequently ignored in serious writing.[2]

Postcard photographers and publishers, on the other hand, reveled in representations of the street, and the resulting image density enables an interrogation of Avenida Revolución that compares to reconstructions of other Mexican border-town main streets.[3] Chapter 6 explores the ways Avenida Revolución can be scripted from postcard imagery. The chapter first assesses the physical and geographic evolution of the street, both the density of development over time and changes to the built environment of the street, block by block. Next follows a half-century postcard assessment of the principal retail establishments of Avenida Revolución, chiefly curio stores, from the early 1900s to the

1950s. Through these historical geographic approaches, a series of interpretive snapshots is created of the changing cultural landscape of the most popular street in the most visited city in the world.

FROM MAIN STREET TO AVENIDA REVOLUCIÓN

At the beginning of the twentieth century, Tijuana was chiefly a town of some two blocks stretching south from the Refugio roundabout according to Orozco's 1889 plan of Pueblo Zaragoza (see fig. 3.2). Buildings were simple wood-frame constructions and included the *aduana* (customs house), the *correo* (post office), Alejandro Savín's bazaar, Jorge Ibs's souvenir shop, and the Hotel Paris (fig. 6.1). The street was wide and unpaved, yet this small cluster of businesses was the inception of Tijuana's main commercial street, a locale that would attract visitors and tourists for generations. The street was named Avenida Olvera after one of the founding families of the town, although postcard publishers most often simply called it Main Street.[4]

Decades later, the character of Avenida Revolución, as it finally became known, was completely transformed. In 1938 a visitor residing in Tijuana recounted how Americanized the border town had become.

> In the border town one usually doesn't encounter the Mexico of the interior. Here one finds the most Americanized section of the entire republic. Were it not for the predominance of the Spanish language one would still think he were across the international boundary [b]ecause the streets, buildings, and many houses are American in design. Even the largest electric signs are in English. On the main drag mama's boy wouldn't feel a bit lonesome. Things are so American.[5]

Most tourist facilities were concentrated along eight blocks, yet tourists still entered the street at the top from First Street and wandered multiple blocks to Eighth Street at the bottom of the avenue (fig. 6.2). Anthropologist John Price described Revolución, the tourist street, as follows:

> Most of the stores along the street sell a wide variety of Mexican crafts: serapes, tire-soled sandals, sombreros, guitars, plaster statuary, paintings on velvet, plastic flowers, chess sets and so on. We counted 126 of these "standard tourist goods" shops along the avenue. . . . In addition, there were 76 specialty shops concentrating on such things as jewelry, liquor, leather goods, wrought iron, and pottery. Some of the shops are along arcades, especially between Third and Fourth Streets, which go back into the block. Avenida Revolucion also has dozens of service shops such as barbers, beauty parlors, shoeshine stands, doctors, lawyers, and marriage and divorce agencies.[6]

FIGURE 6.1 Avenida Olvera, called Main Street by postcard publishers. The avenue was the early twentieth-century nucleus of commercial buildings. Less the Mexican flags flying above, this street scene might have seemed any place in the frontier American West. Published by Eno & Matteson, 4283, San Diego, CA. Manufactured by Curt Teich, C. T. Photochrom, R-39864, Chicago, IL, 1913.

FIGURE 6.2 Avenida Revolución. The transformed main street is complete with some two hundred businesses along an eight-block stretch. Streets are paved, sidewalks are crowded with pedestrians, and Mexican flags fly above businesses, still. México Fotográfico 122, 1940s.

The progression from Avenida Olvera to Avenida Revolución transpired over several decades in the first half of the twentieth century. From the Tijuana Fair in 1915 to Prohibition of the 1920s and finally full-blown post–World War II tourist development, the drag that today is called La Revu by Tijuana residents has witnessed incremental growth era by era. Mexican cultural historian Christian Moisés Zúñiga Méndez has characterized the stages and influences that shaped the image of Revolución.

> El imaginario de la avenida Revolución se construye con historias que se remontan al origen de la ciudad, a la Leyenda Negra y la Ley Seca. . . . Las estampas incluyen las tiendas de curiosidades *curios* donde se venden artesanías provenientes de todos los rincones del país, las margaritas, la ensalada Caesar's y los burros cebra.[7]

When a Mexican scholar recently asked Mexicans in Tijuana what image best reflected their city, they chose Avenida Revolución, the tourist street. Geographer Lawrence Herzog, who has spent a lifetime studying Tijuana, calls Revolución "a grand promenade that sets the mood for a carefully choreographed tourist experience."[8]

Postcards can enhance our understanding of changes along Avenida Revolución over five decades. The Arreola Collection includes 107 postcards that show segments of the street: twenty are real photo postcards, fifty-two are print postcards, and thirty-five are chrome postcards. In 2010 geographer Nick Burkhart drew on the Arreola Collection and the André Williams Collection, using a total of 338 postcards to analyze changes along Tijuana's main tourist street from 1890 to 2000.[9] Table 6.1 shows the number of postcards used by Burkhart to assess eight blocks of Avenida Revolución between 1900 and 1960. Most postcards show the first four blocks of the street, especially during the 1920s, 1940s, and 1950s.

In the first decades of the century, Avenida Revolución was entirely a street of wood-frame buildings (see fig. 3.7). For 1910 Burkhart counted eight of nine buildings on the west side of Revolución between Calles 1 and 2 as constructed of wood. That pattern continued into the 1920s (fig. 6.3). Into the 1930s–1940s masonry construction dominated new development along Avenida Revolución as the tourist street continued to spill south (fig. 6.4).

The 1950s witnessed the greatest transformation of the streetscape of Avenida Revolución. High-rise construction began to appear in the guise of the art deco Hotel Nelson on the northwest corner of Calle 1 and the Silvestre building between Calles 2 and 3 with

TABLE 6.1 Postcards showing Avenida Revolución by street block and decade, 1900–1960

Calle	1900	1910	1920	1930	1940	1950	1960	Totals
1 to 2	8	27	35	18	11	7	3	109
2 to 3	3	6	19	19	19	14	3	83
3 to 4	0	0	0	4	23	16	11	54
4 to 5	0	0	0	0	2	9	8	19
5 to 6	0	0	0	0	0	3	1	4
6 to 7	0	0	0	0	2	3	0	5
7 to 8	0	0	0	0	1	3	1	5
Totals	11	33	54	41	58	55	27	279

Source: Burkhart, "Visualizing Commercial Landscape," (thesis). Based on Arreola Collection and André Williams Collection.

its distinctive Four Roses Whiskey sign above the sky room on the top story (fig. 6.5). Tijuana was entering its golden age of post–World War II tourism.

In his study of changes along Avenida Revolución using postcards to map and assess building transformations, Burkhart found that building changes correlate with specific social events in the first half of the twentieth century. A metric for the velocity of change was calculated using the data of total buildings and changes in the appearance of the structures for some six decades along the most densely built block of the tourist street, Calle 1 to 2.[10] This was also the section of Avenida Revolución most popularly captured by postcard photographers and publishers (see table 6.1). The years from circa 1910 through the 1920s, when Prohibition accelerated visitation to Tijuana, marked the most transformative building period along the first two blocks of Avenida Revolución. The decade of the Great Depression, combined with the repeal of Prohibition in 1933, initiated a decline and then leveling of building activity in this area. With the return of economic vitality in the post–World War II era into the 1950s, construction and building changes revived along the avenue.

PANORAMIC VIEWS AND STREETSCAPES

The decades of the 1940s and 1950s witnessed the greatest population increases in Tijuana to that time. In 1940 the city counted some sixteen thousand residents; that number more than tripled to nearly sixty thousand in 1950 and more than doubled in the next decade

FIGURE 6.3 Wood-constructed buildings on Avenida Revolución. Such buildings, with painted or lighted signs, dominated the streetscape, called Main Street by postcard photographers, in the 1910s–1920s. Photo postcard, 1920s.

FIGURE 6.4 Masonry-constructed buildings on Avenida Revolución. Such buildings, covered by stucco and accented with neon signage, became the norm along southern stretches of Avenida Revolución during the 1930s and 1940s. This view looking north shows the west side of the street between Calles 2 and 3. México Fotográfico 79, 1940s.

FIGURE 6.5 View looking south along the west side of Avenida Revolución from the corner of Calle 1. High-rise buildings such as the Hotel Nelson and Silvestre building were new to the streetscape in the 1950s. Curt Teich, C. T. Art-Colortone, 4C-H709, Chicago, IL, 1954.

to nearly 153,000 (table 1.1). Avenida Revolución emerged as the most popular street for visitors to Tijuana, and postcard photographers and publishers capitalized on the visualization of the drag between Calle 1 and Calle 8, the principal automotive and pedestrian section of the avenue.

Figures 6.6 through 6.9 offer a set of panoramic vistas of this most trafficked stretch of Revolución (see fig. 3.22 to coordinate streets referenced here with locations along the avenue). Figure 6.6 is a 1950 linen postcard view from just above street level looking south from the intersection of Calle 1. Detail is reduced beyond the first block, but the density of autos and sidewalks scattered with pedestrians suggest how active the street was then. Figure 6.7 is a 1940s real photo postcard vista looking south from a rooftop, perhaps the Hotel Nelson, across the intersection of Calle 2 and six blocks beyond to the Jai Alai Fronton on the left (east) side of the street. A burro cart is pictured below near the corner of the Hotel Comercial, and immediately south of this building on the same side of the street is the famous Mexicali Beer Hall. Known as La Ballena (The Whale), it was reputed to have the longest bar in the world. On the right (west) side of the avenue jutting above the roof lines several blocks beyond is the square tower of the Foreign Club Hotel and farther south the bell tower of Caesar's Hotel and Café. Figure 6.8, a 1954 linen postcard view, looks south and was probably taken from the Silvestre high-rise building shown in figure 6.6. The intersection in the foreground is Calle 3, with the Foreign Club Hotel on the west side and a string of curio shops and bars on the east side centered by the bell tower façade of La Misión Café. Beyond, on the same side of the street at the corner of Calle 4, is Los Portales, an arcade of shops. Finally, three blocks farther south is the Jai Alai Fronton. The fourth image in the sequence, figure 6.9, is a chrome postcard panorama looking north from a rooftop at the intersection of Calle 5 during the 1950s. Period two-tone automobiles, bright yellow taxicabs, and pedestrians in clusters crowd the scene. At left is the three-story Hotel Caesar in splendid Spanish Revival architectural style, and at street level facing Revolución is Caesar's Café, made famous though the invention of the salad named after the original owner of the establishment.

MAP AND POSTCARD VIEWS

Besides the panoramic visual sequence of postcard views of Avenida Revolución shown above, there is an additional perspective that enables a visualization of postcard views for the tourist street. In this format, a map of city blocks along Revolución between Calles 1 and 10 is employed to link postcard views with those blocks on the map. Figure 6.10 is a map showing five selected postcard views along the east side of Avenida Revolución, and figure 6.11 is a similar map showing postcard views along the west side of Revolución. The postcards are arranged on the facing pages to the map pages. The map city blocks are

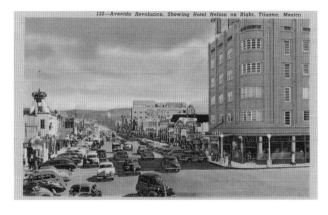

FIGURE 6.6 Published by Cia. Comercial de la Baja California, Tijuana. Manufactured by Curt Teich, C. T. Art-Colortone, OC-H954, Chicago, IL, 1950.

FIGURE 6.7 México Fotográfico, 120, 1940s.

FIGURE 6.8 Curt Teich, C. T. Art-Colortone, 4C-H711, Chicago, IL, 1954

FIGURE 6.9 Fischgrund, 1950s.

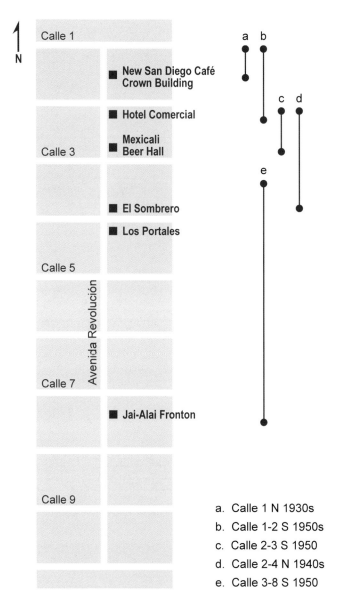

FIGURE 6.10 Map showing geographic locations by city blocks for five postcard views along the east side of Avenida Revolución between Calles 1 and 10, 1930s–1950s. The dot-bar symbols and lettered key below show the geographic range by street blocks, view orientation, and dates for each postcard view. Prominent buildings in the postcard views are positioned on the map. N = looking north, S = looking south. Cartography by Barbara Trapido-Lurie.

FIGURE 6.10 *a*, Businesses along block immediately south of Calle 1. México Fotográfico 36, 1930s. *b*, Businesses south of Calle 1 along the tourist drag. The distinctive crown-topped building is the Club Corona, a bowling alley. México Fotográfico, "Mexfotocolor" 1950s. *c*, View south from Calle 2, showing the Hotel Comercial and the Mexicali Beer Hall. Published by Cia. Comercial de la Baja California, Tijuana. Manufactured by Curt Teich, C. T. Art-Colortone, OC-H950, Chicago, IL, 1950. *d*, Looking north from Calle 4 to Calle 2, with El Sombrero curio store. México Fotográfico, 85, 1940s. *e*, Vista up the street from Calle 4 block and Los Portales arcade to Calle 8 and the Jai Alai Fronton. Published by Cia. Comercial de la Baja California, Tijuana. Manufactured by Curt Teich, C. T. Art-Colortone, OC-H829, Chicago, IL, 1950.

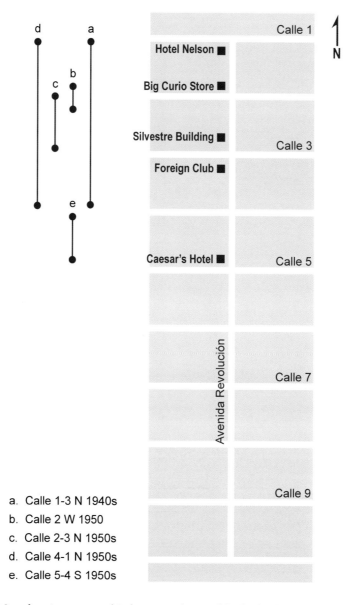

FIGURE 6.11 Map showing geographic locations by city blocks for five postcard views along the west side of Avenida Revolución between Calles 1 and 10, 1940s–1950s. The dot-bar symbols and lettered key below show the geographic range by street blocks, view orientation, and dates for each postcard view. Prominent buildings in the postcard views are positioned on the map. *N* = looking north, *S* = looking south, *W* = looking west. Cartography by Barbara Trapido-Lurie.

FIGURE 6.11 *a*, Businesses between Calles 3 and 1, looking north with the Hotel Nelson under construction at the top of the street. México Fotográfico 25, 1940s. *b*, View of the intersection at Calle 2, looking west with the Big Curio Store on the corner lot. Published by Cia. Comercial de la Baja California, Tijuana. Manufactured by Curt Teich, C. T. Art-Colortone, OC-H948, Chicago, IL, 1950. *c*, Businesses between Calles 2 and 3, looking north with the Silvestre high-rise building at center. México Fotográfico, 145, 1950s. *d*, View looking north from Calle 4 to Calle 1, with the Foreign Club Bazaar and Hotel in the foreground. México Fotográfico 128, 1950s. *e*, View looking south between Calles 4 and 5, with Caesar's Hotel at the southwest corner of Calle 5. Published by A. A. de Martínez, Tijuana, 1950s.

flanked by dot-bar symbols, and lettered keys below show the geographic range by street blocks, view orientation, and dates for each postcard view. The maps show the prominent buildings located on blocks and highlighted in the postcard views.

CURIO STORES

The beginnings of Tijuana are tied to tourism, and a fundamental ingredient in the success of the visitor experience was the souvenir, itself a product of the curio store. Curios, or *curiosidades* as they are sometimes called, can be any number of artifacts, including serapes, baskets, ceramics, leather goods, textiles, and, of course, postcards. Tourists gathered these items as testimonials to and affirmation of their visits to the Mexican border. Curio proprietors boasted about their specialty products, such as Antón's El Charro Stores on Main Street, which claimed, "You haven't really seen Leather Bags until you visit Antón's."

Some of the earliest entrepreneurs in Tijuana were curio merchants. Alejandro Savín's Bazaar Mexicano showcased its 1886 start of business (fig. 6.12), and Jorge Ibs founded the Big Curio Store in 1887, perhaps the most famous curio store in Tijuana (figs. 6.13a, 6.13b). Savín, from La Paz, Baja California, came to Tijuana via San Diego circa 1882,

FIGURE 6.12 Alejandro Savín's Bazaar Mexicano. It may have been the first curio store to open on Avenida Olvera in Tijuana in 1886. Displays in the windows include serapes and embroidery. Visible outside are racks of postcards. Photo postcard, 1910s.

FIGURE 6.13 *a*, George Ibs's curio store, founded in 1887, selling curios, cigars, and post-cards. Published by Newman Post Card Co., no. 5611, Los Angeles, CA, 1900s. *b*, The Big Curio Store, Ibs's business after he changed his name to Jorge. Published by Eno and Matteson, no. 4272, San Diego, CA. Manufactured by Curt Teich, C. T. Photochrom, R-38553, Chicago, IL 1913.

whereas Ibs, from Mazatlán, Sinaloa, ventured to San Diego and then Tijuana circa 1886. Savín and Ibs were fierce competitors. Furthermore, their respective shops were next door to one another on Avenida Olvera (see fig. 6.1). Both merchants capitalized on the tourist trade to Tijuana, yet Savín and Ibs were also savvy businessmen who traded in many goods beyond curios. For example, Ibs started as a merchant selling curios and cigars and advertised his name as George Ibs (fig. 6.13*a*). He later expanded to selling exclusively souvenirs and called his shop the Big Curio Store (fig. 6.13*b*). Savín seemed to have traded in construction materials, beer, tobacco, and clothing. In 1923 Savín rented his Bazaar Mexicano to Japanese merchants, who transformed the building into a billiard hall, and Savín later retired to Los Angeles, where he lived until his passing in 1938. When Miguel González married the daughter of Jorge Ibs, González became a partner in the Big Curio Store, and circa 1909 the store was known as Miguel González Big Curio Store (see fig. 2.4*a*). Ibs departed the tourist business circa 1916 and retired to San Diego, where he lived until his death in 1921.[11]

With the passing of control of the Big Curio Store from Jorge Ibs to Miguel González, the Altar, Sonora, native initiated an advertising campaign in Los Angeles and San Diego newspapers to spread the word about Tijuana as a tourist destination. González leased part of the curio store to Roy Magruder, and this became the border photographer's in-town studio and retail sales outlet (see fig. 2.12). González and Magruder each recognized the power of postcards as advertising for Tijuana and particularly for the Big Curio Store, which proved a backdrop for many photo and print postcards of the era. González further convinced Magruder to print photo postcards of other scenes of 1920 Tijuana as a means of town promotion (see fig. 3.13 and fig. 4.4). When the international boundary was temporarily closed during the outbreak of World War I and tourist visits to Tijuana subsided for a time, González moved to Ensenada and used the Big Curio Store as a warehouse for products, including stacks of unsold postcards.[12]

In 1922 Miguel González in partnership with several other Tijuana merchants formed La Compañía Comercial de la Baja California, a firm established to buy and sell many classes of products, both industrial and retail. The Compañía dismantled the original wooden Big Curio Store and in its place erected a new modern two-story building of masonry and stone. The new Big Curio Store had columns supporting a ground-floor covered arcade with offices above that opened on to a surrounding balcony (fig. 6.14). On September 22, 1925, a fire engulfed the entire west side block between Calles 1 and 2 along Avenida A, and the new Big Curio Store was completely destroyed.[13]

In 1929 Miguel González rebuilt the Big Curio Store and headquarters for the Compañía Comercial on the exact same corner of the previous structure. The new building exhibited a Beaux-Arts façade of stone and marble with Palladian windows and a balustrade; the oval cartouche above the entrance included a clock surrounded by decorative garlands.[14] Above the front door was "Big Curio Store Est. 1887" (fig. 6.15). Large glass

FIGURE 6.14 The Big Curio Store built circa 1922. The building was to inaugurate the forming of the Compañía Comercial de la Baja California. It was destroyed in a 1925 fire. Published by the Big Curio Store, Lower California Commercial Co., Tijuana, 1920s.

FIGURE 6.15 Big Curio Store and offices of the Compañía Comercial de la Baja California located on the northwest corner of Main (Revolución) and Calle 2. The handsome Beaux-Arts building was opened in 1929. Western Publishing and Novelty Co., no. 123368, Los Angeles, CA, 1930s.

windows enabled views of merchandise sold on the ground floor and flooded the interior with daylight. Inside was a decorated high-ceiling space lighted by electrical chandeliers, merchandise cases of curio crafts positioned around a colorful tile floor, and dedicated column displays for postcards (fig. 6.16). This building became a Avenida Revolucíon landmark, reproduced in hundreds of postcards that highlighted the corner and the first two blocks of the tourist street. It stands at this location to this day.

In addition to the Big Curio Store, several other Tijuana merchants produced postcards of their establishments. Two early competitors of Jorge Ibs and Alejandro Savín were the Leader Curio Store and La Sorpresa Curio Store, both on Main Street. By the 1930s Escobedo's Mexican Curio Store and Inzunza's Curio Store opened on Calle 2. Perhaps the most visible competitor to the Big Curio Store was Enrique Silvestre's Big Mexican Curio Store, a curious twist on the name of the former business. Silvestre was a Spaniard who arrived in Tijuana from Barcelona in 1917.[15] His store, operated as Barcelona Comercial, was located on the west side of Avenida Revolución between Calles 2 and 3 (fig. 6.17). Silvestre's Big Mexican Curio Store was a full-service business that, along with all the typical artisan craft products, also specialized in French perfumes (fig. 6.18). Like his curio merchant competitors, Enrique Silvestre developed a successful enterprise that translated into considerable wealth. In the 1950s his business funded an early Tijuana

FIGURE 6.16 Interior of the Big Curio Store illustrating the high ceiling with electrical chandeliers, posh merchandise cases, and dedicated column displays for postcards. Western Publishing and Novelty Co., no. 123357, Los Angeles, CA, 1930s.

FIGURE 6.17 Enrique Silvestre's Big Mexican Curio Store. The store was located on Avenida Revolución between Calle 2 and 3, directly across the street from the Mexicali Beer Hall. No. 129369, print postcard, 1920s.

FIGURE 6.18 Interior of Enrique Silvestre's Big Mexican Curio Store. The store advertised itself as the "Headquarters for highest class and genuine French Perfumes." No 129373, print postcard, 1920s.

FIGURE 6.19 Villa Colonial. With its whimsical art deco façade, the Villa Colonial was an arcade of curio stores set back from the street and enclosed under one roof. The Villa Colonial is located on the west side of Avenida Revolución between Calles 1 and 2. México Fotográfico 88, 1940s.

high-rise structure, the Silvestre Building, which arose on the same property that was the root of his original business on Avenida Revolución (see fig. 6.11c). In the post–World War II era, curio stores saturated Revolución, and their presence became part of the tourist identity of Tijuana.[16]

A specialized type of curio store along Avenida Revolución was the arcade or *pasaje*, literally "passage" but typically used to refer to an arcade of stores. One of the first of this type was the Villa Colonial, a dramatic art deco façade built in 1927 (originally 1924 as the San Francisco Café) during the Prohibition era (fig. 6.19).[17] The Villa Colonial is on the west side of Revolución between Calles 1 and 2 (extant but no longer a curio arcade) and advertised on its street façade "Imports and Curios." A 1950s version of this kind of enclosed space was Callejón Gómez, where *callejón*, or "alley," offered tourists an intimate pedestrian walkway surrounded by independent curio stalls and vendor carts (fig. 6.20). A 1940s example of an outdoor *pasaje*, or arcade, was the Contreras Curio Market, also on Revolución. Perhaps the most famous and popular arcade in Tijuana was Los Portales, built in the 1940s on the east side of Revolución between Calles 4 and 5. Los Portales was a single building divided into many separate stores and fronted by a distinctive arch-covered portico (fig. 6.21). When approaching the arcade from the north, Velazquez Curios greeted the shopper because it used the end of the arcade to advertise

FIGURE 6.20 Callejón Gómez, an enclosed alley off of Avenida Revolución, 1950s. Independent curio stores and vendors filled the space to beckon tourists. México Fotográfico 50, 1950s.

FIGURE 6.21 Los Portales, one of Tijuana's most popular curio arcades. In addition to Velazquez Curios, five separate curio stores were tucked behind the arched portico that faced Avenida Revolución. A burro cart was a near permanent fixture at this location on the corner of Calle 4; the cart photographer is standing in the street to entice passersby. México Fotográfico 97, 1940s.

FIGURE 6.22 Calle 3 west of Avenida Revolución. Such side streets concentrated less well-known curio stores and vendor stalls. México Fotográfico 24, 1940s.

itself by its name on the building. Beyond this curio store were Castro's, Guerrero's, Tampico Hermoso, Maya Curios, and Victor's Curios. The Arreola Collection includes eight separate postcards of Los Portales, suggesting something of its popularity with visitors.

While Avenida Revolución was the premier location for curio stores to access the greatest number of potential customers, side streets off of the main drag also concentrated curio shops. During the 1940s, for example, Calle 3 west of Revolución was a reservoir of lower-end curio stores with shops on one side of the street and stalls on the opposite side (fig. 6.22). East of Revolución, Calle 3 rolled downhill toward the Tijuana River. Nevertheless, an intrepid shopper might find unusual bargains at any of dozens of curio stores and stalls there, including Texcoco Imports, La Bolsa, Azteca Curios, Indio's Place, Vegas Curios, and Sara's Shops (fig. 6.23).

El Sombrero, a Short-Lived Tijuana Curio Store

During the 1940s, when Avenida Revolución was nearing its apex as the tourist mecca of Tijuana, an unusual curio store appeared on the southeast corner of Calle 4 (see figs. 6.10, 6.10*d*). Known as El Sombrero, the shop was distinctive in its architectural façade and unlike anything that had previously graced the famous street. El Sombrero was straight

FIGURE 6.23 Calle 3 east of Revolución. The street dropped toward the Tijuana River yet offered intrepid tourists potential curio store options in lower-end shops. México Fotográfico 13, 1940s.

out of the 1893 Chicago World's Fair, where so-called signature architecture was born and buildings along the Midway Plaisance were gigantic representations of animal and caricatured figures crowded cheek by jowl next to one another. Geographer Barbara Rubin argues that this unique gigantism in world's fair architecture was the inspiration for what evolved as a peculiar form of American roadside architecture where oversized shapes and features of commercial buildings became attention-getting devices to attract customers.[18]

El Sombrero might have been just another curio store such as Rio Rita and Gomez Market next door. What made El Sombrero unique was the giant sombrero on its roof, a massive architectural ornament that gave the store a landmark identity along a street that was already by this time famous for its loud curio store barkers, neon-lighted signs, and colorful burro cart photographers. Within a decade of its founding, an independent photographer sent a snapshot of El Sombrero to the México Fotográfico postcard company headquarters in Mexico City, and almost immediately, real photo postcards of "The Largest Hat in the World" appeared on the postcard racks and spindles in Tijuana curio stores (fig. 6.24). Print postcard publishers followed soon thereafter. The Arreola Collection includes four such examples. Into the 1950s chrome postcard photographers, including California legend Mike Roberts (see fig. 2.32), continued to document El Sombrero.

FIGURE 6.24 El Sombrero curio store. Unusual by the giant hat on its roof, it was a distinctive landmark on Revolución. México Fotográfico 73, 1940s.

Almost as fast as El Sombrero appeared, it disappeared. A late 1950s México Fotográfico chrome postcard showing the businesses along Revolución captured the façades of the Rio Rita and Gomez Market, but El Sombrero was gone, and in its place stood the Hotel Avenida Palace. This brief interlude speaks to the rapid land-use change that could occur along Revolucíon, where the competition for retail space was at a premium. A curio store that failed to attract sufficient customers might fall prey to a higher-value property use if the landlord recognized, as in the case of El Sombrero, that potential lodging revenue surpassed curios sales.

SEVEN

Cabarets

In the opening pages of his book *Poso del mundo*, Ovid Demaris launches the reader into an exotic proposition that a tourist might encounter on the streets of a Mexican border town. The chapter is titled "Cyprian Supermarkets," and the nearly two-page rant presents a situation where a Mexican street hustler tries endlessly to persuade an American visitor to indulge the licentious possibilities of the stereotypical border town. In the end the visitor ignores the enticements, and the street hustler says, "No? Ey, what's the matter meester? You just want to get drunk, or something?"[1] Some three decades later, Humberto Félix Berumen, in his book *Tijuana la horrible*, devotes an entire chapter to the idea of Tijuana as a "Wide Open Town." The Mexican author offers an interpretation of how Tijuana assumed this identity and admits without argument that the origins date to the 1920s and Prohibition.[2] Those so-called Roaring Twenties were the beginning of the period when, as Richard Rodriguez so pointedly observed, "The Tijuana that Americans grew up with was a city they thought they had created."[3] Somewhere between the outrageous tattle of Ovid Demaris, the thoughtful historical reflection of Humberto Félix Berumen, and the keen insight of Richard Rodriguez is the story of Tijuana and cabaret, a word of French origin that has been defined as a restaurant serving liquor and providing entertainment, usually singing and dancing. That perception, drinking welded to unbridled entertainment, and the image it holds on the imagination, is an idée fixe that has haunted the Mexican border town for generations.

At the end of the 1910s, moral reform in the United States set in motion the explosion of attention on Tijuana the following decade. By 1916 twenty-six states legally prohibited liquor consumption and production, and with the passage of the Volstead Act in late 1919 and enforcement of the National Prohibition Act in 1920, the Mexican border became a refuge for Americans seeking legal alcohol.[4] It is, therefore, ironic in the contrived proposition noted above that the final outcome of a failed coercion was simply getting drunk because that was, in large measure, what tipped the glass toward Tijuana's mythic reputation as *la horrible*, an identity shaped in part, but not exclusively, by Americans.

This chapter explores the ways that cabaret as a place construction was packaged in the postcard view of Tijuana. The narrative starts with reflection on Prohibition and its influence on Tijuana to underscore how cabaret was fueled during the 1920s. The story then turns to a postcard visual reconstruction of where cabaret occurred along Avenida Revolución in the 1920s and 1950s, two decades that were pivotal in aligning the image of Tijuana with alcohol, dining, and floorshow entertainments.

PROHIBITION'S EMPOWERMENT

The visitor deluge that engulfed Tijuana started circa 1915 with the spillover tourism of the Panama-California Exposition in San Diego that enabled the Tijuana Fair (see chap. 4). The floodgates opened wide, however, with national Prohibition in the United States in 1920. California, like several other states, had initiated restrictions on alcohol and gambling, notably on horse racing and boxing, as early as the 1910s, yet it was the nationwide proclamation against alcohol production and consumption that turned attention to Tijuana and the Mexican border. While the population in Tijuana grew by more than seven thousand in the decade between 1920 and 1930 (table 1.1), it was the diurnal flow of visitors that changed the character of the Baja border town. On the Fourth of July 1920, 12,654 automobiles and some sixty-five thousand persons crossed the international border to Tijuana.[5] The rush was on. Five years into Prohibition, a newspaper report declared "Tijuana: Built by the Eighteenth Amendment."

> Tia Juana, the sleepy and inconsequential, existed before the eighteenth amendment. It consisted of a shack or two in the midst of a sandy desert. But hectic Tijuana was truly a result of the famous addition to the constitution of the United States as if one of its clauses had specifically provided for the town's erection. Near the original shacks a complete Main street burst into being. It has never been more than a few hundred yards long . . . but it makes up in concentration what it lacks in size. The buildings are mostly one-story affairs of wood, many of them showing that naïve hypocrisy of the old West, the false front, which gives to the near-sighted a faint suggestion of a second story. There has been little variety in the business interests of Tijuana. Something close to 90 per cent of the town's structures are concerned with the distribution of alcoholic beverages, with gambling, and now and then the purveying of food, as side lines.[6]

The allure of Tijuana as a wide-open town spawned an explosion of booster publications, such as Edward C. Thomas's 1922 guide *The Wanderer in Tijuana* (fig. 7.1). Chiefly photographs of scenes around Tijuana, especially bars and cabarets, Thomas introduces the limited text with this declaration.

> There are blocks of buildings where every space is occupied by a saloon. Men and women line up indiscriminately at the bars, drink their drinks, smoke their cigarettes, and solemnly discuss the situation in the old-fashioned style. If the men have no companions they are quickly taken in tow by the girls who are employed by some saloon keepers, and who are obstinately and perennially thirsty.[7]

While sparked by Prohibition, this seemingly overnight sensation developed out of a pull conceived in Tijuana and a push generated in the states. The pull of Tijuana came largely from the recognition by entrepreneurs that a demand for alcohol was created by Prohibition. Property owners especially but not exclusively along Avenida Olvera, soon to be called Avenue A and later Avenida Revolución, built drinking establishments cheek by jowl along two blocks of the town's Main Street. By 1926 Tijuana reported about seventy-five bars including

FIGURE 7.1 *The Wanderer in Tijuana.* The publication promoted the adult entertainment and cabaret scene in 1922. Author's collection.

one—the Mexicali Beer Hall—that claimed to be 229 feet long. One humor postcard in the Arreola Collection shows a man stumbling into a street lined with bars and a caption that reads, "Doing lots of walking in Tia Juana and getting Stiff in all the Joints."

While foreigners were prohibited from owning property in Mexico according to Article 27 of the Mexican Constitution of 1917, Americans typically entered into business partnerships with Mexican nationals to operate Prohibition industries in Tijuana, especially bars, cafés, and gambling enterprises.[8] Tijuana businessmen would later add leverage to their investments through the National Chamber of Commerce formed in 1926. Spearheaded by Tijuana merchants, the chamber responded to local needs to protect business interests. The founding members were chiefly Tijuanense (people of Tijuana), and most were bar and brewery-distillery owners who operated in the town (table 7.1).

In 1923 the territorial government of Baja California Norte further boosted Tijuana through its newly appointed governor, Abelardo L. Rodríguez, whose administration enabled civic improvements in the Baja border town. By the close of the 1920s, Tijuana's major streets were paved, major public streets were lighted, sewer systems were installed,

TABLE 7.1 Selected founding members of the National Chamber of Commerce, Tijuana, 1926

Member	Company
Aldrete, Enrique	Comercio Mixto 5 de Mayo
Aviléz, Alfonso E.	Bancaria del Pacifico
Barbachano, Manuel P.	Compañía Teléfonos y Luz Eléctrica de la Baja California
Beden, Tom	Mint Bar
Calette Anaya, Miguel	Café La Zorra Azul
Cardini, A.	Café La Flor de Italia
Chi Fu, Fernando and Mee Hong, Patricio	San Diego Bar
Cota, Frank B.	Anchor Bar or El Ancla
Escobedo, Alfredo	Café de Luxe
Escobedo, Mariano	Comercial de Tijuana
Figueroa, A.	Cantina El Gato Negro
González, Miguel	Compañía Comercial de la Baja California, and Cevecería de Mexicali
Grande, Luis	Red Mill or Molino Rojo
Jaffe, Herbert L.	Compañía Cervecera Azteca
King, Otto Edmond	Cantina Scandia Barrel House
McKnight, W. B.	Cantina My Place or Mi Lugar
Rakich, John	Pullman Bar
San Clemente, Mariano	Compañía Cervecera de Tijuana
Silvestre, Enrique	Barcelona Comercial
Villa Camus, E.	Cantina Villa Bar
Yasuhara, So	Palacio Real

Source: Piñera and Rivera, *Tijuana in History*, 145–46.

public water supplies improved through construction of a dam and reservoir east of town, and education systems were enhanced.[9]

Beyond initiatives implemented in Tijuana that pulled visitors to the city during the Prohibition era, external factors acted to push Americans, especially Californians, to the border town. San Diego newspapers were flooded with advertisements encouraging visits to Tijuana.[10] In 1924 journalist Aurelio de Vivanco published *Baja California al día/ Lower California Up to Date*, a promotional essay showcasing the potential advantages of investment in Baja, especially Tijuana. The feature was published in San Diego in Spanish and English and included this excerpt.

> Tijuana is a commercially active town where amusement centers are permitted and alcoholic beverages can be bought. In addition, it is located near the border with the United States and it is an essential stopover for tourists that want to obtain there all the things that are forbidden in the neighboring country.[11]

In Los Angeles, Gustavo Solano edited *Baja California Illustrated*, a magazine that reported on business and current affairs. A special issue in 1923 highlighted the bar and saloon scene in Tijuana, specifically the commercial enterprises of Miguel González that included the Hotel Comercial, Mexicali Beer Hall, and the Cervecería de Mexicali.[12]

Another form of advertising that created awareness about Tijuana in the American public consciousness was film. In 1929 a United Artists executive was quoted as saying, "There is a difference between using the name Tia Juana and some other name that is not known, because it has connotations—it has meaning to the audiences and brings a reaction in them that an unknown name cannot."[13] It has been suggested that Tijuana and Hollywood were complicit in a relationship that accelerated the border town's image for popular audiences. In this association, Hollywood stars such as Charlie Chaplin, Buster Keaton, Tom Mix, Jean Harlow, Gloria Swanson, Clara Bow, and Rita Hayworth appeared in Tijuana at the racetrack, the casino, or in a gambling house and elevated the identity of the border town through their very celebrity as objects of public interest.[14]

On top of news reports and film, there was, of course, the postcard as a form of advertising about Tijuana. In Burkhart's accounting of postcards showing Avenida Revolución between 1920 and 1930, the overwhelming number of postcards for this decade pictured the first two blocks of the main street where almost all of Tijuana's bars and cafés were located at the time (see table 6.1). Messages written home about the alcohol-fueled nightlife of Tijuana were legion. One study of a sample of postcards sent from Tijuana concluded that most went to western states and that of those, 76 percent were mailed to California.[15] In the Arreola Collection, several postcards include messages about entertainments in Tijuana. In one example sent to Cedar Falls, Iowa, on June 26, 1923, the author writes, "We are in old Mexico today. Nothing here but saloons, dance halls and gambling houses." In another postcard sent from the Alhambra Café in Tijuana to Muskogee, Oklahoma, and dated July 6, 1923, the author writes "Here we are among all kinds of drinks and all sober—now. Expect to fill up."

To meet the demand for alcoholic beverages, Tijuana merchants launched brewing, distilling, and wine-producing operations. Miguel González, along with associates Luis A. Marín and Heraclio Ochoa, founded Cevecería Mexicali in 1923. The brewery was in Mexicali, Baja California, where a steady supply of water could be accessed and the surrounding valley enabled the cultivation of cereal necessary for commercial production (fig. 7.2). Brewing equipment from Germany was imported, and Canadian brew masters recorded daily production of forty-eight barrels of thirty-two gallons each during the brewing season. Beer was then shipped to Tijuana via the San Diego and Arizona Railway.[16] Mexicali beer was vended in González's two retail outlets, the Mexicali Beer Hall and the Mexicali Beer Garden, and a wholesale outlet, the Mexicali Beer Agency, all located along Avenida Revolución. The great demand for beer in Tijuana resulted in the founding of three additional breweries. Herbert L. Jaffe founded Compañía Cervecera

FIGURE 7.2 Aztec Brewing Company and the Mexicali Brewing Company. Two beers popular in saloons in Tijuana were Mexicali and A. B. C. (Aztec Brewing Company) brands. Both beers were manufactured in breweries located in Mexicali, Baja California, and the product was then shipped by rail to Tijuana for consumption. Published for Lower California Commercial Co., Inc., Tijuana-Mexicali-Ensenada-Tecate, Lower California. Distributed by Western Publishing and Novelty Co., Los Angeles, CA. Manufactured by Curt Teich Company, 104977, Chicago, IL, 1925.

Azteca, which produced the A. B. C. (Aztec Brewing Company) brand, and like Mexicali, the brewery was located in Mexicali, Baja California[17] (fig. 7.2). The third and fourth breweries were Mariano San Clemente's Compañía Cervecera de Tijuana and Cervecería Cardinal; both factories were located on Avenida A between Calle 8 and 9, one block south of the Jai Alai Palace. The enormous popularity especially of the Mexicali brand was enhanced through the production of several colorful postcards that advertised the beer. These were printed in the thousands and published by Miguel González's Big Curio Store (fig. 7.3).

Distilling spirits was another industrial enterprise entered into by Tijuana merchants. The Johnson Distillery was located on the south side of town, and the owners advertised their location on the back of a business card distributed freely to the public. Johnson produced the Spirit of Kentucky bourbon and sold single quarts at the distillery for $1.75, two quarts for $3.00, and four quarts for $5.00. Those who presented the business card at the distillery were entitled to a free drink. Two additional independent whiskey distilleries were located on the far west side of Tijuana.

In addition to beer and spirits, Tijuana was known for wine production. Jesuit priests planted the first grape vines at mission Loreto in southern Baja circa 1700, but the Dominican order introduced vineyards to northern Baja at Santo Tomás south of Ensenada. Following secularization of the missions, Bodegas Santo Tomás assumed the vineyards near Ensenada and in 1888 began producing barrels of wine for commercial consumption. In 1906 Russian immigrants to the Valle de Guadalupe south of Tecate and north of Ensenada planted extensive vineyards. During Prohibition vineyards probably existed on a small scale in each of these areas within reach of Tijuana. In 1926 descendants of Italian immigrants to Baja opened Vinícola L. A. Cetto in Tijuana to produce wine for the Prohibition market.[18]

FIGURE 7.3 Postcard advertising Mexicali brand beer. Such postcards were a popular means of promoting the beverage in Tijuana. Published by the Big Curio Store, no. 15580, Tijuana, 1920s.

STREETSCAPE OF BARS, CLUBS, AND CAFÉS, 1920S AND 1950S

In Dashiell Hammett's 1924 short story "The Golden Horseshoe," Tijuana is depicted as a corrupt border town. In one scene, the main character returns to the town after a short absence and says, "Tijuana hadn't changed much in the two years I had been away. Still the same six or seven hundred feet of dusty and dingy street running between two almost solid rows of saloons—perhaps thirty-five of them to a row—with dirtier side streets taking care of the dives that couldn't find room on the main street."[19] Although fiction, Hammett had spent time in Tijuana and knew of what he wrote. Throughout the 1920s, along Revolución the two blocks between Calles 1 and 2 were alive with bars, clubs, and cafés. By the 1950s, amid the post–World War II boom, Revolución changed significantly with the erosion of saloons and the consequent rise of curio stores (see chap. 6) and restaurants. Nightclubs and bars could still be found, but their character was less oriented to the wide-open nature of the Roaring Twenties and more in line with variety entertainment and floorshows.

Figure 7.4 is a detail from a 1924 map of Tijuana. It shows the built-up parts of the first two blocks—west and east sides—of Avenida Revolución, identified as "Avenida A" on the map. As related by several contemporary observers noted above, bars, clubs, and

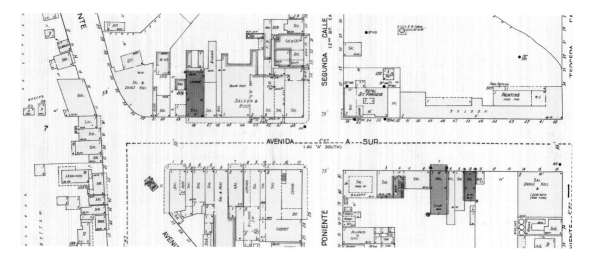

FIGURE 7.4 Map detail of Avenida Revolución in 1924 showing the density of buildings on each side of the first two blocks (from left) between Calles 1 and 3. The construction of structures is as follows: *yellow* = wood; *pink* = brick; *brown* = adobe; and *blue* = concrete. Sanborn Map Company, *Tijuana Baja California Mexico November, 1924*, sheet 2.

cafés crowded each side of the street. Although "bar" often substituted for the Spanish word *cantina* in Mexican border towns, "club" implied a "private" drinking establishment, although rarely so restricted, and "café" during Prohibition meant an adult gathering place for drink and musical entertainment. On the map most drinking establishments are identified as "Sal" for "Saloon." The Arreola Collection includes fifty-four postcards that show cabarets, clubs, and cafés along Tijuana's Main Street (Avenida Revolución) during the 1910s–1920s. Those street views are used below to interpret business changes to the Prohibition townscape of Tijuana's principal avenue.

Arson and accidental fire were said to be common in 1920s Tijuana. The earliest businesses along the east side of Avenida Revolución were destroyed by fire in December 1921. These buildings were chiefly wood structures (see fig. 6.3). Many had sawdust spread on the floors—a potential hazard that eventually resulted in their demise when conflagration occurred. A postcard published sometime after the fire captured the ruins of buildings still smoldering the next day (fig. 7.5). When the business block was rebuilt, new bars, clubs, and cafés came to mark the streetscape. The bars, clubs, and cafés on the east side of Avenida Revolución from Calle 1 to Calle 2 were the Mexicali Beer Garden, Cantina Pullman, the Mint Bar, La Peninsula, Palacio Real, San Diego Bar and Café, and the Red Mill Club. On the corner was the famous Mexicali Beer Garden, owned by Miguel González and the Compañía Comercial de la Baja California. Next door was John Rakich's Cantina (Bar) Pullman, and then Tom Bedin's Mint Bar, followed two doors down by So Yasuhara's Palacio Real. A real photo postcard proof from the 1920s shows some of these establishments (fig. 7.6).

FIGURE 7.5 Day after the December 1921 fire that consumed the entire block of businesses on the east side of Avenida Revolución between Calles 1 and 2. Published by the Big Curio Store, Lower California Commercial Co., no. 15411, Tijuana. Manufactured by H. H. T-Co. (H. H. Tammen, Co.), Denver, CO, 1920s.

FIGURE 7.6 Construction of new bars and a beer garden following the 1921 fire. The fire destroyed businesses on the east side of Tijuana's main street below Calle 1. Surprisingly, the new buildings were once again wood construction; see fig. 7.4. Photograph of postcard proof, 1920s. Author's collection.

168A:—San Diego Bar, Tijuana, Mexico.

FIGURE 7.7 San Diego Bar and Café located on the east side of Avenida Revolución between Calles 1 and 2, 1920s. The windmill on top of the building was a sign that advertised the famous Red Mill or Molino Rojo located two doors to the right on the same block at the corner of Calle 2. Published by M. Kashower Co., no. 23381, Los Angeles, CA.

FIGURE 7.8 Hula girl posed in front of the Anchor Bar. Also known in Spanish as the Cantina Ancla. Photo postcard, 1920s.

Figure 7.7 is a print postcard that shows some of the businesses that were operating on this side of the main street along the block below Calle 1 circa 1920s, including two of the more popular, the Anchor Bar (partly visible on left) and the San Diego Bar and Café. The Anchor was owned by Frank B. Cota and the San Diego by Fernando Chi Fu and Patricio Mee Hong, the latter an example of Chinese entrepreneurs in early Tijuana (see table 7.1). The Anchor Bar promoted a South Seas theme, and figure 7.8 shows a hula girl posed in front of the business welcoming guests to the saloon.

At the corner of Calle 2 at the end of this block was the Red Mill Club, also known as the Molino Rojo, owned by Luis Grande (fig. 7.9). The club takes its name from the legendary Moulin Rouge in Paris, the world famous club built in 1885 that was said to have been the original cabaret.

The west side of Main Street in the 1910s was, like the east side that went up in flames in 1921, chiefly a

Tijuana, Mexico.

FIGURE 7.9 Red Mill Club, also known as Molino Rojo, occupied the northeast corner of Main Street and Calle 2. The club's signature windmill sign was part of its tourist identity. Named after Moulin Rouge, the 1885 Parisian cabaret, at the Red Mill in Tijuana visitors could partake of traditional pisco punch, a strong mixed drink based on Peruvian brandy combined with pineapple and lime juices, sugar, gum Arabic, and distilled water. Published by E. Silvestre, Barcelona Comercial, Tijuana, 1920s.

row of wooden saloons. From Calle 1 at the north end of the block moving south to Calle 2 were the following establishments: Vernon Club, Log Cabin, Palace Bar, Tivoli Bar, San Francisco Bar, Tijuana Bar, and The Big Curio Store. The Vernon Club, a traditional "joy palace" of the era, included live music and exotic dancers (fig. 7.10).

During the 1920s, the west side of Main Street, later known as Avenida Revolución, witnessed the coming and going of numerous drinking establishments and cabaret clubs.

On September 22, 1925, the west side of the street caught fire and burned to the ground (fig. 7.11). Gone were the newly built Compañía Comercial de la Baja California (see fig. 6.14) as well as the original San Francisco Café, Tivoli Bar, and Alhambra Café. In total the conflagration that started in the kitchen of the Vernon Club destroyed fifteen saloons, three cafés, two hotels, two grocery stores, and two butcher shops.[20] To that date it was the greatest fire disaster in the history of Tijuana.

The west side of the first block of Main Street was quickly rebuilt following the 1925 devastation. A prominent new Spanish Colonial–style building, Vick's Place, replaced the former Vernon Club, and both the Tivoli and San Francisco Café were resurrected. The San Francisco Café was reborn in 1927 with a new art deco façade complete with stylized exterior sporting portholes, floral embellishments, and elaborate metal doorways (fig. 7.12).

FIGURE 7.10 Interior of the Vernon Club featuring musicians and exotic dancers that were part of the entertainment at this "joy palace." Photo postcard, 1920s.

FIGURE 7.11 Destruction of the entire block of businesses between Calles 1 and 2 on the west side of Main Street by fire on September 22, 1925. Published by Barcelona Comercial, E. Silvestre, Tijuana. André Williams Collection.

FIGURE 7.12 Art deco–style façade of the rebuilt San Francisco Café, 1927. The decorative exterior made the establishment one of the landmarks of the street for decades, surviving into the 1940s as the Villa Colonial curio arcade (see fig. 6.19). Published by M. Kashower Co., no. 25952, Los Angeles, CA, 1920s.

Continuing south on Main Street, several establishments stood out on the block between Calles 2 and 3. The Mexicali Beer Agency, part of the Lower California Commercial empire headed by Miguel González, abutted Otto Edmond King's Old Kentucky Barrel House with its distinctive façade of barrels lining the cornice of the building (fig. 7.13). Wedged between the Mexicali Beer Agency and the Old Kentucky Barrel House was the Ben-Hur Café (not fully visible in fig. 7.13), an affectation named after the Hollywood silent film epic from 1925. Also on this block were the Aloha Café, Blue Fox Café, or Café La Zorra Azul, owned by Miguel Calette Anaya, and the Midnight Follies Beer Garden.

Whereas most cabaret establishments during the 1920s were located on the first two blocks of Main Street, several outliers could be found farther south on Tijuana's commercial spine. The Last Chance, appropriately, was near the end of the main drag at Calle 3, offering adventuresome Prohibition visitors a final fling before returning to "Santiago" (San Diego) (fig. 7.14). Curiously, as this photo postcard by an unknown photographer reveals, the establishment was called "Ultima Chanza" in Spanish. "Chance" in Spanish is typically *suerte*, which means luck; *chanza* translates to "joke" or "tomfoolery." Presumably, the joke was on any patron who might find this place at the end of the line. Then

FIGURE 7.13 Old Kentucky Barrel House. Yet another distinctive façade along Main Street between Calles 2 and 3. The establishment specialized in wholesale beer barrel sales but also included an open-air bar that served Cardinal Beer. Published by Western Publishing and Novelty Co., Los Angeles, CA. Manufactured and by Curt Teich Company, no. 123371, Chicago, IL, 1929.

FIGURE 7.14 The Last Chance, an outlier away from other bars and cafés on Tijuana's Main Street during the 1920s.

149:—The New Moulin Rouge Cabaret, Tijuana, B. C., Mexico.

FIGURE 7.15 New Moulin Rouge, moved from its previous location as the Red Mill Club, or Molino Rojo at Calle 2 and Main Street to the outskirts of town between Calles 5 and 6. The new cabaret was a complex of multiple buildings, parking lot, and landscaped grounds, and it included a bar, a café, a dining room, and a dance floor. Print postcard published by M. Kashower Co., no. 33506, Los Angeles, CA, 1920s. Photos attributed to Walter Elton Averret.

again, this business could very well have also functioned as a brothel given the woman posed on the boardwalk at the corner of the block.

Another example of an outlier cabaret at the south end of Main Street was the New Moulin Rouge, located on the west side between Calles 5 and 6. This facility as shown in the multiview postcard (fig. 7.15) appears to be a Spanish Colonial–style set of buildings, a layout that could be accommodated on the outskirts of town where space was abundant. The main building appears to have the signature "red mill" situated on its roof so tourists might spot the landmark from a distance. Inside were a bar and café as well as a dining room and dance floor. On the verso of this postcard it boasts that the new cabaret and café cost one hundred thousand dollars and was open night and day. It is likely that the New Moulin Rouge replaced the older Red Mill Club or Molino Rojo that was a popular entertainment spot at the northeast corner of Calle 2 and Main Street (see fig. 7.9). This Moulin Rouge would later become a famous brothel operated by So Yasuhara (who previously owned a bar on Main Street, see table 7.1) before it was retired and converted to a school.

The post–World War II era ushered in a series of changes along Avenida Revolución, as the main street was now called. Gone was the wide-open character of bars and saloons so typical of the Roaring Twenties. Cabarets became tempered, and restaurants began to concentrate along Tijuana's main avenue, where family tourism was drawn to the explosion of curio stores (chap. 6). The 1950s saw a significant boom in Tijuana following the collapse of the tourist economy with the repeal of Prohibition (1933), the Great Depression, and World War II. In 1950, 6.5 million border crossings were recorded between San Diego and Tijuana; by 1960 the number was 20.9 million.[21]

Figure 7.16 is a map of selected cabaret and dining establishments along Avenida Revolución in the 1950s based on a compilation of views from postcards in the Arreola Collection. While cabarets were dispersed for six blocks along the main street, restaurants, at least those that advertised by postcard, are noticeably concentrated on both sides of the street between Calles 3 and 4 and along Calle 4 east and west of Revolución. Of course

FIGURE 7.16 Map showing locations for selected cabarets and restaurants along Avenida Revolución during the 1950s. Source: Arreola Collection. Cartography by Barbara Trapido-Lurie.

other restaurants were found on side streets and even on other commercial avenues such as Constitución to the west of Revolución.[22]

A nighttime photograph from 1949 by Earl Leaf shows how cabarets were squeezed between the competing curio stores along the west side of Avenida Revolución between Calles 2 and 3. The Aloha Café (see fig. 7.16), a cabaret that dates from the Prohibition era, survived although flanked on each side of the 1949 photo by curio shops.[23] The Aloha was something of an institution, and its floorshow was vaunted by generations of regular patrons. A linen postcard colorfully captures its Hawaiian theme and décor (fig. 7.17). The Aloha brokered a variety of floorshows beyond hula girls to embrace Parisian cancan and Mexican favorites like *el jarabe tapatío* (hat dance) and *el baile de la capa* (cape dance). At the Aloha, alcoholic beverages ran the gamut, but specialty tequila drinks were favorites (fig. 7.18).

Another one of the 1950s cabarets located on Avenida Revolución was the Ritz Nite Club, between Calles 4 and 5 and around the corner from La Cigueña or Stork Club. The Ritz, like

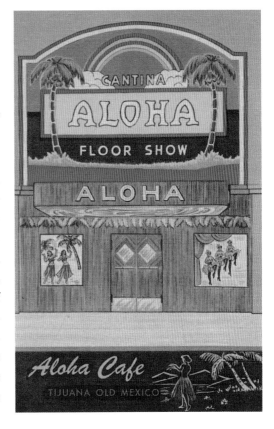

FIGURE 7.17 Colorful linen postcard advertising the floorshows of the Aloha Café. Curt Teich, C. T. Art Colortone, 2C-H1636, Chicago, IL, 1952.

the Aloha Café, was noted for its floorshows, and its neon-saturated exterior showed brightly at night on the crowded main street (fig. 7.19).

Dining out became more common for Americans in the post–World War II era as discretionary income enabled couples and even families to leave home to eat. Unlike previous generations of elite dining, middle-class Americans in the 1950s became especially entranced by themed or concept restaurants that exploited particular foreign settings and cuisines.[24] Mexican food was hardly unknown in the states, particularly among Californians and others from the southwest borderlands. Nevertheless, Mexican food was not always what tourists to Tijuana desired, although it was certainly readily available in many establishments.[25] The allure of eating out in Tijuana was less about the food than the experience that might be enhanced by the exotic, and especially if the eating option offered alcohol as part of that adventure.

An expressly enticing foreign fare popular in Mexican border towns was Spanish cuisine, meaning food from Spain and not to be confused with the early American

Prepared in Fancy Mixed Drinks

TEQUILA is the native drink of Mexico. It is made from the cactus plant.

When drinking tequila straight, always take with lemon and salt to get best results.

SPECIAL DRINKS

Tequila Punch
Lemon Juice
Grenadine
Tequila
Seltzer

Tequila Daisy
Lemon Juice
Grenadine
Tequila

Pancho Villa Cocktail
Lemon Juice
Grenadine
Habanero
Tequila
Aguardiente Parras.

All Mixed Drinks
with Tequila .... .35
10 Year Old Tequila .... .35

Tequila Sunrise
Half a lime
Grenadine
Cassius de Dijon
Seltzer
Tequila

Frank's Bender
Half a lime
Tequila
Fill with 7 Up.

Tequila Sour
Lemon Juice
Syrup
Tequila
Seltzer

Tequila Collins
Half a lime
Lemon Juice
Tequila & Seltzer

WINES
PORT, SHERRY, CLARET OR MOSCATEL .... .25
IMPORTED VERMOUTHS ...... .40

FIGURE 7.18 Postcard menu from the Aloha Café. The cabaret was famous for its floorshows and its variety of tequila-based cocktails. Postcard in the author's collection.

penchant for calling Mexican food Spanish. In Ciudad Juárez, for example, Spanish entrepreneurs were an important part of business enterprise in that Mexican border city, and Spanish restaurants were popular if not common.[26] Tijuana, like Juárez, attracted Spanish immigrants—like Enrique Silvestre from Barcelona—so the appearance of Spanish dining establishments was not a surprise. Emilio Terricabras and Antonio Girbau were proprietors of the Granada Restaurant on Calle 4 east of Avenida Revolución, founded in the 1930s and surviving into the 1950s (fig. 7.16). At the Granada, an advertising postcard showed a Spanish gentleman in traditional dress holding a dispensing flask above his head and pouring wine from the *porron* into his mouth (fig. 7.20). This, the caption on the postcard explains, is how one will enjoy wine in the typical Spanish way at the Granada Restaurant. On the verso of the postcard is printed, "Granada Restaurant, Across from the Foreign Club, Specializing in Real Mexican and Spanish Foods." It might be noted that even in this instance where dining is promoted as being foreign and exotic, the importance of drink is highlighted. This is the legacy of cabaret, a restaurant where liquor is served along with entertainment, and the entertainment at the Granada was to imagine oneself in Spain and drinking wine from the *porron*.

At the opposite extreme from the exotic was the familiar, a testament to the transformation that had taken place on Revolución from the days of Prohibition. The Capri Café Restaurant was an eatery located on Avenida Revolución between Calles 3 and 4 (fig. 7.16). An advertising multiview linen postcard shows the modern metal and glass exterior and three inset views of the interior (fig. 7.21). In keeping with the aesthetic of the 1950s, the Capri was an upscale coffee shop with counter, table, and booth seating as well as, importantly, a separate cocktail lounge. The restaurant specialized in Mexican,

FIGURE 7.19 Bright neon fountain sign of the Ritz on Avenida Revolución. Published by Ames Color, S13826, Escondido, CA, 1950s.

FIGURE 7.20 Advertisement for the Granada illustrating the typical way of drinking Spanish wine with a special dispensing flask called a *porron* as an inducement to attract diners. The restaurant was on Calle 4 east of Avenida Revolución. Curt Teich, C. T. Art-Colortone, 4A-H1999, Chicago, IL, 1934.

American, and Italian cuisines and, according to printing on the verso of the postcard, was "Open 24 Hours," the implication being that one could depend on food—and further drink—after a late night of cabaret in Tijuana. The Capri, unlike the Granada, was an establishment familiar to American tourists, with its coffee shop décor and versatility in its multiple food offerings for couples as well as families.

ZONA NORTE

In 1952 it was reported that an estimated six hundred people under eighteen years of age crossed without parental chaperone into Tijuana each week. The report went on to signal that Tijuana sheltered an estimated three thousand prostitutes, marijuana peddling

FIGURE 7.21 Capri Café Restaurant. A recognizable space for most American tourists to Tijuana, its coffee shop appearance provided counter, table, and booth dining options that could accommodate families, yet it contained a separate cocktail lounge and was open twenty-four hours. Mexican, American, and Italian food choices made for variety among patrons. Curt Teich C. T. Art-Colortone, 6C-H53, Chicago, IL, 1956.

was common, and pornographic literature was readily available.[27] This sordid announcement paints a portrait of a long-standing reputation that dogged Tijuana for much of the twentieth century, a "black legend," as the Mexicans call it, one inextricably linked to the perception of lewd bravado. It is, perhaps, this perception that led Fernando Jordan to proclaim in his 1951 book, *El otro Mexico*, that "Tijuana es . . . una calle nocturna donde un cabaret sigue un bar . . . al bar un hotel y luego otro cabaret y otro bar. . . . El Turista se va y de Tijuana recuerda solamente esa calle."[28]

In the years following the Second World War, the *calle nocturna* metaphor of Tijuana might have been supposed to be the more risqué cabarets of Avenida Revolución, like La Cigüeña (Stork Club), which advertised "Girls, Girls, Girls," or the Bambi Night Club, whose advertising postcard featured a scantily clad young woman, "Gi Gi," intertwined with the innocence of Walt Disney's fawn. Yet the truly "dark street" of the city was a short stretch of Avenida Revolución north, not south, of Calle 1 that came to be known as the Zona Norte, although it also went by the name Chihuahuita. The Zona Norte represented the old Tijuana of Prohibition and the war years, "a small, somewhat isolated vestige of Tijuana's more sordid past," but one, it was said, which "feeds many families."[29]

While the Zona Norte was an established red-light district, it developed an unsavory reputation among U.S. military personnel who frequented Tijuana during and notably following the World War II years. One of the explanations frequently given for the revival of tourism in Tijuana following the Second World War is the popularity of military visitors to the Mexican border town. San Diego's U.S. Naval Station and Oceanside's Camp Pendleton Marine Corps Base emerged as major installations after the war where thousands of young men were posted for temporary duty.[30] Anthropologist John Price quoted one Mexican informant who said, "During the war we had thousands of sailors in their uniforms every night. They came with a few months [*sic*] pay and spent it wildly." Following the war, U.S. military personnel were prohibited from wearing uniforms while on leave visits to Mexico and were restricted from entering houses of prostitution. Yet they still came to the Zona Norte.[31]

The Zona Norte featured a number of clubs and bars, but its reputation was fixed as the place where prostitution was legal and accessible. When the New Moulin Rouge in Tijuana (fig. 7.15) closed down, the name in Spanish—Molino Rojo—was applied to what became one of the most notorious brothels in the Zona Norte.[32] This district, like others known as *zonas de tolerancia* across the Mexican border, never attracted the postcard photographer and, therefore, popular imagery that might have been widely distributed was not forthcoming.[33] There was, however, another form of underground publication that gained notoriety via the more risqué cabaret clubs of Tijuana. The decidedly raunchier of these printed materials became known as Tijuana Bibles.[34] The more tame versions were so-called modern dictionaries like the one published by the Aloha Café. These small handbooks, usually of only a few pages, were chiefly alphabetical lists of terms defined with sexual innuendo such as "Adultery—Two wrong people doing the right thing" or "Mistress—Something between a mister and a mattress." Not surprisingly, few popular postcard images of clubs and bars in the Zona Norte circulated. Their scarcity leaves a visual gap in the story of cabaret in Tijuana. Nevertheless, sufficient numbers of postcards survive to enable a reconstruction of the legendary cabaret businesses of the most visited Mexican border town.

EIGHT

Landmarks

In his pathbreaking book *The Image of the City*, Kevin Lynch defined *landmarks* as physical elements that can vary widely in scale yet maintain singularity, meaning they hold some aspect that is unique or memorable.[1] In his book *Close-Up: How to Read the American City*, Grady Clay refined the landmark to a *fix*, which he defined as a location that fastens our view because of its particular quality. In the European heritage tradition of the city, for example, the temple, the arch, the palace, the cathedral, and the piazza are fixes that focus our view of a townscape.[2] Landmarks or fixes, cities create spaces that are prominent and that seize our attention because of their monumentality, their physical uniqueness, or the historical memory associated with them. In this regard Tijuana is no different from the grand cities of Europe or modern urban centers of America. Landmarks are created and attain singular status in place according to memory and meaning.

This chapter describes some of the most recognized landmarks that achieved meaning in Tijuana's past. Some no longer survive in the landscape of the border town, whereas others have persisted into the present. Several of these landmarks were monumental structures while others were modest by comparison. They, nonetheless, reinforce how landmarks can attribute meaning and sustain memory regardless of their physical stature. The landmarks discussed below include bullrings, the Tijuana Racetrack and Monte Carlo Casino, the Mexicali Beer Hall, and the Agua Caliente Casino and Resort, all of which have been erased from the Tijuana townscape, and the Foreign Club (name only), the Jai Alai Fronton, and Caesar's Hotel and Café, which survive to this day. These particular landmarks were selected because of their repeated representation on postcards, which suggests something of their popularity. In the end, however, it is the memory of these landmarks and the meanings ascribed to them through time that are of the greatest significance.

The discussion and illustrated format below loosely follows the location of each landmark in the Tijuana townscape, a brief historical chronicle of the landmark, and reproduction of postcard examples and other ephemera with captions to illustrate the landmark in time and place.

TIJUANA BULLRINGS

The first significant landmark of Tijuana was, arguably, the bullring. Bullfighting is a
traditional sport of Mexico, inherited from Spain, and many border towns as well as
towns and cities across the country have bullrings, or *plazas de toros*, as they are formally
known. Bullfights have been staged in Tijuana since the late nineteenth century. The first
bullring was erected in the early twentieth century on Avenida Olvera and occupied a
city block between Calles 3 and 4. The ring was financed and built by the Spanish *torero*
Antonio González Rubio and the Mexicali merchant José R. Alvarez.[3] Rebels combatting
federal troops in Tijuana burned the first bullring to the ground in 1911 (see chap. 1).

A new and slightly larger plaza de toros was built near the same location—then identified as Avenue B—and that ring is visible on the outskirts of town in the 1920s in
figures 3.6, 3.11, and 3.12. The wooden structure is documented in more than a dozen
print and photographic postcards in the Arreola Collection. Figure 8.1 is a 1910s photo

FIGURE 8.1 Exterior of Tijuana's second bullring, a wooden structure built in the 1910s, then
on the southern outskirts of town. Photo postcard, 1910s.

FIGURE 8.2 El Torero de Tijuana, built in 1938 on Agua Caliente Boulevard at the southeastern edge of town. México Fotográfico 48, 1940s.

postcard view of the exterior of this bullring. The plaza was said to accommodate two thousand spectators. This bullring survived at the location near Calle 5 and Avenida B until the mid-1930s.[4]

In 1938 a new bullring—El Torero de Tijuana—was constructed facing Agua Caliente Boulevard on the southeast edge of town not far from the original location of the Agua Caliente Resort, which had closed to casino gaming only three years previously (fig. 8.2). This plaza is visible on figure 3.18, an aerial view of Tijuana in 1948. The Torero de Tijuana bullring is captured in more than two-dozen print, photo, and chrome postcards in the Arreola Collection. During the 1950s the arena was considered the city's "downtown bull ring." At that time Tijuana's population hovered close to 150,000, and when the city expanded west to the sea, a new bullring was opened in 1960 overlooking the Pacific Ocean.[5] Nevertheless, the downtown bullring continued to stage bullfights into the 1960s but closed and was finally removed from the site under great protest in 2007.[6]

TIJUANA RACETRACK AND MONTE CARLO CASINO

By the 1910s horse racing and other forms of gambling were being closed down in many American states. California's Santa Anita and Tanforan tracks in Los Angeles and San Francisco, respectively, had been shuttered. In Baja California discussions ensued about the prospects of establishing racetracks and casinos, but internal political rivalries and opposition from nearby American towns stalled initiatives. In 1915 acting governor of Baja California, Esteban Cantú, awarded a racing contract to the Tijuana Jockey Club, which was managed by an American in San Diego and backed by financial interests in Dallas, Texas. The Jockey Club hired and funded two Californians to organize and build a racetrack in Tijuana: Jim Coffroth, a San Francisco boxing promoter, and Baron Long, a social glad-hander from Los Angeles with a passion for thoroughbred horses.

Astonishingly, a *hipódromo* was built in just sixteen days with materials from San Diego and labor from Tijuana. The one-mile oval track was formed proximate to the border crossing. A long walkway connected the crossing to a grandstand that accommodated three thousand fans (see fig. 3.8). Below the stands were a large café and slot machines, and nearby were stables for one hundred horses. Because the track was built close to the Tijuana River and across the stream from the town, a low levee was constructed to protect the track from potential flooding. The Tijuana Racetrack opened New Year's Day, 1916. Repeated torrential rain events within weeks of the opening and a flood that breached the levee destroyed the track and most buildings, although the grandstand remained intact. The racetrack closed until it was rebuilt and reopened that April.[7]

The racetrack attracted tens of thousands of spectators and generated dozens of popular postcard images. The Arreola Collection includes some ten photo and print cards that highlight the facility. Not uncommonly, print postcards were made from original photographic postcards. Figure 8.3 is a Detroit Publishing Company "phostint" print postcard

72188 RACE TRACK, TIA JUANA. MEXICO

FIGURE 8.3 Print postcard of Tijuana Racetrack following a race and showing horses, riders, and crowd at the winner's circle below the judging stand. Detroit Publishing Company, no. 72188, 1920s.

made from a photo postcard produced in the 1920s. In the print postcard, graphic designers generalized some features from the photo card and added other elements like the
crowd at the finish line, whereas the original photo postcard showed only the horses with
riders crossing the line.

Despite interruptions by World War I (1917–1919), a track fire (1924–1925), and a second flood (1927), thoroughbred racing at Tijuana continued for more than two decades.
Several innovations can be attributed to the Tijuana Racetrack, including the first scratch
rule, the first starting gate with individual stalls for horses, the first photo finish, and the
first hundred thousand dollar purse. The track closed after the 1929 season because a new
track was being built nearby at the Agua Caliente Casino and Resort, and investors in the
Tijuana Racetrack decided to invest in that new venture. The racetrack was never used
again, and the grandstand and out buildings were dismantled as squatters moved into
the area.[8] Figure 3.18, the 1948 aerial photograph of Tijuana referenced above, shows the
abandoned oval on the flats where the Tijuana Racetrack was once positioned.

In 1917, following the opening of the Tijuana Racetrack, another border baron, as
American entrepreneurs of the era became known, moved next door to the track. Carl H.
Withington, a Bakersfield bordello owner who became notorious for his adventuresome
investments in Southern California, relocated his pleasure palace businesses to Mexicali
in 1914 under an agreement with Esteban Cantú, the acting governor of Baja California.
Withington, smelling opportunity from the Tijuana Racetrack crowd that typically retired
to San Diego following races, bought the gambling rights from Antonio Elosúa's Monte
Carlo, which was part of the Tijuana Fair, and, with Cantú's blessing, built a new casino
on the border immediately west of the Tijuana Racetrack (see fig. 3.8).[9]

Withington's Monte Carlo Casino was an elaborate wooden structure that cost one
hundred thousand dollars to build and included a garden balcony that overlooked the
Tijuana Racetrack. The castle-like Monte Carlo Casino was walking distance from the
border crossing as well as proximate to the San Diego and Arizona Railroad depot (see
fig. 5.6). Crowds of visitors were drawn to the Monte Carlo, and dozens of popular postcard images were made, often capturing a sea of autos in the car park and pedestrians
strolling into or out of the site (fig. 8.4). Withington stocked the floors of the Monte
Carlo with gambling machines and provided inexpensive meals to keep patrons inside.
A dance hall provided an entertainment option, and even bullfights were staged at the
site, although no large plaza was ever built.

In 1920 Withington enabled an addition to the Monte Carlo Casino, a single-story
hotel named the Sunset Inn (see fig. 3.8). The lodging was run by Baron Long, who had
previously partnered with Coffroth to build the Tijuana Racetrack and who had experience as an innkeeper and manager of the U. S. Grant Hotel in San Diego. Because visitors
to the Monte Carlo and Tijuana Racetrack passed by the Sunset Inn, the first property

FIGURE 8.4 Monte Carlo Casino. The casino was a palatial extravaganza next door to the Tijuana Racetrack. The casino was close to the border and the San Diego and Arizona Railway depot (note the white sign). Photo postcard, 1920s.

encountered on crossing the border and the last one on return, the entertainments and lodgings became popular with regulars to the casino and track.[10]

The ensemble of the Tijuana Racetrack, the Monte Carlo Casino, and the Sunset Inn created a festival landmark immediately across the boundary for visitors to Tijuana between 1916 and 1929. During the racing season, thousands might visit the facilities on a single day, and postcard photographers such as Roy Magruder were early chroniclers of the crowds of visitors who thronged the gambling, drinking, and cabaret entertainments of this landmark space (fig. 8.5).

MEXICALI BEER HALL

Infamous is the word popularly associated with the Mexicali Beer Hall, an institution in Tijuana for nearly half a century. The establishment was also one of the most celebrated images in Tijuana postcards. The Arreola Collection includes some thirty separate representations in photo, print, and chrome formats and with both exterior and interior views. Exactly when the hall was constructed is not certain, but it was probably in the 1920s.[11] Miguel González, who founded the Cevecería Mexicali in 1923, was the proprietor, and

FIGURE 8.5 Tijuana Racetrack and Monte Carlo Casino. The racetrack and casino became signature landmarks only five hundred yards from the border outside Tijuana. This 1920s photo postcard attributed to Roy Magruder shows the western end of the one-mile oval racetrack, the grandstand and Jockey Club, the Monte Carlo Casino, and the Sunset Inn surrounded by hundreds of parked automobiles. Beyond the racetrack is the Tijuana River, and across and to the west, the village of Tijuana, which is not visible in this view. Border Studio, no. 4.

the Mexicali Beer Hall became famous for its exclusive serving of Mexicali beer, which it advertised on signs above the roof of the bar, at ten cents for a tall glass, thirty-five cents for a small pitcher, and seventy-five cents for a large pitcher.[12]

The Mexicali Beer Hall was located on Avenue A, later Revolución, at the corner of Calle 3, on the east side of the street, next door to the Hotel Comercial, which was also owned by Miguel González (see fig. 6.10 and fig. 6.10c). The bar gained a reputation as the longest bar in the world—approximately 229 feet—and its Spanish nickname was La Ballena (The Whale)[13] (fig. 8.6).

The single-story wooden structure occupied most of the block (see fig. 7.4), and many of the postcard images show the length of the bar with autos parked in front diagonally at curbside. On the north end of the bar proximate to the 1920s Hotel St. Francis (later the Hotel Comercial) was a separate entrance and outdoor section for families (fig. 8.7). At the south end of the bar on the corner of Calle 3, one of Tijuana's burro carts became a permanent fixture in the 1940s to take advantage of potential customers as they exited the hall (fig. 8.8).

Figure 8.9 is an interior view of the Mexicali Beer Hall, a long, cavernous space that gained it the first nickname, the Long Bar. By the 1940s the interior accommodated

FIGURE 8.6 Mexicali Beer Hall. It was first called "the long bar" and was reputed to be the longest bar in the world at 229 feet. Print postcard published by Enrique Silvestre, 1920s.

FIGURE 8.7 Mexicali Beer Hall looking south, showing the family entrance in the 1920s. The bar advertised beer by the glass and by small and large pitchers.

FIGURE 8.8 Burro cart photographer and a food vendor strategically positioned in front of the Mexicali Beer Hall to capitalize on customers who entered and exited the long bar. México Fotográfico 53, 1940s.

FIGURE 8.9 Mexicali Beer Hall. A cavernous space, it became known in Spanish as La Ballena (The Whale). This 1920s print postcard shows the long bar and mostly male patrons. Published by The Big Curio Store, Lower California Commercial Company, Tijuana, 1920s.

FIGURE 8.10 Musical entertainment at the Mexicali Beer Hall, 1940s. Published by Cia. Comercial de la Baja California, Tijuana. Manufactured by Curt Teich, C. T. Art-Colortone, 1B-H234, Chicago, IL, 1941.

FIGURE 8.11 Mexicali Beer Hall, called the Longest Bar in the World, during the post–World War II era. Patrons, both male and female, could then be seated at tables as well as the bar. Published by Cia. Comercial de la Baja California, Tijuana. Manufactured by Curt Teich, C. T. Art-Colortone, OC-H964, Chicago, IL, 1950.

FIGURE 8.12 Mexicali Beer Hall. The hall survived into the 1960s. Although a curio store cut into its corner space at Calle 3 and Avenida Revolución, the burro cart and water tower remain fixtures of the postcard view from earlier times. Published by Thompson Photo Service, P10655, San Diego, CA, 1950s. A "Plastichrome" postcard manufactured by Colourpicture, Boston, MA.

entertainment space as seen in a linen postcard featuring a marimba band and advertising beer prices reduced for the Christmas holiday season (fig. 8.10). During the post–World War II era, the hall continued as a popular venue attracting large crowds at tables as well as the bar (fig. 8.11).

The Mexicali Beer Hall survived into the 1960s, but in the 1970s it was torn down and replaced by a Woolworth's store. Figure 8.12 is a 1950s chrome postcard view of the bar. The long physical nature of the establishment can still be seen, but other businesses began to encroach on the space, evident in the curio store on the corner of Calle 3. The burro cart photographer remains in place, and the tin man water tower, seen in so many postcard views of the hall from the street, survives. A three-dimensional advertising billboard for Mexicali beer broadcasts from around the corner.

When the Mexicali Beer Hall closed its doors, a broadside titled "The Long Bar Closing Out Sale" was circulated. The sheet advertised liquor and glassware for sale at discount prices and the following declaration.[14]

WE ARE POSITIVELY RETIRING FROM BUSINESS!

THE LONG BAR, ONE OF TIJUANA'S LAND-MARKS, IS GOING

Visit us; look at yourself for the last time in the gallery of funny looking-glasses, which, together with our low prices and excellent quality of liquors that we sell, has been the principal attraction of our establishment. Upon retiring, we wish to express to our faithful customers, in particular, our heartfelt appreciation of the many years of their patronage and to assure them that we go out of business with a feeling of fulfillment: the deep satisfaction that we have always given them the best in return.

FAREWELL!!

FOREIGN CLUB

Many associate the past glamour of Tijuana with the world famous Agua Caliente Casino and Resort, a landmark of significance discussed separately below. However, before the popularity of Agua Caliente, there was the Foreign Club, a casino and rendezvous spot for the high rollers of Prohibition-era Tijuana. From 1917 to 1935, the Foreign Club catered to a tony crowd of visitors, and while the club is long gone, the name still survives as a hotel and cabaret on Avenida Revolución and Calle 3. The Foreign Club was a fashionable venue for postcard photographers and publishers. The Arreola Collection includes some twenty-one separate photographic, print, and chrome postcards of the site as well as related ephemera such as a menu, brochure, souvenir photo folder, and matchbook covers.

As noted in chapter 7, drinking restrictions in California were ahead of national Prohibition, and consequently, many entrepreneurs sought out Baja California to reestablish cabaret entertainment. Chief among these businessmen were Marvin Allen, Frank Beyer, and Carl Withington, who formed the A. B. W. syndicate that owned the Monte Carlo, Tivoli Bar, and the Foreign Club in Tijuana along with the Owl Café in Mexicali. When Withington died, Wirt G. Bowman joined the enterprise, and he and James Coffroth assumed the operation of the Foreign Club.[15]

The original Foreign Club was located on the corner of Main Street and Calle 3 in Tijuana, across the street and catercorner from the Mexicali Beer Hall (see fig. 6.11). It advertised as the "in town" counterpart to the Sunset Inn located next to the Tijuana Racetrack. The Foreign Club was a single building in early Mission Revival architectural style with Arts and Crafts highlights and a stylized white picket fence that cordoned off its street perimeter (fig. 8.13). With increased popularity, by the 1920s the Foreign Club expanded to a larger central building and several out buildings (fig. 8.14). The complex even included a separate curio store that advertised Mexican silver jewelry, amethysts, serapes, drawn work, leather, basketry, carved canes, and Aztec feather cards (fig. 8.15). The main ballroom featured a dance floor, orchestra stage, art nouveau wall décor and lighting, and linen-clothed table seating (fig. 8.16).

Circa 1927 the original Foreign Club burned down, a tragedy all too common in early Tijuana. The owners wasted little time rebuilding and hired renowned San Diego architect Frank Stevenson to design a new and more elegant compound. The new Foreign

FIGURE 8.13 Foreign Club. The earliest upscale casino and cabaret in Tijuana, the Foreign Club was located at the corner of Main Street and Calle 3. Photograph attributed to Enrique Silvestre, 1910s.

FIGURE 8.14 Foreign Club expanded to multiple buildings in a large compound during the 1920s. Published by M. Kashower, Co., no. 33844, Los Angeles, CA, 1920s.

FIGURE 8.15 Foreign Club Curio Store. A retail business included in the cabaret compound, the store vended Mexican curio crafts to guests. Published by M. Kashower, no. 33838, Los Angeles, CA, 1920s.

FIGURE 8.16 Foreign Club Dining Room with dance floor, orchestra stage, and art nouveau decorations. Published by M. Kashower, no. 38394, Los Angeles, CA, 1920s.

Club was a stylish Spanish Revival structure with a tower, arcade, and red-tile roofline (fig. 8.17). Reminiscent of so many emblematic Spanish pinnacles, the tower became a symbolic logo for the club and was featured on stationery, matchbook covers, and postcards. Floorshow entertainment became a staple of the new club, which advertised its Café de Luxe Mexican Revue on postcards it published and distributed, announcing the club atmosphere as "quaint . . . for devotees of dining, dancing, and diversions."

From 1932 to 1933, the most popular dancers at the Foreign Club were Spaniard Eduardo Cansino and his teenage daughter Margarita. Eduardo's Irish wife, Volga, and the Cansino family resided in Chula Vista, across the border south of San Diego. Cansino's spirited choreographies became recognized by visitors to Tijuana, and Margarita was quickly discovered and emerged as a celebrity in her own right in Hollywood, taking her mother's maiden name— Haworth—and becoming Rita Hayworth.[16]

Keeping with the club's elegance, dining was a first-class experience. The 1930s menu cover was a colorful artistic rendering of a Lady-of-Spain figure shadowed by a Spanish guitarist (fig. 8.18a). Meals ranged in price from a dollar to a dollar and a half, and the à la carte menu offered Spanish (Mexican) and Italian dishes along with meat

FIGURE 8.17 Tower of the new Foreign Club, a symbol of the enterprise embedded in the shield seal of the club. This 1930s postcard published by the club accentuates the Spanish Revival façade of the building and the entertainment divas of the Café de Luxe Mexican Revue.

entrees, seafood, hors d'oeuvres, cold dishes, salads, soups, sandwiches, potatoes and vegetables, eggs and omelets, and desserts (fig. 8.18b). The beverage menu offered a staggering list of French, German, Italian, and Mexican wines; Mexican and European beers, ales, and stouts (fig. 8.18c); and every imaginable spirit, including American and Scotch whiskies, French brandy and cognac, English gins, Jamaican rum, Danish aquavit, and Mexican tequilas as well as liqueurs and cordials, ports, sherries, vermouth, bitters, and aperitifs.

The new Foreign Club burned down in 1935. Yet again, another more modern Foreign Club was constructed on Avenida Revolución (see fig. 6.11). The modern Foreign Club encompassed property fronting Calle 3 and featured a hotel with a tower and arcade as reminders of the previous incarnation and the Foreign Club Bazaar, a dining, dancing,

FIGURE 8.18   Foreign Club Menu, 1930s. *a*, cover. *b*, á la carte menu. *c*, wine list. Author's collection.

and cabaret section that fronted Revolución with ground-level curio stores (see fig. 6.11*d*). The Foreign Club Hotel was a popular Tijuana lodging into the 1950s and 1960s. Centrally located, the hotel claimed itself air conditioned and luxurious at moderate rates of five-dollar singles, six-dollar doubles, and eight-dollar suites where "your discriminating taste will be gratified by superb appointments and modern décor . . . your yen for comfort amply satisfied by peerless service."

AGUA CALIENTE CASINO AND RESORT

In his chronicle of Agua Caliente Tijuana, historian Paul Vanderwood notes, "Where else in the world might one mingle so openly with neither fanfare nor modesty among royalty, movie stars, ambassadors, ministers of government, Hollywood moguls, and pure-blooded thoroughbreds (horses as well as their owners)?"[17] Agua Caliente was called the "Playground of the Hemisphere" and "America's Deauville in Old Mexico." By many accounts it was considered *the* landmark in the history of Tijuana.

The Agua Caliente (Hot Springs) was part of the original Rancho de Tía Juana owned by the Argüello family. Since the early 1920s, a crude two-story hotel, cabaret, and casino existed at the springs. The hot springs property was sold to Abelardo L. Rodríguez in 1926, along with partners Baron Long, Wit Bowman, and James Crofton, the so-called border barons, who raised $750,000 to build the resort. The investors contracted a young San Diego architect, Wayne McAllister, to design a Spanish-themed tourist development on some six hundred acres three miles south of the international boundary west of the Tijuana River and southeast of the town of Tijuana[18] (see fig. 3.22, which shows the former location).

Construction at the Agua Caliente site was launched in 1927, and the property was inaugurated June 23, 1928. The initial resort included a hotel, casino, restaurant, outdoor pool, indoor spa, tennis courts, lushly landscaped garden and grounds, and dog track (*galgódromo*). In 1929 a horse track (*hipódromo*) and championship golf course were added in addition to a series of independent residential bungalows. The site included an airport and two special train depots with track connected to the San Diego and Arizona Railway that coursed east of the Tijuana River (fig. 8.19).

Spanish Revival architectural style was a thematic signature of San Diego and Southern California. Wayne McAllister, along with his aspiring architect fiancée and later wife Corinne, worked to design the Spanish Revival plan with flourishes of Arts and Crafts, Renaissance, and Moorish elements. Once complete, Agua Caliente was praised by architectural critics as a marvel.[19]

Not surprisingly given the enormous popularity of Agua Caliente, the resort generated hundreds of postcards, making the landmark the most frequently represented image

FIGURE 8.19 Agua Caliente Casino and Resort circa 1930. From "Agua Caliente America's Deauville in Old Mexico" (brochure). Author's collection.

of Tijuana. The Arreola Collection alone includes eighty-five photographic, print, and chrome postcards of the hotel, casino, grounds and gardens plus twenty-eight additional postcards in all formats that show the dog and horse racetracks. Postcards were published by individuals, small printing firms, and, most importantly by large companies including the Agua Caliente Company, México Fotográfico, Western Publishing and Novelty, and M. Kashower Company.

The following vignette provides a glimpse of some of the highlights of Agua Caliente. The range of postcard images is overwhelming, so the illustrations presented here are but a sampling. While photographic postcards exist, many more print postcards were manufactured in part, no doubt, because publishers wished to emphasize the dazzling colors of tiles, flower gardens, and the picturesque that was rendered with greater ease in print format than in black and white. Selected details in the figure captions are from several key sources.[20]

Agua Caliente survived and flourished during the Great Depression and the repeal of Prohibition in the United States, but it began to teeter with the election of Mexican president Lázaro Cárdenas in 1934. Cárdenas set in motion a series of national reforms that ultimately led to the demise of "America's Deauville in Old Mexico." When Cárdenas closed down casino gambling in Mexico, he initially spared Baja California Norte in part, it has been argued, because the casino tax revenue benefitted the federal coffers. Nevertheless, Cárdenas dropped the hammer on July 20, 1935, when he issued an edict that closed casino gaming in Baja. The border barons decided that without casino profits, all other aspects of Agua Caliente were untenable. The entire resort was shuttered at

FIGURE 8.20 Campanile, or Tower of Chimes. The single most emblematic landmark of Agua Caliente, it was photographed and reproduced many times over in postcards and other imagery. The eighty-foot tower of Moorish inspiration was the gateway beacon of the development, and vehicles passed under its arched base to move into the resort complex. A revolving light at the top warned and directed airplanes to the nearby landing strip. Bells in the tower chimed on the hour until they were moved to the steam plant chimney that was disguised as a Muslim minaret because guests complained about the constant ringing when trying to sleep late after a night of cabaret. Published by the Agua Caliente Company, 1930s.

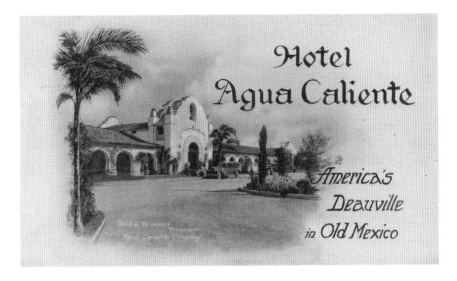

FIGURE 8.21 Hotel Agua Caliente featured as the cover postcard of a folder of eleven different cards bound together but capable of being separated individually to message and post. The hotel accommodated five hundred guests, and rooms were individually embellished with each having an outside exposure. The Agua Caliente garden and grounds were designed by George Body, who previously worked on the Panama-California Exposition at Balboa Park in San Diego in 1915. Published by the Agua Caliente Company, 1930s.

FIGURE 8.22 Casino at Agua Caliente. The casino required formal dress to enter. Gaming proved a critical revenue source for the Agua Caliente Company, generating profits that could be reinvested in the continued expansion of facilities. Western Publishing and Novelty Company, Los Angeles, CA. Manufactured by Curt Teich Company, no. 123384, Chicago, IL 1929.

FIGURE 8.23 Olympic-size swimming pool known as The Plunge. The facility included a spa (see fig. 2.29), bathhouse, mud baths, and a massage parlor. Western Publishing and Novelty, Los Angeles, CA. Manufactured by Curt Teich Company, no. OA3649, Chicago, IL, 1930.

181A:—The Patio Dining Room, Agua Caliente, Tijuana, B. C., Mexico.

FIGURE 8.24 Patio Andaluz adjacent to the main restaurant at Agua Caliente. The patio was an outdoor dining area where guests could be entertained by musicians and dancers. M. Kashower Company, no. 32985, Los Angeles, CA, 1930s.

X-49 MAIN DINING SALON, CASINO, HOTEL AGUA CALIENTE, TIJUANA, MEXICO

FIGURE 8.25 Main dining salon at Agua Caliente with orchestra stage on right and dance floor at center. The elaborate interior décor was designed by Louis Sherman and spared no expense to impress guests. Western Publishing and Novelty Company, Los Angeles, CA. Manufactured by Curt Teich Company, no. 4104–29, Chicago, IL, 1929.

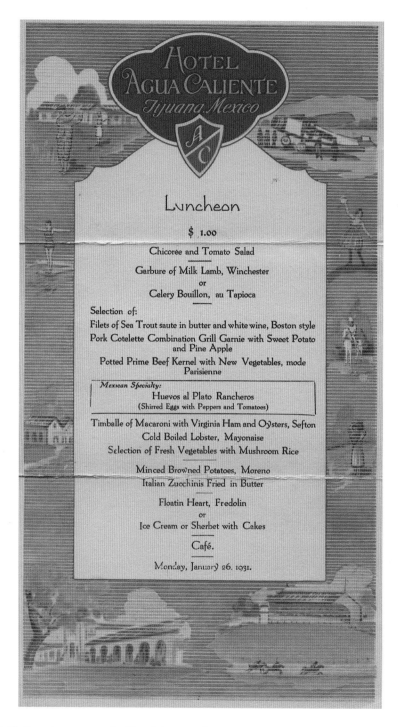

FIGURE 8.26 Lunch menu at the Hotel Agua Caliente, January 26, 1931. The caption to this trifold postcard sent to South Norwalk, Connecticut reads, in part, "Mother and I had lunch here. . . . They claim it's the most beautiful place in the world. . . . It's the Monte Carlo of North America." Author's collection.

FIGURE 8.27 Greyhound racing at Agua Caliente. Its track preceded the later construction of the horse track (see fig. 8.19). Photo postcard, 1920s.

FIGURE 8.28 Agua Caliente Racetrack. The track was opened in late 1929 to considerable success. The facility was larger and more elegant than the 1916 Tijuana Racetrack and included a large grandstand that could accommodate 4,500 spectators, a Jockey Club house with veranda seating and imported Italian marble decoration, and extensive mature palms and exotic plantings. The racetrack and grounds cost two million dollars to build. Published by the Agua Caliente Company, 1930s.

FIGURE 8.29 Eighteen-hole championship golf course at Agua Caliente. The course was added in 1929. This photograph shows Bernice Wall, a nationally competitive golfer from Wisconsin, putting out in a special tournament arranged in November 1930. The Campanile or Tower of Chimes entrance landmark is visible in the background along with the golf clubhouse. Author's collection.

FIGURE 8.30 Caliente Racetrack, 1950s. The track survived the 1937 shuttering of the Agua Caliente Casino and Resort. During the 1950s, thoroughbred horses raced in the day and greyhounds ran at night, ensuring a stream of gaming patrons at Tijuana's historic landmark. Chrome postcard, 1950s.

midnight December 18, 1937, and horse racing on the track was temporarily suspended. The economic chaos created by closing Agua Caliente sent shockwaves across Tijuana and into San Diego, where unemployment soared and financial supply linkages were crippled. Nevertheless, Cárdenas expropriated Agua Caliente, transforming the facilities into an industrial trade school; only the horse track was allowed to remain (see map that shows the racetrack in the 1950s–1960s, fig. 3.22).[21]

Closing Agua Caliente probably underscored political rivalry, because Cárdenas was at odds with the so-called Sonoran clique of Plutarco Elías Calles and Abelardo L. Rodríguez, the latter a partner in the Agua Caliente operations and beneficiary of the capital profits from the enterprise. The Agua Caliente racetrack continued to operate through various unsavory business owners with shady political alliances into the 1950s and beyond.[22] The popularity of the Caliente Racetrack (Agua was dropped from the name), where horses raced in the day during the season and dogs raced at night under the stars, continued into the post–World War II era (fig. 8.30).

CAESAR'S HOTEL AND CAFÉ

Caesar's is without argument the most celebrated hotel and café in Tijuana, both historically and to the present. The story centers on Caesar Cardini, an Italian immigrant to the United States who opened a restaurant in Tijuana and reputedly invented the Caesar Salad. There are several interpretations to the salad story, but postcards—there are a dozen in the Arreola Collection—and local histories enable a reasonable reconstruction of the circumstances surrounding the landmark restaurant in the border city.[23]

Abelardo Cesare "Caesar" Cardini (1896–1956) immigrated to the United States with brothers Alessandro, Nereo, and Gaudencio. Caesar operated a restaurant in Sacramento, California, but relocated to San Diego and, along with brothers Alessandro and Gaudencio, opened a restaurant in Tijuana. This restaurant, called Caesar's Place, was opened in 1923 and was located behind the Foreign Club on Callejón de Travieso near Avenida B. Circa 1927 Caesar opened with two new partners an establishment known as Hotel Caesar's Place on Avenida A (Revolución) at the northwest corner of Calle 5 (see fig. 6.11). This establishment became a popular venue in Tijuana and was shown on both photographic and print postcards of the era (fig. 8.31). The two-story hotel and restaurant was built in Spanish Colonial architectural style. It enclosed a courtyard terrace for outdoor dining and was said to be the location where Cardini first served the Caesar Salad.

Sometime in the 1930s, a second Caesar's restaurant opened in Tijuana attached to Miguel González's Hotel Comercial (built in 1928) on the southeast corner of Avenida A (Revolución) and Calle 2. This business was known as Original Caesar's Place and may have been the relocated restaurant from Callejón de Travieso, although that cannot be

FIGURE 8.31 Hotel Caesar's Place opened on the corner of Avenida A and Calle 5 circa 1927. This location persists to the present as Caesar's Hotel and Café and is reputed to be the restaurant where Caesar Cardini first served the Caesar Salad. Published by M. Kashower Company, no. 36020, Los Angeles, CA, 1930s.

confirmed. The Original Caesar's Place operated under Caesar Cardini and his brothers because Caesar split with his partners from Hotel Caesar's Place, which continued to operate successfully but without Cardini. The Original Caesar's Place did appear in both print postcards and a photograph circa 1930s. The Original Caesar's Place was popular with tourists for several years and offered floorshows, strolling musicians (mariachis), and, of course, Caesar's signature salad. Circa 1936 the Cardini brothers closed the Original Caesar's Place at the Hotel Comercial. Caesar returned to San Diego to open a new restaurant called Caesar Cardini Café, but the venture closed within one year.

The Hotel Caesar's Place on Revolución and Calle 5—owned then by Cardini's original partners, Giuseppi "Joe" Ferraris and Clement Monaco—continued to operate as Hotel Caesar. It transitioned through several owners into the post–World War II period and was remodeled and expanded to include a gift shop as well as a café (fig. 8.32). Print postcards from the 1950s touted Hotel Caesar's dining as the "Originator of the World Famous CAESAR SALAD" and showed that the hotel continued to serve the item in its Gold Room restaurant (fig. 8.33).

The Hotel Caesar was remodeled again in the mid- to late 1950s, enclosing the façade of the Revolución side of the three-story building (fig. 8.34). A large banner announced

FIGURE 8.32 Hotel Caesar at the corner of Revolución and Calle 5. Shown here is the remodeled Hotel Caesar's Place from the 1920s (cf. fig. 8.31). Caesar Cardini split with his founding partners in the 1930s, but the Hotel Caesar continued to operate and to offer the famous Caesar Salad in its restaurant. México Fotográfico, 57, 1940s.

FIGURE 8.33 Gold Room in the Hotel Caesar. The Gold Room continued to serve Cardini's Caesar Salad, evident from the salad mixing bowl and preparation bowls on the empty table on the right. Published by Elmo M. Sellers, no. 81297, Los Angeles, CA, 1950s.

FIGURE 8.34 Hotel Caesar remodeled in the 1950s. The hotel continued to advertise to visitors Caesar's Bar Restaurant Grill as the place where the Caesar Salad was invented. Foto Enrique Asin, C8751, printed by Colores Naturales, 1950s.

a New Caesar's Bar Restaurant Grill in the hotel where the Caesar Salad continued to celebrate Cardini's "invention."[24]

JAI ALAI *FRONTÓN*

"Faster than ice hockey more thrilling than baseball or football." So read a billboard in front of the Tijuana Jai Alai Palace as it was being constructed in the 1920s (fig. 8.35). *Jai-alai* (pronounced "hi'li") translates to "merry festival" in the Basque language. The lightning-fast court game is said to have its origin in *pelota*, a handball game traditionally played in a three-walled outdoor court in the Basque regions of Spain and France. In the 1800s baskets, or *cestas*, were added so that the velocity of the thrown ball accelerated, and jai alai was born.

The court, called a *cancha*, is typically an indoor rectangle about 176 feet long with forty-foot-high front, side, and back walls and one sidewall open. In many parts of the Spanish-speaking world where jai alai is played, including Mexico, the court and/or the building (palace) that encloses the court is called a *frontón*. The game includes multiple players called *jugadores de pelota* (ball players) in teams, although single matches are possible (fig. 8.36). Similar to racquetball, a game starts with a serve in which a ball is thrown against the front wall and must be retrieved by an opposing player on the fly or on one bounce and returned to the wall in a continuous motion. The ball (*pelota*) is

FIGURE 8.35 Jai alai *frontón*, or palace, under construction in Tijuana. México Fotográfico 27, 1920s.

FIGURE 8.36 Jai alai players. Jai alai is typically played in teams with players volleying the ball (*pelota*) thrown at high speed against the walls of the court by a *cesta* (basket) until a player misses or fouls. Attributed to Mike Roberts Color Production, no. C4314, Berkeley, CA, 1950s.

FIGURE 8.37 Tijuana's Jai Alai Palace in Moorish architectural splendor. Opened in February 1947, it became for several decades the epicenter of the sport on the border. Photo postcard, 1950s. Attributed to Guy Sidney Sensor.

FIGURE 8.38 Statue celebrating the jai alai player standing on top of the globe and stretching his *cesta* to the sky. Designed and presented by Eduardo Corella. It became a signature symbol of the Tijuana *frontón* in dozens of postcards. Foto Enrique A. De Frias, Colores Naturales, no. C11451, 1950s.

roughly the size of a baseball and is made of enclosed hard rubber traditionally covered in stitched goatskin. When thrown with the *cesta*, a roughly two-foot-long curved wicker basket framed in wood, it can reach speeds in excess of one hundred miles per hour. Players continue to volley until the ball is missed or goes out of play (there are foul zones on the walls). Points are scored, and the first team to reach seven wins. For audiences, the thrill beyond watching is to bet on teams organized in round-robin tournaments called quinielas, where teams of two—one frontcourt and one backcourt player—compete with up to eight different teams rotating in and out as points are won and lost.[25]

Jai alai got its start in Tijuana in 1926 when Mariano Escobedo initiated the construction of the *frontón* (see fig. 8.35). The Great Depression and then World War II, when materials became difficult to procure, delayed building the jai alai palace, and construction was not completed for two decades. The *frontón* was finally inaugurated in 1947.[26] Jai alai quickly gained a following as a new sport-gaming enterprise in Tijuana. The *frontón* was built on Avenida Revolución between Calles 7 and 8 (see fig. 6.10), and it became the epicenter of the sport, attracting locals and Americans from across the border. The Tijuana jai alai *frontón* that came to be known locally as El Palacio (the Palace) was a spectacular Moorish-styled structure seemingly imported from Spain's Alhambra. The brick building was stucco coated a creamy white, and the rooflines were peppered with tiny minarets (fig. 8.37). Arches and tile were decorative highlights inside and out, including the main side entrance facing Revolución. A decorative fountain graced the entrance to a café attached to the front of the palace. A large red neon sign on the front exterior signaled Jai Alai Games. Palms ornamented the street side of the building. The palace survived a disastrous 1957 fire only to be rebuilt in the same year.[27]

The popularity of jai alai in Tijuana is borne out by the many postcard images made of the *frontón*. The Arreola Collection includes thirty-six postcards in all formats—photo, print, and chrome—that show the palace. Chrome postcards featuring a statue of a player perched on top of the world, standing on one foot, and stretching his *cesta* to the sky were notably common (fig. 8.38). The life-size monument to jai alai made by Eduardo Corella was surrounded by a shallow fountain and positioned in the parking lot near the café entrance to the palace for all to see.[28]

Jai alai slowed as an attendance sport when satellite betting made it unnecessary to visit the palace in Tijuana. Player strikes added to the decline. By the 1990s, Mariano Escobedo Jr., who inherited the *frontón* from his father, closed the facility to games and began to rent the space for alternative entertainment events.[29] Today the palace is called "El Foro" (The Forum). While it survives as a landmark in Tijuana, increasingly its colorful past slips away as the generations who knew it during its heyday fade.

PART III

Mexicali

Mexicali debío haber nacido . . . en 1902. . . . derivándolo como el nombre de Caléxico, del anagrama MEX-ico CALI-fornia. . . . Por lo tanto las ciudades de Mexicali, del lado mexicano, y Caléxico del norteamericano, son con razón HERMANAS GEMELAS.

—Celso Aguirre Bernal[1]

NINE

Mexicali Town Plan and Townscape

Mexican American border town names have a history of complementarity, to wit, the Texas-Tamaulipas towns of Los Dos Laredos and the Sonora-Arizona towns of Ambos Nogales. The origin of the town name Mexicali, that is, a play on the name of its cross-border neighbor, Calexico, is yet another example of this twinning but with a twist. As Mexicali historian Celso Aguirre Bernal notes, the town is rightly a sister city of Calexico, California.[1] The towns of Mexicali and Calexico were founded and platted just two years apart; however, their historical developments followed separate trajectories, a common experience among border towns that emerged from a similar root. Yet Mexicali's Baja rival has not been its twin sister Calexico but rather its distant cousin, Tijuana. It is, therefore, ironic that Mexicali, a town for most of its history in the shadow of Tijuana, has been a more populated place—a bigger place but a town less well known— than its celebrated Baja neighbor for most of the decades of this study (see table 1.1).

This chapter introduces the geographical foundations of Mexicali from its small-town origins to its historical maturity as a major city of Baja California using postcard views and maps to understand that transformation. The story of Mexicali is explored through two time frames: the 1900s–1910s and the 1920s–1950s. In each chronicle, emphasis is given to the look of major streets and landmarks of Mexicali to the extent that they were captured in postcard representations and to how those features were arranged in the mapped space of the city, its townscape. A third section in this chapter will describe the varied residential landscapes of Mexicali as shown in postcards.

FROM INSTANT TOWN TO EARLY MORPHOLOGY

In his 1909 recollection of the platting of the border town of Calexico, Charles R. Rock- wood proclaimed, "Calexico just happened." In fact, the founding of Calexico and its twin town of Mexicali was a tortured process of land acquisition and railroad accommodation involving many actors, several governments, and a decade-long undertaking. From land originally granted to Guillermo Andrade, a Mexican citizen with financial interests in the United States, and transferred to American investors through multiple exchanges, property holders circa 1901 decided to found two towns, speculate lot sales, and give birth to Calexico and Mexicali.[2]

Historical record suggests that squatters were already living on the Mexican boundary before the towns were platted. Settlers were attracted to the site because reclamation efforts in the region had already begun before 1900. The first residents, Mexicans and Native Cocopah, inhabited a few ramadas and were, therefore, said to be "sin orden y sin ley" (orderless and lawless).[3] The California Land Company–Imperial Land Company acquired 463 acres south of the international boundary and platted the initial outlines of Mexicali in 1902. Engineer and investment partner Charles Rockwood drafted the plat map for the Mexican border town, which was published by the Emerson Realty Company of Los Angeles (fig. 9.1).

Rockwood's map shows Mexicali spread out hard against the international boundary with plaza spaces buffering the town lots from the border. The plan showed no recognition of the New River that flanked the west of the town, but it did locate the original railroad corridor anticipated for the Southern Pacific that intended to route into Mexico from the Imperial Valley in California (see chap. 1). That initial routing was abandoned

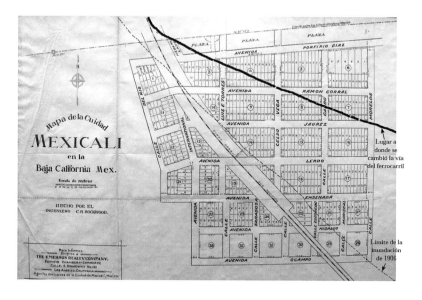

FIGURE 9.1 *Mapa de la Ciudad Mexicali en la Baja California, Mex.* Original plat map of Mexicali drafted by Charles R. Rockwood in 1902. The original location of the Southern Pacific Railroad corridor was rerouted after the 1906 flood as an alignment north and east across the grid. Entire blocks of Mexicali west of the inundation line were lost. After Charles R. Rockwood, 1902, in Alfonso Herrera Moreno, "Antecedentes urbanos de Mexicali." Author's collection.

when a flood erased much of the western edge of Mexicali and forced realignment across the grid of the town (the black line addition to fig. 9.1). Rockwood's plat called for 460 lots, and the official survey was recognized by Mexico and the date of the town's founding set in 1903. In 1904 Mexicali counted some two hundred inhabitants concentrated in thirty dwellings strung along a single street, Avenida Ramón Corral (later Avenida Reforma). The flood of the New River in 1905–1906 forced a reconfiguration of Mexicali because whole blocks west of the original railroad alignment were lost (see dashed line "Limite de la inundación" on fig. 9.1). A 1906 historic photograph shows the style of adobe and simple wood-frame houses that were scattered along Mexicali's single main street as the floodwaters encroached (fig. 9.2).[4]

Developments that followed the inundation were the construction of the municipal waterworks, the realignment of the railroad corridor, and construction of a new depot.[5] Before the flood Mexicali secured water via a conduit that crossed the border from Calexico. The Mexican town built its own facility circa 1910, and the waterworks occupied a parcel of land near the boundary line. A tin man water tower, as well as a similar one across the border in Calexico, would survive for many decades. Each became a distinctive landmark visible throughout the towns. Certainly the most disruptive change from Rockwood's original map of Mexicali was the realignment of the railroad corridor after the disastrous flood. When the breach that caused the flood was finally repaired in early 1907, Mexicali started to rebuild. Whereas some of the original blocks had been completely spared from the floodwaters, whole sections of Mexicali on the western edge fronting New River were completely eroded. This caused the Southern Pacific railroad to seek a

FIGURE 9.2 New River flood pushes on to the main street of Mexicali in 1906. The first dwellings in the town were simple adobe and wood constructions. Author's collection.

new high-ground alignment that would cut diagonally across the reconfigured town grid (see fig. 9.1). The new rail corridor was a single right-of-way flanked on each side by a new road, called the Inter-California (after the Southern Pacific line) and today known as Avenida López Mateos. A new depot was constructed at the intersection of this new road with Calle Altamirano (see fig. 1.14).

Mexicali regained its footing between 1907 and 1910 as the town population more than doubled to over four hundred and then exploded in the 1910s to nearly seven thousand (table 1.1) as cotton farming boomed in the Mexicali Valley (fig. 9.3). The modified town plat would be known as the Primera Sección (First Section) to differentiate it from later additions. Avenida Porfirio Díaz, one block below the international boundary, emerged as the main street (fig. 9.4).

Several streets were renamed during this period. East–west Avenidas Porfirio Díaz and Ramón Corral, for example, became Madero and Reforma, respectively. North–south Calles Luis E. Torres, Celso Vega, and Carbó became Zorrilla, Azueta, and Altamirano, respectively. A new street, Calle Melgar, was carved through block 4 of Rockwood's plat between Zorrilla and Azueta, stretching from the international boundary to Avenida Reforma.[6] Figures 9.5 and 9.6 show Calle Azueta (formerly Celso Vega) looking north toward the border line. As Mexicali matured, commercial buildings increasingly were

FIGURE 9.3 Wagons loaded with cotton line up along the international border. Cotton cultivation boomed in the Mexicali Valley during the first two decades of the twentieth century, driving the Mexican border-town population to near seven thousand. Photo postcard, 1910s.

FIGURE 9.4 Avenida Porfirio Díaz. This dirt road emerged as Mexicali's main street in the 1910s. False-front wooden buildings were scattered along the avenue. Electrical power came to Mexicali from Calexico in 1905. Photo postcard, 1910s.

FIGURE 9.5 Calle Azueta looking north to the boundary line several blocks beyond, near the water tower located across the line in Calexico. Rafael Castillo Foto., no. 18, 1910s.

FIGURE 9.6 Calle Azueta only a block from the borderline. The water tower at far right is actually in Calexico. The Hotel Intercolonial and street businesses like La India, a small general store, catered chiefly to men who crowded the streets of Mexicali. Photo postcard, 1910s.

built with brick rather than wood, suggesting a modern face to the fast-growing Mexican town. Mexicali streets were bustling with activity and dominated by men.

The decade of the 1910s witnessed a cavalcade of private and public construction in Mexicali as the town pulled itself up from the muddy inundation of the previous years. By this time, most of the land in the Mexicali Valley had transferred to the California-Mexico Land and Cattle Company, the Mexican-chartered subsidiary of the Colorado River Land Company directed by Harrison Gray Otis of Los Angeles. Irrigation farming focused on cotton expanded across the region, and Mexicali boomed in conjunction with this development.[7]

One of the first projects in keeping with the tradition of Mexican town founding was to create a plaza space. Because Rockwood's original plat allowed multiple lots dedicated to potential plazas, Mexicali selected the parcel between Calles Azueta and Altamirano and fronting Avenida Porfirio Díaz (later Madero) to construct its principal plaza. The rectangular space was christened Chapultepec Park in 1915 and has historically been known in Mexicali as the Parque (Park) (fig. 9.7). This, perhaps, was an intentional misnomer, because in traditional Mexican towns and cities, the plaza is a central townscape feature, whereas a park or *alameda* is typically found elsewhere in the urban plan. Given Mexicali's close relationship with Calexico and the strong influence of American town planning ideas in the original Rockwood design, it may have been no accident at all. Nevertheless, the formal name of Niños Héroes de Chapultepec, honoring a memorial in Mexico City's major public park, gave the space Mexican legitimacy. Its layout was that

FIGURE 9.7 Mexicali's Chapultepec Park. The town's first formal plaza, it was positioned next to the international boundary and displayed all the traditional elements of a Mexican plaza. The water tower in the upper right is across the border in Calexico. Photo postcard, 1910s.

of classic Mexican plazas, with its landscaped greenery, walk paths, benches, lighting, enclosure, and *kiosco* (bandstand).[8]

Facing Chapultepec Park on the west near Calle Celso Vega (later Azueta), Mexicali erected its municipal palace, another traditional landmark of a Mexican town. The palace, initially constructed of adobe and wood in 1908, was completed in 1915 but rebuilt in stone and concrete after several earthquakes threatened the earlier building. The municipal palace was razed in 1926 when the decision was made to relocate the government building, and a hotel was constructed in its place.[9] More significant than the municipal palace, perhaps, was the construction in 1916 of the Escuela Cuauhtémoc, in part because it still stands today but also because of the symbolic attachment to the structure positioned on Calle Altamirano facing the park on its east flank.

The Escuela Cuauhtémoc is considered one of the most important buildings in Mexicali, and the structure is included in the national catalog of historic properties of Baja California (fig. 9.8). Symbolically, the school, designed by Eduardo Trujillo, is a representation of the importance of education in the history of Mexicali. The two-story structure built of wood frame and cement embraced many neoclassical architectural elements such as columns, cornice moldings, and balustrades. Its position at the end of the town plaza afforded a view looking west along the borderline. The school's balcony became a popular platform for political speeches. Escuela Cuauhtémoc was enabled, in large measure, because of the political will of Coronel Esteban Cantú, governor of the northern district

FIGURE 9.8 Escuela Cuauhtémoc on inauguration day September 16, 1916. Iris Studio. Carol Hann Collection.

of Baja California, whose leverage and financial connections benefitted many construc-tions in the border towns of Baja.[10]

The 1910s witnessed the construction of additional public buildings such as the Cárcel Municipal (city jail) and the Cuartel Zaragoza de Mexicali (military garrison). An impos-ing public structure, the Cuartel was built by Esteban Cantú and exemplifies how Mex-icali benefitted from what historian Celso Aguirre Bernal called the "década de Cantú" when the *coronel* was more than a governor and more like a patriarch. Because Cantú maintained an armed force, he needed a garrison to house his troops. The adobe-block constructed Cuartel was completed in 1913 (fig. 9.9). The garrison walls included rooms that opened onto a central patio. The structure was located on the original block 18 of Rockwood's map and faced east on to Calle Carbó (later Calle Altamirano) just below Avenida Lerdo. The Cuartel remained at this location until it was demolished in 1943.[11]

Like other Mexican border towns, Mexicali erected a plaza de toros, or bullring. The first wooden ring was located on the northeast corner of Avenida Lerdo and Calle Carbó (Altamirano). This bullring burned to the ground in 1916, and a new ring built nearby in 1917 lasted only a short time before it was relocated.[12] The third plaza built in 1919 near the outskirts of town was typical of early wooden bullrings on the border and attracted visitors, Americans and locals alike, who filled the bleachers to watch the popular sport—the contest between man and beast (fig. 9.10).

FIGURE 9.9 Cuartel Zaragoza de Mexicali. An adobe structure built in 1913 to house Esteban Cantú's army, it was a landmark fixture in central Mexicali near the intersection of Calle Altamirano and Avenida Lerdo until it was demolished in 1943. Rafael Castillo Foto., no 6, 1910s.

FIGURE 9.10 Mexicali's third bullring. A wooden structure built near the outskirts of town circa 1919, it was popular with locals and outsiders. Photo postcard, 1920s.

MEXICALI EXPANDS, 1920S–1950S

By 1920 Mexicali was six times more populated than Tijuana, a consequence of the cotton boom in the region that brought labor and opportunity to the Mexican border town. Over the next two decades, Mexicali's population would triple to nearly nineteen thousand as the town consolidated its position as a central place in the Mexicali Valley. In the single decade of the 1940s, Mexicali exploded to near sixty-five thousand inhabitants, and by 1960 it would again nearly triple its population to become the largest place in the state (table 1.1). This growth trajectory both increased the density of development in the original core of Mexicali (Primera Sección) and pushed its built landscape to multiple new additions over the years. Postcards, again, were testimony to this expansion and reveal the transforming townscape of Mexicali over some four decades. This section highlights select streetscapes and landmarks that characterized Mexicali from the 1920s to the 1950s and combines historic maps with postcard views to create a visual narrative of Baja California's major border town during an era of unprecedented expansion.

Figure 9.11 is a 1921 map of Mexicali, and comparison of the physical limits of this map with Rockwood's 1902 map (fig. 9.1) illustrates that an entire new section of the town had been added on the northeast quadrant. This addition, the urban extension of the Primera Sección, is called the Segunda Sección.[13] The district of some fourteen blocks stretched east from Calle Morelos to Calle Oriente and from the international boundary south to Avenida Ocampo. This addition did not conform perfectly to the grid of the original section, so several avenues—such as Reforma, Juárez-Obregón, and Lerdo—were not congruent; Avenida Francisco Madero (formerly Porfirio Díaz) remained intact because it aligned with the international boundary. New north–south streets on the map of Mexicali were Calles Mexico, Bravo, and Oriente.

To illustrate the changes in the townscape from 1910s to 1930s Mexicali, consider a comparison among figures 9.12*a*–*c*. The figures are all postcard views looking east along Mexicali's main street, Avenida Porfirio Díaz (later Madero), from a point where it intersects the railroad corridor. The small triangular block shown on the 1921 map (fig. 9.11, section 2) is the location of the Imperial Hotel, the main structure shown in each of the postcard views. This distinctive building, located near the early crossing to Calexico, was known as El "Flat Iron" Mexicalense after its resemblance to New York City's famous landmark. Figure 9.12*a* is the earliest view circa 1910s, and it shows the Hotel Imperial in a modified Mission Revival architectural style positioned on the triangle block with distinctive portico-covered sidewalks to combat the fierce sun of Mexicali (where summer temperatures easily reached into triple digits). The hotel rooms are visible on the second floor, but below were commercial offices for a bank, a newspaper, and other businesses. Avenida Porfirio Díaz was then unpaved. Across the street from the hotel was new construction, a *cine* (cinema) that would become the Teatro México, the first movie house

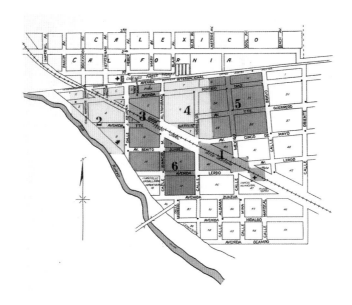

FIGURE 9.11 Map showing the extension of fourteen blocks in the northeast quadrant to the original plat of Mexicali. Compare to figure 9.1. Sanborn Map Company, *Mexicali Baja California Mexico December, 1921*, index sheet.

FIGURE 9.12 *a*, View looking east along Avenida Porfirio Díaz, 1910s. The Hotel Imperial occupies the triangle block to the right of center, and new construction is ongoing across the unpaved street. Print postcard published by Pacific Novelty Company, no. 4759, San Francisco and Los Angeles, CA, 1910s.

FIGURE 9.12 *b*, View looking east along Avenida Madero, 1920s. The Hotel Imperial Cabaret and increased auto traffic suggest this view was taken during the height of Prohibition. Print postcard published by Lower California Commercial Co., Tijuana-Mexicali-Ensenada-Tecate, 1920s. Original photo is a postcard attributed to Rafael Castillo.

FIGURE 9.12 *c*, View looking east along Avenida Madero, 1930s. The Hotel Imperial has removed its Cabaret sign. Avenida Madero is now paved, and decorative streetlights line the middle of the avenue. México Fotográfico 2, 1930s.

in Mexicali. Down the avenue just visible at left is a corner of the Escuela Cuauhtémoc that sits on the east end of Mexicali's plaza.[14]

Figure 9.12*b* is a 1920s view from nearly the same vantage point as the previous figure, again showing an eastward looking view along Avenida Madero (formerly Porfirio Díaz). More parked cars and the large sign on the roof of the hotel that spells "Cabaret" are clues to the fact that this postcard was made during the Prohibition era (1920–1933). The street remains unpaved, and buildings with porticos across Av. Madero are now completed. The thick patch of vegetation down the street on the left is Mexicali's plaza, Parque Chapultepec.[15]

Figure 9.12*c* is a 1930s view of Avenida Madero, once again looking east from the railroad corridor. The steadfast Hotel Imperial no longer sports its roof sign announcing Cabaret, a clue that this view is post-Prohibition. Further, Avenida Madero was paved in 1927, and in this postcard view decorative streetlights can be seen staggered down the middle of the street to a vanishing point. On the north side of Madero one block east where Calle Azueta intersects the main street is a two-story tile-roof building, the Hotel Comercial that was first built as the Hotel Aldrete in 1928 on the site of the original municipal palace.[16]

The 1920s witnessed a building boom in Mexicali, much of it tied to Prohibition palaces, which will be discussed in chapter 11. Nevertheless, new constructions to service the growing residential population of the border town were evident in postcard views. For example, the Municipal Market was built in 1924 to accommodate wholesale fruit, vegetable, and meat sales. The single-story building with large arched doorways was snapped by Calexico photographer Rafael Castillo and published as one of his many real photo postcards (fig. 9.13). Along one side of the market building are several flatbed trucks that transported products from Mexicali's farming hinterland to the *mercado* for sale and distribution to retail stores. The Mercado Municipal, a government-owned facility, was located on Avenida Obregón and Calle del Arbol, major boulevards in the city as evident from the paved street, curbing, median, and landscaping visible in the Castillo photo postcard. The Mercado Municipal building burned down in 1927 and was rebuilt. It burned a second time in 1954 and was rebuilt again in 1955.[17]

On January 1, 1927, at 12:17 a.m., an earthquake measuring 5.8 on the Richter scale rocked the Imperial Valley in California, and the shock wave extended across the border into Mexicali. About one hour after the first jolt, a single major aftershock of equal magnitude struck the region and was followed over the course of days by many minor aftershocks. Earthquakes, or *temblores* as they are known in Spanish, are not unusual in the Mexicali border region because the famous San Andreas Fault system extends into the Imperial Valley and then runs southeast across the international boundary through the Mexicali Valley and into the Gulf of California (called the Sea of Cortéz in Mexico). In Calexico some twenty homes were destroyed by the 1927 quake, and estimates of damage

FIGURE 9.13 Mercado Municipal. Mexicali's wholesale city market was built in Mission Revival architectural style in 1924. Photo postcard by Rafael Castillo Foto., no. 9, 1920s.

in 1920s dollars reached one million. The impact in Mexicali was more significant. Some four hundred private residences were affected, chiefly in Pueblo Nuevo, where poorly constructed dwellings of adobe suffered the greatest damage. Along major streets in town, such as Avenida Reforma, Avenida Teniente Guerrero, and Calle Melgar, smaller buildings, notably those built of unreinforced brick, crumbled, and postcard photographers were there to document the damage (fig. 9.14). On Avenida Madero, street lamps in the middle of the road collapsed.[18]

While Mexicali continued to grow into the decade of the Great Depression, its development slowed appreciably compared to earlier leaps. The decade of the 1940s, by comparison, witnessed a sizable rebound, with population more than tripling from about nineteen thousand to nearly sixty-five thousand (table 1.1). This acceleration was even greater in the decade of the 1950s when Mexicali exploded to about 175,000 inhabitants. These cycles of growth brought peripheral geographic expansion to the townscape. Postcards and historic maps help illuminate these changes.

Figure 9.15 is a tourist map of Mexicali from 1951. This map enables a comparison with the 1921 map showing the Primera Sección (fig. 9.11) to assess additions made to Mexicali over a quarter century. Calle Oriente, the eastern boundary of the town in 1921, became Calle del Arbol. Using this street as a benchmark, the 1951 map shows that a letter system has been put in place to name streets east of this line; eleven new Calles, A–K, now define the eastern quadrant of the city known formally as the Segunda Sección.[19]

FIGURE 9.14 Damage to a building façade in Mexicali caused by the January 1, 1927 earthquake that struck the Imperial Valley in California and extended into the Mexicali Valley. Photo postcard, January 1, 1927.

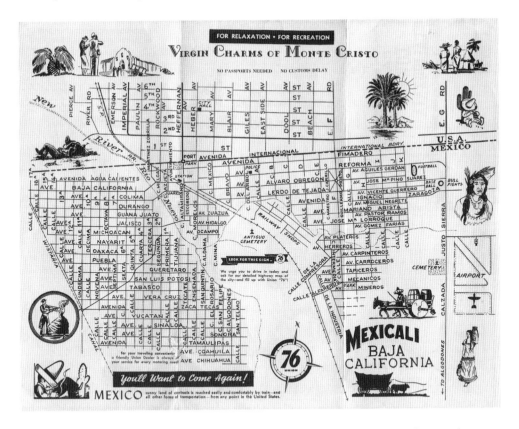

FIGURE 9.15 Mexicali, Baja California, tourist map showing the expansion of Mexicali into the Segunda Sección, the eastern quadrant of the city, and the inclusion of Pueblo Nuevo, the large residential area west of Río Nuevo, known formally as the Tercera Sección (Third Section). Published by Renié Map Service, Union Oil Company of California, *Baja California Road Map*, 1951. Author's collection.

On this eastern periphery, Mexicali stretched even farther, beyond the alphabet streets to the Calzada Justo Sierra, a north–south road that was then seemingly isolated from development. Typical of peripheral land uses, a second cemetery for the city was located on this outer limit, suggesting that development had yet to arrive. The Segunda Sección also reaches south beyond the *desagüe*, a water drainage feature shown on the 1951 map as a dotted line rambling east to Calzada Justo Sierra. Sixteen new avenues now crossed west to east through this new addition, including several major ones—Avenida Ignacio Zaragoza, Avenida Mariano Arista, and Avenida José Maria Lorroque—beyond the former southernmost avenue, Lerdo. In an arc of industrial land use just north and east of the old cemetery (labeled Antiguo Cemetery) on the 1951 map are railroad shops, which suggest how Mexicali's 1948 connection by rail to the mainland of Mexico via Sonora state had enlarged its rail transportation presence from earlier days when rail access to Yuma, Arizona, to ship produce seemed the only concern (see chap. 1).

Beyond the expansion of Mexicali on its eastern flank, the 1951 map shows the addition of a large residential quarter west of Río Nuevo (New River). This district is Pueblo Nuevo, a peripheral zone that began as a series of squatter settlements circa 1918.[20] The first families to locate in Pueblo Nuevo were challenged not only for services and housing, most of which was self-constructed of gathered materials, but also by the neighborhood's location across the river from the center of Mexicali. This siting forced residents to cross the water divide in shallow watercraft until a primitive bridge was constructed to link the two districts in 1919. By 1924, Pueblo Nuevo was a recognized part of Mexicali—the Tercera Sección. As infrastructure improved, a new bridge was built connecting the suburb to the town center. This bridge became known locally as Puente Blanco because it was painted white (fig. 9.16). This postcard from the Arreola Collection of more than four hundred postcards of Mexicali (table 2.1) is the only view suggestive of Pueblo Nuevo, a statement perhaps of how alien this district was to postcard photographers.

Nevertheless, Pueblo Nuevo became a substantial residential area of the city, absorbing thousands of the migrants who crowded into Mexicali during its explosive growth phases in the 1940s. By the 1950s Pueblo Nuevo was an area somewhat larger than the historic core of Mexicali and the first and second sections combined (see fig. 9.15). Its north–south avenues were named alphabetically after selected states of Mexico. The original grid of Pueblo Nuevo streets east to west were numbers in sequence.

Circa 1950, Mexicali stretched for about one and a half miles along the international boundary and reached close to a half mile south from the borderline. The town had transformed to a city, and selected streets and landmarks became popular postcard views. One of the major west–east avenues of Mexicali is Avenida Reforma, a street called Avenida Teniente Guerrero for a short time in the 1920s and earlier known as Ramón Corral (see fig. 9.1). Three postcard views taken from near the intersection of Reforma and Calle

FIGURE 9.16 Puente Blanco, a substantial bridge built to connect the center of Mexicali with the peripheral settlement of Pueblo Nuevo in 1924. Print postcard published by Lower California Commercial Co., Tijuana-Mexicali-Ensenada-Tecate, 1920s.

Azueta create a set of changing views of Mexicali's commercial landscape over several decades into the 1950s.

Figure 9.17*a* is the earliest view in the sequence of postcard views of Avenida Reforma (then called Teniente Guerrero). The view is looking east toward the railroad tracks (with magnification, boxcars are visible in the center distance) with the wide swath of the unpaved avenue flanked by wooden storefronts and some masonry structures. To the left of center is a two-story white building labeled La Casa Blanca Café, a popular restaurant.[21] Figure 9.17*b* is a photo postcard view some two decades later in which it can be seen that Reforma is paved and commercial businesses with porticos line each side of the avenue. The Casa Blanca, with a changed façade, is faintly visible down the street on the left. Streamline Moderne and art deco architectural flourishes are visible for some buildings like the Iris and Botica Moderna on the left. Finally, figure 9.17*c* is a 1950s view from the same vantage point. The portico street front remains, but several buildings have added upper floors, suggesting increased density of the streetscape as commerce intensified. The Iris is now a cinema, and next door the Hotel Reforma occupies two properties at the corner.

With the growth of population, Mexicali retail expanded to serve a larger clientele. Two of the most famous landmarks of this era were La Maderería del Valle and La Nacional (fig. 9.18). La Maderería del Valle was a lumber and hardware outlet near the intersection of the railroad corridor and Avenida Reforma. Affiliated with the Calexico

FIGURE 9.17 *a*, Avenida Reforma (then Teniente Guerrero) looking east from near Calle Azueta (then Celso Vega), 1920s. La Casa Blanca Café, a white building, is visible at left of center. Print postcard published by Pacific Novelty Company, no. 4745, San Francisco and Los Angeles, CA 1920s.

FIGURE 9.17 *b*, Avenida Reforma looking east from near Calle Azueta, 1940s. Arcaded porticos in front of businesses were common in Mexicali to combat intense sun and heat. México Fotográfico 79, 1940s.

FIGURE 9.17 *c*, Avenida Reforma looking east from near Calle Azueta, 1950s. Commercial streetscape is denser a decade later, with many businesses adding a second story. México Fotográfico 113, 1950s.

FIGURE 9.18 La Maderería de Valle lumber and hardware store and La Nacional clothing store. Both were popular with Mexicali residents during the 1940s–1950s. México Fotográfico, 1950s.

Lumber Company, La Maderería sold all manner of household products and construction materials useful to *Mexicalense* (people of Mexicali), many being recent arrivals from small towns and rural areas of the republic. La Nacional, located on the corner of Calle Altamirano and Avenida Juárez, was said to be a favorite clothing store of farmers in the Mexicali Valley.[22] Both La Maderería and La Nacional exhibit art deco and Streamline Moderne architectural details, including rounded cornices and fountain signage that were popular in Mexico during the 1940s–1950s (see also fig. 2.19).

A popular landmark in tourist imagery of Mexicali during the 1950s was Nuestra Señora de Guadalupe church. The *parroquia*, or parish church, of Mexicali was first built in 1918, and historic photographs of the building show a simple wooden structure located on Calle Morelos at its intersection with Avenida Reforma (then Avenida Ramón Corral). In the early 1940s a campaign to raise money to rebuild the church was launched, and in 1949 the new structure with a Mission Revival architectural façade was inaugurated.[23] The church became an instant landmark, and postcard photographers began to include its façade in popular representations (fig. 9.19). The Arreola Collection includes eighteen separate postcards of Nuestra Señora de Guadalupe in photographic, print, and chrome formats.

In the World War II era, Mexicali's bullring was relocated to its fourth location, on the eastern edge of the city. As described above, the city's third plaza de toros had been relocated from Calle Morelos next door to the church to a new area in the railroad corridor

FIGURE 9.19 Nuestra Señora de Guadalupe. Mexicali's *parroquia* was originally a simple wooden structure. In 1949 a rebuilt façade in Mission Revival style with a single bell tower appeared at the intersection of Calle Morelos and Avenida Reforma. México Fotográfico 31, 1950s.

FIGURE 9.20 Fourth Mexicali bullring, located on the eastern edge of the city, relocated there circa 1942 and known as Plaza de Toros Mexicali. México Fotográfico 13, 1940s.

above Avenida Zuazua circa 1919 (see fig. 9.11). In 1942 this ring was again relocated to the Hidalgo Park area on the far northeast edge of the city where Avenida Zaragoza meets Calzada Justo Sierra (see "Bull Fights" on fig. 9.15). This arena was a large wooden structure enclosed by a wall and named Plaza de Toros Mexicali (fig. 9.20). While bullfights remained popular in Mexicali during the 1950s, the arena itself was little photographed by postcard photographers, and the Arreola Collection has no chrome postcard images of the Plaza de Toros Mexicali.[24]

HOUSESCAPES OF MEXICALI

Beyond the commercial streetscapes and institutional landmarks were the residential neighborhoods where Mexicalense lived. Typical of Mexican border towns, the range of housescapes, or dwelling types, could vary from quite primitive to luxurious and even avant-garde.[25] Architectural styles and building materials were usually imported from the United States, although adobe was an early medium (see fig. 9.2). Later brick (see fig. 9.14) and cement block became common and were made locally. Even before rail connections, lumber was being imported to Mexicali from across the border.

A 1921 Sanborn Fire Insurance Map for Mexicali shows that the preponderance of built structures were frame (fig. 9.21). On the map, yellow designates wood-frame construction.

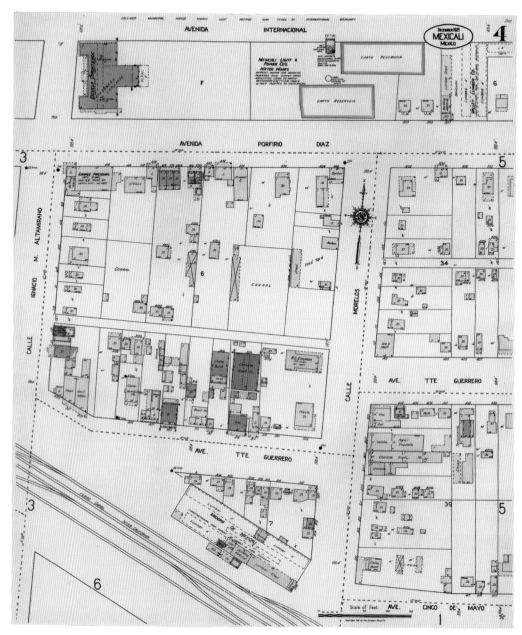

From the collections of the Geography and Map Division, Library of Congress.

FIGURE 9.21 Several blocks in the Primera Sección of Mexicali illustrate the preponderance of wood-frame (yellow) construction versus fired brick (red) or concrete (blue). Lot sizes were generous, and property owners could build multiple structures, including commercial, without zoning enforcement. Sanborn Map Company, *Mexicali Baja California Mexico December, 1921*, sheet 4.

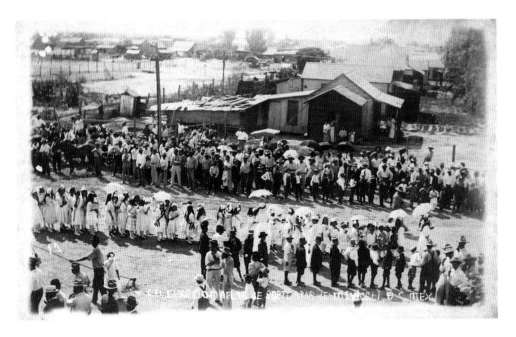

FIGURE 9.22 Mexican Independence Day parade down a residential street in Mexicali circa 1910s. Behind the crowd is a typical residential lot with simple wooden dwelling and attached peripheral buildings, including an unattached outhouse (privy). Lumber for early houses in Mexicali was imported from across the border. Photo postcard, 1910s.

It is not surprising, therefore, to see residential dwellings of simple wood-frame construction in early photographic postcards. The style of housescape illustrated in figure 9.22 was probably the most common form of residential dwelling found in all parts of Mexicali from the early 1900s into the 1920s.

With greater wealth among select residents, examples of Arts and Crafts bungalow-style constructions (figs. 9.23a and 9.23b) that were especially popular in California appeared in some neighborhoods such as Colonia Nueva, one of the subdivisions in the Segunda Sección of Mexicali east of Calle Morelos.[26]

Housescapes began to alter significantly in the post–World War II period as Mexicali continued to spill east of Calle de Arbol (Oriente) (see fig. 9.15). In these near eastside neighborhoods, homes mirrored what one might have encountered in middle-income American suburban communities. Houses were set back from paved streets, and sidewalks fronted properties. House styles were modern, mass-planned boxes with carports and sometimes two-story elevations (fig. 9.24). Housescapes might include ornamental plantings, yet unlike their American counterparts that favored open front-yard spaces, Mexicalense continued the national practice of enclosure with front-property fences.

FIGURE 9.23 *a*, Arts and Crafts house styles, typical of homes built in the Segunda Sección of Mexicali east of Calle Morelos in the 1920s. Photo attributed to Rafael Castillo. *b*, One century later, a surviving example of an Arts and Crafts home on Calle Morelos between Avenida Reforma and Avenida Obregón. Photo by author, 2020.

FIGURE 9.24 Residences in Colonia Moderna. A post–World War II neighborhood in Mexicali, these housescapes mirrored those common to American middle-class suburbs with sidewalks, property setbacks, ornamental landscaping, and modern house plans. México Fotográfico 116, 1950s.

FIGURE 9.25 Spanish Revival elite home in Colonia Moderna, Mexicali, 1950s. México Fotográfico 114, 1950s.

FIGURE 9.26 A Mexican modernist-style home in a new subdivision in Mexicali. México Fotográfico 88, 1950s.

In the most elite districts of Mexicali's eastside neighborhoods, upscale architect-designed homes were popular. Spanish Revival, a style then found in upper-income areas of Southern California, was a standard statement of affluence in the Mexican border town.[27] Red-tile roof, white stucco exterior, a circular tower projecting to the street, a balcony, arched windows, chimneys, and wrought iron fence enclosure met all the elements necessary in Colonia Moderna (fig. 9.25). If traditional affluent style was not statement enough, there was always the truly exceptional, a Mexicali version of Mexican modernism that shouted au courant (fig. 9.26). Mexicali had arrived—from early twentieth-century adobe and frame to mid-twentieth-century concrete, glass, and steel housescapes.

⟩⟩ TEN ⟨⟨

Boundary, Boulevard, and Railroad Corridor

Mexicali from its founding was stamped with two distinctive lines: an international boundary on its northern reach and a railroad right-of-way that
extended northwest to southeast across the grain of the street grid (fig. 9.1).
Later, when the Mexican border town pushed east into a new addition, another linear
alignment, Avenida Álvaro Obregón, was etched into the Mexicali townscape, a boulevard in the Renaissance meaning of that word. These spaces—a boundary, a boulevard,
and a railroad corridor—would become early physical imprints in the Mexicali urban
scene. Beyond landscape signatures, these features carried a symbolism through their
design and representation in the townscape. They created and manifested different landscape elements that can be documented through historic maps and picture postcards.
This chapter revisits these landscapes to uncover their origins, reconstruct selected
phases of their evolution, and present an interpretive assessment of the spaces as landmarks of twentieth-century Mexicali.

BOUNDARY

Whereas every Mexican border city includes an international boundary, only a handful
were created nearly simultaneously along a land border with an American counterpart
community. Two towns of the Sonora-Arizona boundary, Los Dos Nacos and Ambos
Nogales, are examples of this nearly simultaneous creation.[1] Only Mexicali, on the Baja
California border, was actually platted at nearly the same time as its American twin,
Calexico, thereby making the boundary from the beginning an indelible divide.

Figure 10.1 is an 1889 map showing the international boundary where Mexicali-
Calexico would be platted some years later. The map illustrates the borderline, two des-

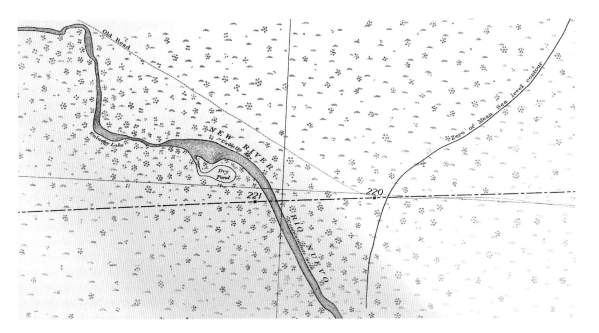

FIGURE 10.1 Map detail from 1889 U.S.-Mexico boundary resurvey showing the site where Mexicali would be platted in 1902 and Calexico in 1904. Two border monument locations, the New River/Río Nuevo, a mean sea-level contour line, and two old road alignments fill out the otherwise blank space. International Boundary Commission, *Boundary Between the United States and Mexico*, Map No. 3.

ignated locations of border monuments (220 and 221), and the course of the usually dry New River/Río Nuevo that crosses the boundary. When the California Land Company purchased property at this location and Charles Rockwood drafted the plat for the town site of Mexicali in 1902, the international boundary was the divide between it and Calexico, the American town across the border that would appear in 1904.[2]

Following the disastrous 1905–1906 inundation in the region, the United States and Mexico agreed to a restoration of monument 221. Located nearest the New River/Río Nuevo, the monument had become unstable from the floodwaters that had eroded its base. The U.S. Department of State published a short report with photographs and a sketch map documenting the restoration process.[3] The restored concrete monument, with its two-foot base and pyramidal column encasing plates that declared the original 1852 survey boundary, was later reproduced as a print postcard by a Calexico drug store (fig. 10.2).

At Mexicali and Calexico, the international boundary became a feature of visual importance to early photographers like Schuyler Bunnell, whose 1911 panoramic image of the towns (see fig. 1.9) was made into a double folded postcard.[4] Photographic postcards showing the borderline at Calexico-Mexicali became popular images. Figures 10.3*a* and 10.3*b* are 1910s photo postcards emphasizing the boundary zone from opposite

INTERNATIONAL MONUMENT. BORDER OF U. S. & MEXICO.
CALEXICO, CAL.

FIGURE 10.2 Restored international boundary monument 221 on the border between Calexico and Mexicali, near the New River/Río Nuevo. Published by White Cross Drug Store, Calexico, CA, and manufactured by the Albertype Company, Brooklyn, NY, 1910s.

perspectives. Figure 10.3*a* looks east into Mexicali from just above the borderline. The flood plain of the Río Nuevo is at the upper right, and the railroad alignment can be seen at the upper left. The two-story white building to the left of center is the Pullman Palace Hotel, and a scattering of other buildings can be seen in the foreground and background of the image. Figure 10.3*b* is a photo postcard view looking west from above the boundary line with part of Calexico at right and part of Mexicali at the left of the line, which is obscured by trees along an irrigation ditch. At the upper right in Calexico next to a flagpole is the U.S. customs house just north of the crossing, whereas the Mexican guardhouse is not visible through the thicket of trees south of the line. The Pullman Palace Hotel in Mexicali is also visible in this view as is the famous Owl Café next door. The initial alignment of the railroad entering Mexicali is visible (with magnification) between the buildings and marked by a crossing sign above the M in Mexico on the postcard. While it is likely that figure 10.3*b* was a photograph taken from a perch on Calexico's water tower, it is uncertain where photographer Sholin was located when figure 10.3*a* was taken. Because a historical account identifies that there were structures in Calexico near the line in the early twentieth century, it is possible that the photographer climbed to the roof of one of these buildings to snap the image.

A decade later the towns of Calexico and Mexicali had developed considerably, and postcard photographers remained fascinated with oblique views of the boundary line. Figure 10.4 is a print postcard showing almost the same view as the one in figure 10.3*b*. In the 1920s postcard, however, a wire fence has replaced the trees along the boundary, and the built environment of each town is entirely changed from the 1910s postcard view. Not surprisingly, the photographer was probably perched on the same Calexico water tower as the earlier photographer to make the photograph that was the basis of the print postcard.

In 1918 a meeting of William Stephens, Governor of California, and Esteban Cantú, governor of the northern district of Baja California, was convened on the international

FIGURE 10.3 *a*, View looking southeast into Mexicali from a point above the international boundary west of the crossing. The Río Nuevo is seen below the high bank at upper right, and the railroad alignment across the grid of Mexicali appears at upper left. Photo postcard no. 220 by Sholin, 1910s. *b*, View looking southwest across the international boundary with Calexico shown on the right and Mexicali on the left. The borderline is obscured by trees and is paralleled by an irrigation ditch on the U.S. side. Photo postcard, 1910s.

FIGURE 10.4 View looking southwest across the boundary line showing parts of Calexico and Mexicali. The borderline is now a wire fence. Published by Pacific Novelty Company, no. 5751, San Francisco and Los Angeles, 1920s.

boundary between Mexicali and Calexico (fig. 10.5). Conducted in the thirty-foot neutral strip on the boundary line, that gathering proved a ceremonial event with American and Mexican flags draped over a canvas awning and Americans and Mexicans collected in their respective territories to witness the meeting.[5]

The first *aduana*, or customs house, in Mexicali was established in 1903 at a site on Avenida Ramón Corral (later Avenida Reforma) and Calle Celso Vega (later Calle Azueta). This location was compromised by the flood of 1905–1906 and resulted in the *aduana* being relocated proximate to the border crossing on Avenida Porfirio Díaz (later Avenida Madero) between Calle Melgar and Calle Azueta. At this time, the customs house was part of the municipal palace, or city hall. In 1930 the customs house was again relocated to Avenida Obregón and Calle Mexico. A new *aduana* was built at Calle Martínez Zorrilla and Avenida Internacional on the boundary in 1952.[6]

While the *aduana* was a symbolically important landmark of Mexicali, its multiple locations meant there were few repeat postcard images made of the buildings. Instead, postcard imagery tended to focus on the gate crossing, or *garita*. Before the 1905–1906 inundation, the first crossing between Mexicali and Calexico was a ground-level bridge that enabled traffic to move across the boundary over an irrigation ditch that paralleled the border. This crossing was labeled Heber's Lane in Rockwood's 1902 plat after Anthony H. Heber, an official of the land company that platted Calexico and

FIGURE 10.5 William Stephens, Governor of California, and Esteban Cantú, governor of the northern district of Baja California, meet on the boundary line dividing Calexico and Mexicali, June 11, 1918. Photo postcard, 1918.

Mexicali (see fig. 9.1). Figure 10.6 is a print postcard showing this bridge before the flood, which resulted in the abandonment of this crossing and relocation of the *garita* to the east.

An early photo postcard credited to the *Calexico Chronicle* shows the first crossing structure at Mexicali's new *garita* established circa 1907 (fig. 10.7), a simple frame building that was burned down by *insurrectos* in the 1911 rebellion (see chap. 1). The next image representing the *garita* is a 1920s print postcard that shows the guardhouse as a small wooden building on the international boundary with a flag standard to designate its authority (fig. 10.8). This view shows the crossing street called Calle Melgar, which was not indicated on the original town plan but was subsequently added to the town's street grid. There was no formal gate or arched entry at the crossing at this time.

By the mid-1920s the gate crossing between Calexico and Mexicali emerged as a popular view in many images (see fig. 2.27). Figure 10.9 is a print postcard view looking north from Mexicali to the crossing and beyond to Heffernan Avenue in Calexico. The border is now decorated with an arched metal sign that reads United States looking north and Mexico looking south. On the Mexicali side of the boundary, a small kiosk is positioned in the middle of Calle Melgar to monitor cross-border traffic. Buildings on the Mexicali side of the boundary display the popularity of porticos that were common for commercial structures in the town center to shade pedestrians from the intense sun of the desert environment. The Mexicali *garita* during this era never closed, and the crossing view was

FIGURE 10.6 First crossing between Calexico and Mexicali, a bridge over an irrigation ditch that paralleled the boundary. This crossing was abandoned following the flood of 1905–1906. This view is looking north into Calexico. Published by M. Rieder, no. 21039, Los Angeles, CA, 1900s.

Boundry Line Garrita Burned
by Insurrectos Feb. 11. 1911

Calexico Chronicle Photo

La Garrita de Mexicali. Destruido
por Incendio Feb. 11. 1911

FIGURE 10.7 Mexicali guardhouse (*la garita*) at the international boundary. In 1911 rebels destroyed the *garita* during a conflict with federal forces. Photo postcard, *Calexico Chronicle*, 1910s.

FIGURE 10.8 A second Mexicali *garita*. The guardhouse is the small frame building at right on the international boundary. Calle Melgar was a new street created for this crossing. Print postcard published by Imprenta Nacional, Mexicali, 1920s.

FIGURE 10.9 International crossing looking north from Mexicali into Calexico. By the 1920s, an arched metal sign was a fixture at the boundary, and a small kiosk had been constructed in the middle of Calle Melgar on the Mexicali side of the line. Print postcard published by Curt Teich Company, C. T. American Art, no. 104970, Chicago, IL, 1925.

FIGURE 10.10 Mexicali *garita* looking south along Calle Melgar with the kiosk at left and the guardhouse and immigration office on right. México Fotográfico 27, 1930s.

widely distributed when *National Geographic Magazine* published a photograph of the now famous metal sign and the street leading into Mexicali in 1942.[7]

The Mexicali *garita* continued as a postcard fix into the 1930s and 1940s. The Arreola Collection includes twenty photo postcards of the crossing taken from both the U.S. and Mexico sides of the boundary. Many of these were published by México Fotográfico, but several were issued by Frashers Foto of Pomona, California. Figure 10.10 is an example of one of the MF photo postcards. It shows the kiosk on the Mexicali side of the boundary in the middle of Calle Melgar and, on the right, the same guardhouse viewed in Figure 10.8. The building then began to function as an immigration station for crossers who required permits to travel beyond the border zone. In the background is the large sign signaling the A. B. W. Club that during late Prohibition and after had been the legendary Owl Café (see chap. 11). Figure 10.11 is a close-up view of the Mexicali *garita* seen from the Calexico side of the border. A large sign advertising Mexicali Beer on the roof of a money exchange house (*casa de cambio*) is shadowed by the 1920s arched metal sign announcing Mexico.

In 1933 President Franklin Roosevelt announced the Good Neighbor Program, a foreign policy intended to improve relations with Latin America, including Mexico. The main principles were to encourage nonintervention and promote cooperation between the United States and its Latin neighbors. In Calexico-Mexicali, this was celebrated as Good Neighbors at the Gate during the Calexico winter festival known as the Desert Cavalcade. Figure 10.12 is a print postcard showing civilian and military officials of Mexico

FIGURE 10.11 Mexicali *garita* seen from the Calexico side of the border with the American kiosk on the left at the end of U.S. Highway 99. Photo postcard, 1940s

FIGURE 10.12 Good Neighbors at the Gate, a Calexico-Mexicali ceremony celebrating the cooperative foreign policy initiated by the United States during the Franklin Roosevelt administration. Print postcard published by Cavalcade Views, Calexico, CA, 1940s.

FIGURE 10.13 Four-portal underpass added to the crossing on the Mexican side of the boundary. This addition was intended to better monitor the increased automotive traffic brought on by a fourfold increase in Mexicali's population that resulted in greater cross-border exchange with the United States. México Fotográfico, 10, 1950s.

and the United States meeting at the international boundary in a ceremony honoring the famed Spanish colonizer Juan Bautista De Anza.

During the 1950s Mexicali added some forty-five thousand residents to its population (table 1.1). Cross-border traffic, both pedestrian and automotive, surged and, as a consequence, a concrete four-portal underpass was erected on the Mexican side of the boundary to monitor more closely and control crossings (fig. 10.13). The 1950s witnessed the continued popularity of postcard views of the *garita*. The Arreola Collection includes a dozen photo postcards showing this crossing during that decade. The period also brought a new landmark to the Mexicali crossing, the Hotel del Norte, erected at the corner of Avenida Madero and Calle Melgar. The hotel built in 1948 was originally a three-story structure with distinctive modernist exterior window frames to combat solar exposure and included a ground-floor portico, by now de rigueur for Mexicali commercial buildings (fig. 10.14). Testifying to the popularity of the lodging, the Hotel del Norte later added a fourth floor, although more recent postcards show that top floor was removed.[8]

Circa 1960, the old 1920s arched metal sign that announced Mexico when entering Mexicali from Calexico was removed, erasing a landmark of the international boundary that had survived almost four decades. In its place, the Mexican government erected a flagpole with a colorful shield showing the Mexican national emblem, an eagle on a cactus with a snake in its mouth (fig. 10.15). On the portals of the concrete underpass

FIGURE 10.14 Hotel del Norte. The hotel was erected near the Mexicali crossing in 1948 at the corner of Avenida Madero and Calle Melgar. It became a modernist landmark with distinctive window frames and a Streamline Moderne curved façade. México Fotográfico 109, 1950s.

FIGURE 10.15 Border-crossing gate circa 1960s with a Mexico national shield attached to a flagpole in front of the 1950s four-portal underpass. Black sign above announces the peso-to-dollar exchange rate of about 12 to 1. Chrome postcard published by Papalera Internacional, Mexicali, 1960s.

two lighted signs with Mexico against a backdrop of the Mexican flag were added to the entrance. These ornamentations would survive another decade or so until the *garita* experienced further changes to its landscape when the Calle Melgar crossing was closed and massive new crossing buildings were erected and put in place west of the original gateway.

BOULEVARD

The word *boulevard* is associated with a broad street or avenue that is median divided and landscaped with trees. Historically, it was both a pedestrian and a carriage street. The origin of the word is tied to eighteenth-century French urban avenues that were extensions of the city into the countryside. Consequently, the boulevard was part of an addition. Boulevards became specific elements of European cities and spread around the world to many urban places in the nineteenth century. Among Mexican border cities, one of the more famous boulevards is part of Avenida 16 de Septiembre in Ciudad Juárez, an extension of a historic street into a new elite development on the east side of that city.[9] In the early 1920s, when Mexicali created its Segunda Sección east of the historic core of the town, one street, Avenida Álvaro Obregón, became the boulevard of the city.

Although Avenida Obregón was a separate street east of the railroad diagonal below Avenida Reforma and above Avenida Lerdo, the true boulevard nature of the avenue started at Calle del Arbol (previously Calle Oriente). This was an auspicious name, "Tree Street," given the historic association of boulevards with ornamental landscaping. Mexicali's boulevard was unusual, however, because its end point some six blocks beyond Calle del Arbol was the monumental Palacio de Gobierno, the government house built to celebrate Mexicali as the capital of the District of Baja California Norte.

Figure 10.16 is a detail from a 1925 map of Mexicali that shows the focal point at the end of Avenida Obregón (then called Avenida Cinco de Mayo and Independencia) where the Palacio de Gobierno was fixed at the center of a grand space surrounded by plazas marked by *X*'s. South of the *palacio* and plazas, a smaller block was subdivided into a plaza and garden. The residential blocks that flanked Obregón were set back from the median-divided avenue and fronted by sidewalks and trees to create the symbolic pedestrian path typical of historic boulevards (fig. 10.17).

The construction of the Palacio de Gobierno was started under the governorship of Esteban Cantú in 1919 and completed in 1922. The building was contracted to Henry Clarke Construction Company of Los Angeles, California, and executed in a Beaux-Arts style using reinforced concrete rather than stone. The two-story palace enclosed a central courtyard with a prominent fountain surrounded by an arcade.[10] The exterior

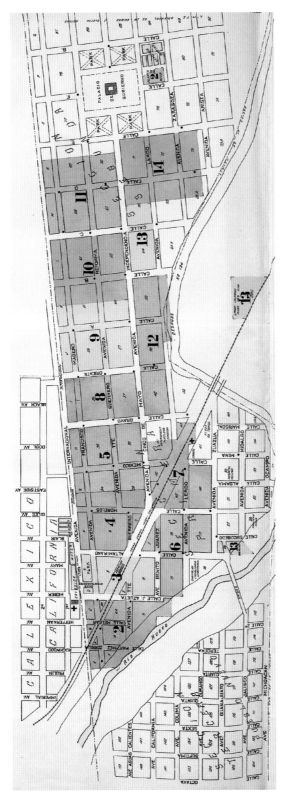

FIGURE 10.16 Mexicali's boulevard, Avenida Obregón, part of the city's Segunda Sección eastside addition. When this map was drafted, the street was named Avenida Cinco de Mayo–Avenida Independencia. The avenue ended at the Palacio de Gobierno complex completed in 1922. Detail from Sanborn Map Company, *Mexicali Baja California Mexico May, 1925*, Index sheet. Courtesy of The Sanborn Collection at California State University, Northridge.

FIGURE 10.17 Avenida Obregón, Mexicali's boulevard, looking east to the Palacio de Gobierno. Published by M. Kashower Company, no. 32948, Los Angeles, CA, 1920s.

FIGURE 10.18 Mexicali's Palacio de Gobierno shortly after it was completed in 1922. Rafael Castillo Foto., no. 3, 1920s.

FIGURE 10.19 Monument of Mexican president Álvaro Obregón positioned in front of the Palacio de Gobierno in 1929. The surrounding grounds of the palace were planted with a series of gardens that became popular entertainment spaces for local events and for visitors. México Fotográfico 54, 1930s.

façade included three central balconies that looked west down Avenida Obregón. The surrounding grounds were landscaped and ornamented to enhance the attractiveness of the site (fig. 10.18).

The spaces surrounding the Palacio de Gobierno on its south and east were developed into a series of gardens that became popular with locals and visitors to Mexicali. Dances and ceremonial events were often staged in these outdoor spaces. Since the Palacio de Gobierno was completed during the administration of Mexico's president Álvaro Obregón, a life-size statue of the Sonoran native was positioned on a pedestal in a circular street directly in front of the palace grounds in 1929 (fig. 10.19).[11]

In many respects, the boulevard and the palace acted as a physical spine and social center for Mexicali in this era. Avenida Obregón was the premier neighborhood of Mexicali in the 1930s–1940s (fig. 10.20). Many of the most celebrated families of the city resided at addresses on Obregón, and selected upscale commercial businesses, such as El León de Oro (The Golden Lion) restaurant were situated nearby. Skirting the Palacio de Gobierno to the north and east were a popular outdoor theater, the city's most prominent hospital, and a recreational polo field.[12]

FIGURE 10.20 Avenida Obregón, the boulevard of Mexicali, a median-divided, tree-lined automotive and pedestrian causeway, or *calzada* as it was sometimes called in Spanish. This view is looking west from the Palacio de Gobierno. México Fotográfico 82, 1940s.

RAILROAD CORRIDOR

The influence of railroads on Mexican border towns was considerable, both economically and spatially. Border towns that serviced ranching, mining, or trade hinterlands benefited from the tariff collections enabled by railroads that crossed the border. Places like Nogales and Agua Prieta in Sonora, Ciudad Juárez in Chihuahua, and Piedras Negras in Coahuila became wealthy towns where magnificent customs houses testified to the revenue stream that grew out of railroad commerce. In some towns, the railroad was a peripheral land use that circumvented the city and rarely interfered with urban commerce. In at least two towns, Ciudad Juárez and Nogales, the railroad extended perpendicularly from the international boundary through the center of the historic core of the city. In Naco, Sonora, and Mexicali the railroad alignment cut against the grain of the street grid and created chaos in the land use patterns of each town.[13] This disruption was less critical in Naco, a small place, but in Mexicali the railroad corridor created a diagonal across the townscape that divided what became a large city. That unusual crease in the urban fabric remains to the present.

The Mexicali map in figure 10.16 shows the railroad corridor, identified as the Ferrocarril Inter-California, running diagonally across the otherwise north–south and east–

FIGURE 10.21 Mexicali's railroad corridor near the border crossing was the commercial center of the town circa 1910s. Photo postcard, 1910s.

west streets of the border town. This large cut through the center of Mexicali evolved, not surprisingly, as an industrial corridor serviced by the railroad. An early photo postcard of a stretch of this corridor nearest the border crossing (section 2 on fig. 10.16) labeled this district the "business center" of town (fig. 10.21). In the photo postcard, the railroad track bisects the view. Businesses such as the Pullman Palace Hotel, the Owl, and the San Diego Bar are positioned on the south side of the tracks and largely open property with an occasional unidentified structure on the north side.

Beyond the early businesses that paralleled the railroad alignment near the crossing, a concentration of industrial uses emerged southeast of Calle Morelos (sec. 7 in fig. 10.16). This was Mexicali's cotton processing center, where the earliest mechanical gin operations were located (fig. 10.22).[14] The cotton cultivation that supported the growth of Mexicali in the 1910s gave rise to the first industrial landscapes of the town. North of the railroad track was the Globe Mill Oil Company (oil processed from cotton seed), and facing this complex south of the railroad corridor was the Mexican Chinese Ginning Company; both operations were started in 1916. Postcard photographers were not completely allergic to these landscapes, and real photo postcards would occasionally appear testifying to the importance of these spaces (fig. 10.23).

Mexicali's railroad corridor attracted other peripheral land uses like bullrings (discussed in chap. 9), a flour mill, and the *cárcel municipal*, or city jail. The *cárcel* had been relocated in 1916 to the railroad corridor from two previous locations. Like the Cuartel

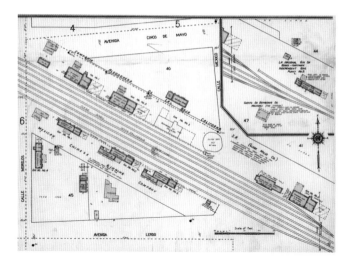

FIGURE 10.22 Mexicali's first industrial landscape, a section of the railroad corridor east of Calle Morelos, as shown in this 1921 Sanborn fire insurance map. Northeast of the tracks is the Compañía Algodonera de la Baja California, also known as the Globe Mills Company. To the southwest is the Mexican Chinese Ginning Company. Sanborn Map Company, *Mexicali Baja California Mexico December, 1921*, detail sheet 1.

FIGURE 10.23 First-generation *despepitadora* (cotton gin mill) located along the railroad corridor in Mexicali. Industrial landscapes did not entirely escape the eye of some postcard photographers. The two-story building in the far background was the first *cuartel de bomberos* (fire station). Iris Studio, 1910s.

Zaragoza de Mexicali (fig. 9.9), the jail was adobe block, but its façade was plastered and carved to suggest stone with a crenelated cornice that was intended to give the appearance of a castle.[15]

More significant to the economy of Mexicali were the locations of breweries that shipped product out of town on railroad cars and thus needed to be close to the rails. As discussed previously (chap. 7), breweries in Mexicali were organized and built by financial interests in Tijuana and Mexicali to service the saloons in those cities. The first brewery in Mexicali was the Cervecería Azteca, constructed in 1922 near the bridge crossing of the Río Nuevo on the southeast edge of town (see location near sec. 6 in fig. 10.16). The Aztec Brewing Company hired a St. Louis brew master to produce A. B. C. Beer, a popular Bavarian-style beverage on the Baja California border during Prohibition. The brewery was a large industrial facility where the main building, designed in a Mission Revival architectural style, stood prominently next door to a cantina (fig. 10.24) and nearby beer garden where locals could enjoy the product in an appropriate setting.[16] Although the brewery was not directly on the railroad corridor, its proximity only blocks away allowed for easy transport of beer in barrels and cases to loading docks near the tracks so it could be shipped by rail west to Tijuana drinking palaces. The Aztec Brewery was one of the buildings significantly damaged by the 1927 earthquake (fig. 10.25), but the facility was quickly rebuilt and continued to produce beer.

FIGURE 10.24 Cervecería Azteca. Mexicali's first brewery was built in 1922 on the south edge of town and proximate to the railroad corridor. México Fotográfico 21, 1920s.

FIGURE 10.25 Aztec Brewing Company severely damaged by the 1927 Mexicali earthquake. The rebuilt facility continued to produce A. B. C. Beer that was consumed locally and shipped to distant locations in Baja California. Photo postcard, January 1, 1927.

Mexicali's railroad corridor, of course, was foremost a railroad alignment, and it provided passenger service as well as freight transport. The main depot had been built along the tracks in 1908 (see fig. 1.14) where the corridor intersected Calle Altamirano (then Calle Carbó) (see "station" in fig. 9.15). The wooden building and adjoining structures became a central location for the operations of the railroad while the administrative offices were located in another part of Mexicali.[17] Figure 10.26 is a 1927 aerial photograph showing the railroad corridor through part of Mexicali. The depot is visible near the center of the image behind a series of stationary boxcars. To the east beyond the station in the aerial photograph is the edge of the railway shops district shown on the 1951 map (fig. 9.15).

A roadway, Avenida López Mateos—a name attached in the 1960s to honor Antonio López Mateos, Mexico's president from 1958 to 1964—parallels the railroad corridor in Mexicali. During the 1940s the rails were also used for regional transport by a kind of motorized *tranvía*.[18] This unusual vehicle was a 1930s sedan in which the automotive wheels were replaced with railroad wheels so the car could motor on rails. A passenger trailer also mounted with railroad wheels was attached to the vehicle to create what might be called a *tren tranvía* (motorized train), which could operate as a passenger carrier. The tren tranvía was in service between Mexicali and Puerto Peñasco, Sonora, via the Ferrocarril Fuente Brotates a Puerto Peñasco (see fig. 1.12). This *tren tranvía* operated out of Mexicali from 1940 to 1948 before full train service was completed between the mainland of Mexico and Baja California via the Ferrocarril Sonora-Baja California (see chap. 1).[19]

FIGURE 10.26 Aerial view looking northeast across Mexicali in 1927. The railroad corridor is shown as it cuts across the grid of streets at a forty-five-degree angle. The depot is situated north of the tracks near the cluster of boxcars. The dark set of cultivated fields at the bottom of the image is the Río Nuevo. The international boundary is visible just north of Parque Chapultepec, where the distinctive Escuela Cuauhtémoc is located in the upper left of the photograph. Aerial shot of Calexico and Mexicali after the 1927 earthquake (photograph). Author's collection.

FIGURE 10.27 Mexicali's railroad corridor looking southeast in the 1960s. The diagonal alignment is interrupted for automotive traffic at major street crossings. Chrome postcard published by Papelera Internacional, Mexicali, 1960s.

Passenger train service operates still in Mexicali; the historic railroad corridor remains in place and continues as a diagonal divide in the border city. Figure 10.27 is a chrome postcard that shows how the corridor appeared in the 1960s. Sometime in the 1970s, Mexicali beautified the alignment with palm trees in an effort to soften the harsh industrial nature of the corridor.

ELEVEN

Cabaret, Chinatown, and Curio Street

In 1914 California toyed with a statewide prohibition ordinance, Amendment 47, which would have restricted the number of saloons and blocked any future wet or dry vote for eight years. The proposed amendment was defeated, but two years later the Golden State, along with eighteen others, adopted prohibition laws in advance of national Prohibition. The Volstead Act was passed in 1919, and it began to be enforced in early 1920. In California the moral reform wave pushed the legal production and consumption of alcoholic beverages into the Baja California border towns, and Mexicali became a center for cabaret entertainment. During the same era, the Chinese district of Mexicali, the largest concentration of this population group in any Mexican border town, emerged as a distinctive community, marking Mexicali as an ethnic border town unusual in Mexico to the present. Mexicali's Chinatown, known as La Chinesca, became notorious in the early decades of the twentieth century as a place of vice and associated adult entertainments, but it was also a separate enclave community within Mexicali. With the tamping down of the cabaret, gambling, and casino economies of the border in the mid-1930s, Mexicali's tourist sector turned to the popular curio trade that emerged in many Mexican border towns. While underdeveloped compared to other border places, the curio trade in Mexicali concentrated on one street, Calle Melgar, which was proximate to the border crossing and gave easy access to Americans and other visitors who walked across the line to participate in the largely post–World War II tourist retailing.

This chapter navigates among these economic and cultural geographic drivers in Mexicali using postcards, historic maps, and related ephemera to enable a visual historical perspective of these past landscapes of the Baja border town. Mexicali proved something of an aberration compared to Tijuana. This chapter explores that theme through the lenses of cabaret, Chinatown, and curios.

CABARET MEXICALI

Almost from the start, Mexicali was branded a center of vice and nocturnal diversions. Part of the explanation, no doubt, had to do with the simple geography of spatial proximity: Mexicali was only a pedestrian stroll from Calexico across the line. There was also the social distance of crossing the boundary into a different space that was, in the expression of the day, "wide open." Prohibition in the states was not only a restriction in alcoholic beverage production and consumption, it was a moral restraint that adults could cast aside by visiting Mexicali, where anything and everything seemed possible. By 1920 religious organizations in California were calling for the state to close access to Mexican border towns like Tijuana and Mexicali, which were seen to be dens of iniquity full of gamblers, prostitutes, and boozers. Newspaper accounts claimed that one billion dollars would pour across the border, where "The great hegira is on and already these towns are filled to the limit with throngs of the thirsty, willing to pay big sums for the pleasure banned by law on American soil."[1]

In Mexicali, this collection of drinking, gambling, and prostitution services was already an established activity more than a decade before national Prohibition. Avenida Porfirio Díaz, the Mexican border town's main street, was a magnet for such services circa 1909 when there were thirty-six cantinas for eight hundred residents, and local newspapers across the border were calling for Mexican president Porfirio Díaz to clean "The Nuisance at Mexicali."[2]

Figure 11.1 is a detailed land-use map from 1921 that shows five blocks of Mexicali focused on the intersection of Avenida Porfirio Díaz and Calle Melgar and straddled by the railroad corridor. Visitors to Prohibition-era Mexicali were greeted on Calle Melgar alone by six saloons, one cabaret, and one restaurant that also included cabaret. On the northeast corner of Calle Melgar and Avenida Internacional was the Climax Café, a popular cabaret that featured a curved Streamline Moderne façade with arched portico and a roof capped by a large "Drink Mexicali Beer" sign that lit up the night (fig. 11.2). Next door on the same side of the street was the Gambrinus Café, another bar with entertainment, whose colorful stained-glass doors and decorative façade were classic art deco style (fig. 11.3). On the opposite side of Calle Melgar was the famous San Diego Café flanked by four additional saloons. The San Diego was especially known for its dining, dancing, and cabaret floorshow (fig. 11.4). The interior was neon lit with ceiling fans, linen-clothed tables, and a prominent dance floor (fig. 11.5). The Café appeared in dozens of postcards and remained one of the longest-surviving businesses in Mexicali. A 1950s photo postcard shows its distinctive tiled roof, portico, and block glass windows (fig. 11.6).

As tourists crossed Avenida Porfirio Díaz, the black of night became bright by illuminated signs and façades for the various clubs and cabarets of Prohibition-era Mexicali. On the triangle block facing the railroad corridor (see fig. 11.1) was the Hotel Imperial

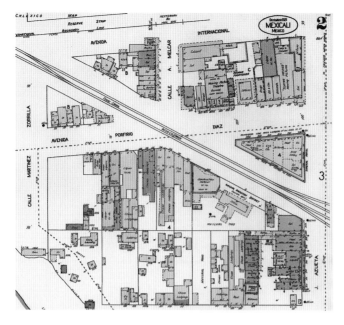

FIGURE 11.1 Mexicali's Prohibition-era landscape featured saloons and cabaret on the first block of Calle Melgar, the gateway street connected to Heffernan Avenue in Calexico across the boundary. Detail, Sanborn Map Company, *Mexicali Baja California Mexico December, 1921,* sheet 2.

FIGURE 11.2 Climax Café with its Moderne façade and arched portico. The establishment greeted tourists to Mexicali as soon as they crossed the line. Published by M. Kashower, no. 21388, Los Angeles, CA, 1920s.

FIGURE 11.3 Gambrinus Café. Next door to the Climax Café on Calle Melgar, it projected art deco elegance with its neon-lighted sign, stained-glass doors, and draped curtain that shielded the west-facing establishment from the setting sun mirrored on its façade. Published by M. Kashower, no. 32953, Los Angeles, CA, 1920s.

with its rooftop cabaret sign, and nearby was the high-profile sign of the A. B. W. Club. Between the two were the twin bell towers of the Spanish Revival façade of the Southern Club (fig. 11.7; see also fig. 2.15). Mexicali became famous for its so-called White Way of lighted cabarets—a kind of vernacular landscape map of the night that guided visitors from one joy palace to the next. By 1926 Mexicali hosted eighty-five cantinas, cabarets, and associated centers of adult entertainment.[3]

Mexicali's "White Way" cabarets included El Gato Negro (The Black Cat), a club in Chinatown on Calle Azueta across the street from the famous Owl Café. The Black Cat was a billiard parlor and cabaret restaurant. Next door was the Chinese-operated Hotel Peninsular, where Chinese prostitution was promoted and where opium den experiences could be arranged for slumming visitors to Mexicali (fig. 11.8).[4]

The "White Way" clubs of Mexicali were not restricted to the gateway zone of Calle Melgar and Avenida Porfirio Díaz or La Chinesca but could be found across the town. They also included the previously mentioned

FIGURE 11.4 San Diego Café, 1940s menu advertised dining, dancing, and cabaret floorshow, only steps from the international crossing. Author's collection.

La Casa Blanca Café, situated at the intersection of Avenida Reforma and the railroad corridor, and The Palace, a cabaret and cantina also located on Reforma (fig. 11.9).

The Owl: Vignette of a Mexicali Cabaret

"Famous from the Yukon to Panama City, the history of the Northern District of Lower California has centered around the Owl to some extent since its construction."[5] Circa 1913, three cabaret operators—Marvin Allen, Frank B. Beyer, and Carl Withington—were forced out of Bakersfield, California, by reform movements and relocated their business enterprise, the A. B. W. Corporation, to Mexicali. Withington had operated a club in Bakersfield known as the Owl, so in celebration of that past, the A. B. W. Company named the new cabaret established in Mexicali "El Tecolote" (The Owl). The owners,

FIGURE 11.5 Interior of the San Diego Café in Mexicali showing linen-clothed tables, neon lights, and the dance floor. México Fotográfico 65, 1940s.

FIGURE 11.6 Exterior of the San Diego Café, a restaurant-cabaret on the international boundary looking south into Mexicali. The café was one of the longest-lived survivors of the Mexicali cabaret scene lasting from before Prohibition into the 1950s. México Fotográfico 32, 1950s.

CALLE PRINCIPAL ASIA LOS CABARETS, MEXICALI, BAJA CAL. MEXICO

X-75 PRINCIPAL STREET SCENE AND CABARETS, MEXICALI, LOWER CALIF MEXICO 104968

FIGURE 11.7 Cabarets of Mexicali featured brightly lighted signage to steer Prohibition-era visitors from one club to the next along a "White Way." Western Publishing and Novelty Company, Los Angeles, CA. Manufactured by Curt Teich, no. 104968, Chicago, IL, 1925.

PORTION OF "WHITE WAY", MEXICALI, MEXICO

FIGURE 11.8 El Gato Negro (The Black Cat) Cabaret. A billiard parlor and restaurant next to a Chinese-operated hotel that arranged Chinese prostitutes and visits to opium dens for slumming American visitors to Mexicali. Print postcard published by Lower California Commercial Company, Tijuana-Mexicali-Ensenada-Tecate, 1920s.

FIGURE 11.9 Palace Cabaret and Cantina. Nighttime photography became something of a specialty of Mexicali postcard photographers who documented the "White Way" cabarets of the border town. Foto. Iris, 1910s.

FIGURE 11.10 Original Owl Café located on Avenida Porfirio Díaz in Mexicali after damage by earthquakes that struck the region on June 22, 1915. Photo postcard, 1915.

Allen, Beyer, and Withington (A. B. W.), reputedly paid Esteban Cantú, then governor of the northern district of Baja, eight thousand dollars a month for the exclusive rights to gambling and prostitution in Mexicali. The Owl became the most heavily taxed enterprise in Mexicali during Cantú's reign, contributing disproportionately to the town's revenue stream.[6] The Owl would become the most famous cabaret in the town and, some might say, one of the most celebrated, even infamous, on the Mexican border.

The original Owl Café opened its doors circa 1914 on Avenida Porfirio Díaz in Mexicali. It was a choice location, directly south of the new border crossing and next to the railroad tracks. The cabaret thrived there. On June 22, 1915, at 7:59 p.m., an earthquake measuring 6.1 on the Richter scale centered across the boundary in California's Imperial Valley rocked Mexicali. This was followed an hour later by a second jolt measuring 6.3. The Owl and other joy palaces in Mexicali were at peak business hours, so the first quake sent people out of buildings into the street only to see them return shortly to resume their activities. When the second, more powerful quake struck, building walls collapsed and falling material seriously injured several and caused six deaths.[7] The Owl was sig-

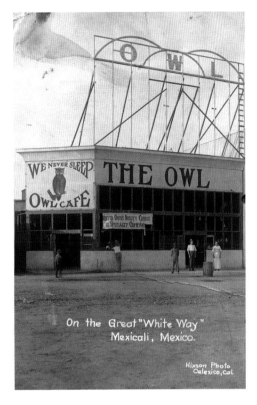

FIGURE 11.11 Entrance to the Owl Café showing a rebuilt façade with its distinctive slogan "We Never Sleep." Like other cabarets in Mexicali, the Owl promoted itself on the "White Way" of nighttime illuminated clubs in the city. Hixson Photo, Calexico, CA, 1910s.

nificantly damaged by the two quakes (fig. 11.10). The cabaret rebuilt quickly, creating a new façade with its signature logo "We Never Sleep" painted above its entrance (fig. 11.11).

The Owl was forced to relocate from Avenida Porfirio Díaz to Mexicali's Chinatown, an action that was anticipated even before the 1915 earthquake because local interests on both sides of the border had been lobbying for years to clean up the concentration of cabarets at the border gateway. On May 31, 1916, Cantú requested (it was not mandatory) that cabarets relocate from Mexicali's gateway and ordered that a string of lights and a fence surround the new district in Chinatown.[8] The next day, June 1, 1916, the Owl opened at a new site on the northeast corner of Calle Azueta and Avenida Teniente Guerrero in Mexicali's Chinatown (fig. 11.12).

The Owl's new fifty-thousand-dollar building in Mexicali's Chinatown allowed the cabaret to expand its physical facilities. Figure 11.13 is a detail from the 1921 Sanborn

FIGURE 11.12 The Owl in 1916 relocated to the corner of Calle Azueta and Avenida Teniente Guerrero, south of the railroad tracks in Mexicali's Chinatown. The new Owl is visible right of center with its tall sign. This view looks south on Calle Azueta. Iris Studio, 1917. André Williams Collection.

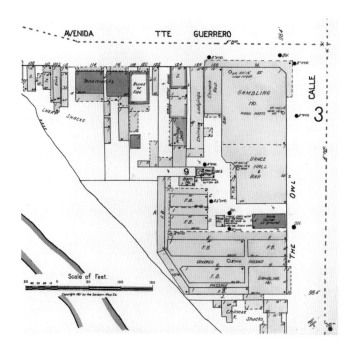

FIGURE 11.13 Detail from 1921 Sanborn fire insurance map showing the Owl's new location since 1916. The cabaret occupied most of the city block between Calle Azueta and Avenida Teniente Guerrero in Mexicali's Chinatown. The expanded facilities included a large gambling house, dance hall and bar, separate smaller gambling hall for "colored" clients, and extensive residential quarters (F. B.) for prostitutes. Sanborn Map Company, *Mexicali Baja California Mexico December, 1921*, sheet 2.

fire insurance map that reveals the larger foot-print of the enterprise. The gambling house and dance hall/bar occupied half the block frontage along Calle Azueta. Down the block was a smaller gambling house, known as the Little Owl, operated exclusively for a "col-ored," or black, clientele. The Hop Lee Chi-nese restaurant was a separate entrance on Avenida Teniente Guerrero. Because the Owl had exclusive rights to prostitution in Mexicali, it maintained an extensive housing quarter for female workers. Behind the dance hall and bar, the properties labeled "F.B.," or female board-ing, contained 104 separate rooms and accom-modated 312 registered prostitutes, mostly American women from California—mainly San Francisco—but very few Mexican women, testifying to the demand by American visitors.[9]

The main frontage of the cabaret faced Avenida Teniente Guerrero and was largely a glass window façade that proclaimed it The Owl Theatre. Beyond the many entertainments offered at the Owl, the building itself, like oth-ers on Mexicali's "White Way," was its own advertisement. To celebrate its grand opening in 1916, the cabaret added to its ordinary roof sign a magnificent lighted fountain that could be seen from across the border (fig. 11.14). The

FIGURE 11.14 Night view of the Owl Theatre, as the new cabaret became known in Mexicali. The large fountain sign illuminated the night, directing visitors to one of the most famous Prohibition-era joy palaces of the Baja border. Photo postcard attributed to Foto., Iris, 1916.

interior of the Owl was said to accommodate three thousand visitors. Jack Tenney, who composed the famous song *Mexicali Rose*, played piano in a seven piece band at the Owl and recalled the cabaret as "rough and unattractive" yet profuse with large potted imi-tation palms. The main gambling house featured thirty-five poker tables and others for keno, twenty-one, and monte (fig. 11.15). There were six roulette wheels and faro tables, where, it was said, the odds were eighteen to one in favor of the house (fig. 11.16).[10]

The Owl had its own barbershop and photography studio for special occasions and tourists. Besides Hop Lee's Chinese restaurant, there were many others within easy walk-ing distance of the cabaret. Jazz musical performance was a mainstay at the Owl, and floor-shows featuring exotic dancers, including African American performers, were legendary in the dance hall.[11] The bar was large and made famous in many popular postcards such as

FIGURE 11.15 Main gambling hall at the Owl in Mexicali. Photo postcard, 1910s. Carol Hann Collection.

FIGURE 11.16 Faro table in the main gambling house at the Owl in Mexicali. Photo postcard published by Zuckerman Bros., 1910s.

THE OWL THEATRE

Allen, Beyer & Withington   MEXICALI, MEXICO   P. O. Box 341, Calexico, Cal.

A GRAND ORCHESTRA OF NINE PIECES
FINEST DANCE FLOOR ON THE RIALTO
=== FEATURE ACTS DIRECT FROM THE ===
ORPHEUM AND PANTAGES CIRCUITS
Six New Motion Picture Films Daily

The Largest Gambling House in the World
WE NEVER SLEEP

FIGURE 11.17 Advertising postcard for the Owl Theatre distributed by Allen, Beyer, and Withington—the A. B. W. Corporation—who used a post office box mailing address in Calexico. The theater showed movies daily. Print postcard published by the A. B. W. Corporation, 1910s.

Rafael Castillo's well-known image (see fig. 2.16), which was pirated by other postcard publishers. The popularity of the Owl was regularly promoted by the A. B. W. Corporation through advertising postcards that drew attention to its large dance floor, grand orchestra, gambling house, and theater that screened motion pictures daily (fig. 11.17).

The new Owl was Mexicali's premier cabaret for nearly a decade, but fires would ultimately plague the Chinatown site. Although part of the Owl had been rebuilt from a 1920 fire, on June 27, 1922, the Owl again caught fire and this time was completely destroyed—a $250,000 loss. Arson was suspected. The Calexico fire department could not control the blaze, which threatened other nearby buildings.[12]

A year later, in June 1923, the A. B. W. syndicate announced that another new Owl would be built with a 100 ft. frontage on Avenida Madero south of the railroad corridor and facing the main gate crossing to Calexico. It is pictured in the background of figure 11.7. The new $125,000 building would be built of reinforced concrete with a steel ceiling and fireproof roofing (fig. 11.18). The 1923 Owl would accommodate gambling, a cabaret dance floor, a bar and café, and a boxing arena, but

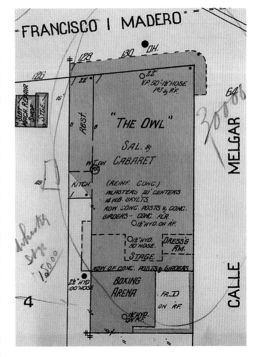

FIGURE 11.18 1923 Owl relocated to the corner of Avenida Madero and Calle Melgar. The concrete (blue color code on the map), fireproof building was a standard cabaret but included a boxing arena in the rear. Detail, Sanborn Map Company, *Mexicali Baja California Mexico May, 1925*, sheet 2. Courtesy of The Sanborn Collection at California State University, Northridge.

MX1:—"El Tecolote" The Owl Bar, Mexicali, B. C., Mexico.

FIGURE 11.19 A. B. W. Club, formerly the Owl, in the second half of the 1920s when the cabaret was moved to a location closer to the crossing and near the railroad track. Published by M. Kashower, no. 21385, Los Angeles, CA 1920s. This print postcard is an exact color reproduction of Rafael Castillo's photographic postcard titled "A. B. W. Club, Mexicali, B. C.," Foto. 22, 1920s, in the author's collection.

FIGURE 11.20 El Tecolote, known as the A. B. W. Club, in a nighttime view recalling the "White Way" of Prohibition-era Mexicali. Photo postcard, 1930s.

FIGURE 11.21 El Tecolote, Mexicali, 1940s. The Owl, divorced from its A. B. W. association and its distinctive owl roof sign eliminated, still managed to sport an owl, now relegated to a silhouette on the cornice above the portico at left. Photo postcard, 1940s.

no prostitution. Carl Withington, speaking for the company, announced that all concessions had been secured from the federal and local governments.[13]

To disassociate itself with its notorious past, the Owl was renamed the A. B. W. Club when it relocated to its new site near the border crossing. The new location rested next to the railroad tracks not far from its original situation on Avenida Porfirio Díaz (now called Avenida Madero). While the older nocturnal diversions including prostitution were legally restricted, the A. B. W. Club continued to be called the Owl or Tecolote, and drinking and floorshow entertainment remained its daily fare. Postcard publishers were loyal to the cabaret, producing print versions of the A. B. W. Club with its distinctive owl roof sign (fig. 11.19). Photo postcard publishers also found retro appeal in the new Owl and capitalized on the old "White Way" slogan by producing night scenes of the A. B. W. Club into the 1930s (fig. 11.20).

The Great Depression, along with local changes, brought a temporary cessation to the A. B. W. Club. In February 1931 rumor had circulated that the Owl was facing financial difficulty due to reduced attendance and competition from cabarets that had recently been allowed gaming permits (no longer the exclusive privilege of the Owl). The curtain fell later that year, and in August the A. B. W. Company announced that the Owl would close because it could not meet the increased taxes and permit fees demanded by the local and federal governments.[14] New investors rallied, and the Owl continued operation as the A. B. W. Club with a grand gala opening in December 1932. But once again, fire brought destruction when the club burned, only to be rebuilt yet again. The Owl then lost its gambling privilege in 1935 with the legal reforms initiated under the Lázaro Cárdenas administration.[15]

The 1940s brought Mexican federal restrictions to cabaret licensing, but the Owl continued to operate by the name El Tecolote. While a Maya Beer brand now highlighted its roof sign, a silhouette outline of the bird could still be found along the cornice line of the portico (fig. 11.21). By the 1950s few remembered the wild nights at the Owl of Mexicali during Prohibition. Gambling, however, did return to Mexicali via wire-service betting, no doubt less exciting than the gambling-house days of old.[16]

LA CHINESCA

Mexican border towns like Agua Prieta and Nogales in Sonora as well as cities of Mexico's Pacific coast had their Chinese populations or districts, but only Mexicali seems to have used the word "La Chinesca" to identify its Chinatown. A visitor to the quarter in 1925 writing for the popular magazine *American Mercury* identified Asian as the distinguishing quality that separated Mexicali from all other Mexican border towns.[17] In his pioneering study "Mexicali's Chinatown," geographer James Curtis declared, "Only in the context of a particular set of intersecting local and external factors that operated largely between the first and third decades of the twentieth century is it possible to understand the Chinese settlement in Mexicali and environs."[18]

Those intersecting local and external circumstances were, respectively, the need to bring labor to the Mexicali Valley to reclaim the Colorado River Delta for cultivation and the Colorado River Land Company (CRLC), a syndicate controlled by Harrison Gray Otis and Harry Chandler (his son-in-law), publishers of the *Los Angeles Times*, who set the process in motion. Otis and his group of investors recognized the burgeoning money-making possibilities of growing cotton in the California deserts, a scheme that could help supply the immense demand for the raw material in China and Japan during the early decades of the twentieth century. The CRLC entered the scene by acquiring some 832,000 acres of the massive Andrade tract, more than 80 percent in the Mexicali Valley stretching from the Sierra de Cocopah in the west to the Colorado River in the east (see fig. 1.10). At first the CRLC failed in its efforts to persuade Mexican workers to settle the Mexicali Valley because better working conditions existed north of the border. The syndicate turned, instead, to Chinese labor because Mexican President Porfirio Díaz had recently signed a treaty of commerce and immigration with China. In the United States the Chinese Exclusion Act of 1882 restricted access to Chinese labor. Once the region began to recover from the earlier Colorado River floods, Otis initiated the direct recruiting of labor in China with advertisements placed in Canton and Hong Kong that offered opportunities to work, rent, and own land in Baja California.[19] The CRLC program to lease land to Chinese workers, who were granted favorable immigration status to enter Mexico, caught fire, and soon Chinese from other regions, such as Sonora and Sinaloa in Mexico as well as parts of California, migrated to the Mexicali Valley. Between 1910 and 1919, an estimated five thousand to eleven thousand Chinese resided in and around Mexicali.[20]

Chinese merchants were given certain immigration privileges, and almost from the founding of Mexicali, the ethnic group became a presence in the border town. By the 1920s Chinese were concentrated in the southern part of the Primera Sección, which had the highest density of buildings in the city.[21] Figure 11.22 is a detail from the 1921 Sanborn fire insurance map of Mexicali that shows the extremely high density of buildings on the principal block of La Chinesca, bounded on the west and east by Calle Azueta and Calle Altamirano and north and south by Avenida Teniente Guerrero and Avenida Benito Juárez, respectively. The Sanborn Company mapmakers labeled "This Whole Block is Occupied Entirely by Chinese." Most buildings were frame (yellow), although a few were adobe (brown) and several along the northeast corner of the district that fronted the railroad corridor were brick (pink).

Chinese residents, largely a male society then, lived in a variety of accommodations shown on the Sanborn map as bunkhouses and shacks. Wealthy merchants were more likely to reside in residences above their stores, many of which were masonry construc-

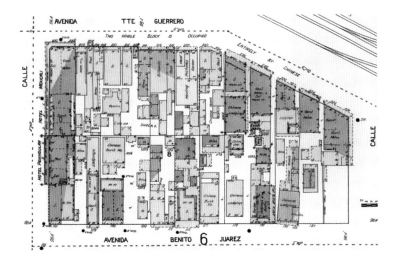

FIGURE 11.22 Detail map showing the heart of La Chinesca, Mexicali's Chinatown in 1921. The Chinese quarter of the city was the most densely populated section of the border town. Sanborn Map Company, *Mexicali Baja California Mexico December, 1921*, sheet 2.

tion. Typical of Chinatowns across the American West during this era, social institutions included merchant and benevolent associations often identified by a *tong* (hall) building. Mexicali's Chinatown contained an opera house, a movie theater, a Masonic temple, and a Methodist Episcopal Church,[22] although not all of these were located in the area shown on the map figure 11.22. Restaurants, billiard parlors, general merchandise stores, and laundries were more common enterprises (fig. 11.23). Businesses were often organized by families or hometown regions, and more than thirty different associations were active in Mexicali in the 1920s.[23]

The 1921 Mexican census documented thirty-two distinct Chinese farming operations with eighty-one thousand acres under cultivation in the Mexicali Valley.[24] Chinese merchants in Mexicali were major suppliers of fresh produce for the city, and their wholesale and retail operations figured in some postcard photographs in the early years of the twentieth century. An image by Calexico photographer Rafael Castillo shows merchant houses and Chinese businessmen unloading shipments in front of a barber shop and tailor (fig. 11.24). Another photo postcard by an unknown photographer features a street scene in La Chinesca with sidewalk vegetable vending, a trade common to the streets of Chinatowns across North America (fig. 11.25). Other postcard views of La Chinesca in the Arreola Collection show street scenes and social institutions of the community.

On May 22, 1923, one of the most disastrous conflagrations in the history of Mexicali swept across La Chinesca. The fire, which was estimated to have resulted in damages of approximately two million dollars, was started in a movie theater when an electrical short ignited and the frame building began to burn.[25] The daytime fire spread quickly, aided

FIGURE 11.23 Chinese businesses, Mexicali's Chinatown. Photo postcard, 1910s. Carol Hann Collection.

FIGURE 11.24 Chinese merchant houses in La Chinesca, Mexicali's Chinatown. Rafael Castillo Foto., no. 11, 1910s.

FIGURE 11.25 Chinese vegetable vendors on the streets of La Chinesca in Mexicali. Photo postcard, 1920s.

by strong winds. The only structures saved from flames were the Hotel Mexicali and the Hotel Peninsular (brick buildings) on Calle Azueta (see fig. 11.22). Much of the rest of the heart of the quarter was burned to the ground. Two photographic images capture the before and after of the destruction. Figure 11.26 is a news photograph taken of the ABC Club on April 21, 1923, with the caption that noted that the building, located in a Mexican city, was a Chinese concern whose principal customers were thirsty Americans. Figure 11.27 is a photo postcard by an unknown photographer showing the ABC Club in Mexicali's Chinatown on fire May 22, 1923.

La Chinesca was rebuilt, but the 1925 Sanborn fire insurance map published two years after the devastating blaze showed that empty properties on the block remained. Many of the new buildings had been constructed of masonry (pink) or concrete (blue) (fig. 11.28).

Fires continued to plague La Chinesca. In 1931 eleven buildings burned to the ground, and an early morning blaze on September 26, 1945, again destroyed an entire business block between Avenida Reforma (formerly Avenida Teniente Guerrero) and Avenida Juárez and between Calle Azueta and Calle Altamirano in Mexicali's Chinatown, the exact same location as the devastating 1923 disaster.[26] A newspaper account suggested that once again the fire started in a movie theater. The intensity of the conflagration was exacerbated by the stocks of alcoholic beverages, lard and grease in restaurants, and cotton goods stored in warehouses in the district.

FIGURE 11.26 ABC Club on the ground floor of the Him Sang Lung Company in Mexicali's Chinatown, April 21, 1923. Pacific and Atlantic Photos, Los Angeles and New York. Author's collection.

Mexicali exploded as a population center of the Mexicali Valley into the 1950s, and its Chinatown was continually rebuilt. In fact, the number of Chinese in Mexicali probably increased dramatically in the postwar years because many Chinese farmers were displaced from holdings in the valley with the growth of Mexico's *ejido* program that returned land to Mexicans.[27] A consequence was the expansion of tourism in Mexicali, some of which attracted visitors to La Chinesca, considered an exotic locale on the border. The main street of Mexicali's Chinatown, Avenida Juárez, witnessed new construction that presented a mixture of curious façades with distinctive Chinese rooflines and imparted a Grant Avenue, San Francisco, Chinatown ambience (fig. 11.29). One particular location, Callejon La Chinesca (the Chinese Alley), became a popular destination where Chinese restaurants and local services crowded into a tight corridor suggestive of an earlier Chinatown of the imagination (fig. 11.30). This alley actually shows on the 1925 Sanborn fire insurance map, figure 11.28, where it extends west to east from Calle Azueta to the middle of the block. In 1925 the alley was lined principally with saloons, but in the post–World War II years it transitioned to a mixture of eateries and local services. To the

FIGURE 11.27 ABC Club burning in the Mexicali Chinatown fire that devastated the quarter on May 22, 1923. Photo postcard, May 22, 1923.

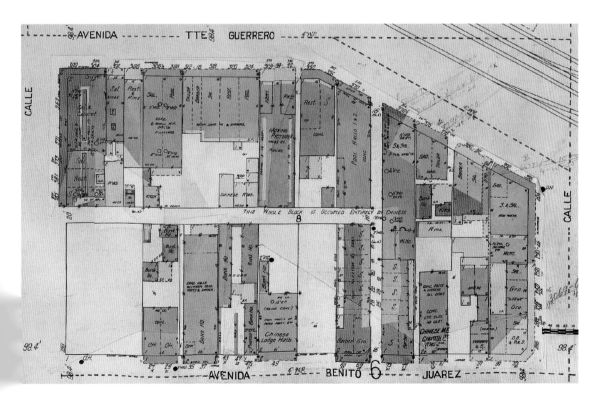

FIGURE 11.28 Detail map showing La Chinesca rebuilt from the May 1923 fire. New buildings were chiefly masonry and concrete, but large sections of the quarter remained empty. Sanborn Map Company, *Mexicali Baja California Mexico May, 1925*, sheet 3. Courtesy of The Sanborn Collection at California State University, Northridge.

FIGURE 11.29 Avenida Juárez, the main street of Mexicali's Chinatown in the 1950s, where building façades started to display Chinese architectural flourishes. México Fotográfico, 1950s.

FIGURE 11.30 Callejon La Chinesca, Chinatown Alley, was an especially popular destination for Mexicali visitors in search of Chinese restaurants and local color. México Fotográfico 30, 1950s.

present, Chinese eateries populate La Chinesca and attract their share of travelers who are drawn to the historic district.[28]

CALLE MELGAR, MEXICALI'S CURIO STREET

Curio shopping has been a mainstay of Mexican border towns since the late nineteenth century. In some towns, shops were concentrated around a main plaza as were the early curio stores in Reynosa. In other border towns particular streets emerged as the major concentration of curio stores, such as those found on Avenida Juárez in Ciudad Juárez, Avenida Obregón in Nogales, and Avenida Revolución in Tijuana.[29] In many border towns the curio shopping street was no more than a few blocks located close to the port of entry or border crossing. Historically, the importance of the curio street in a border town has depended on the size of the town and, more importantly, to its proximity to an American population center that could act as the main source of consumer shoppers.

Mexicali developed a curio street, Calle Melgar, which connected the *garita* to the main commercial street of the town, Avenida Madero. Nevertheless, gauged by the number of curio stores and in light of the size of the Mexican border town, curio shopping in Mexicali has been limited. As evidence of this paucity, consider that Mexicali curio store postcards are rare in the Arreola Collection. Even considering the possible exception of Calle Melgar, the principal curio shopping street of the town, the number of shops is but a handful. By comparison, curio stores in Nogales, Sonora, in the 1950s were plentiful even though Mexicali was a bigger town many times over. Part of the explanation has to do with the relative proximity of a tourism-consuming population. While Calexico and other towns of the Imperial Valley provided day-tripping curio shoppers, Mexicali's extreme isolation from the larger population centers of Los Angeles and San Diego meant that it had no direct center across the international boundary that could sustain heavy tourist traffic.

It should be acknowledged, of course, that tourism in Mexicali has historically been tied to cabaret more than to the curio trade. Nevertheless, from its beginnings, Mexicali was perceived as exotic Mexico, and tourists visited the desert town. Mexicali's early appeal to outsiders was probably a result of its proximity to cross-country railroad stops in the Imperial Valley. Figure 11.31 is a print postcard showing two women flanking "Old Borrego," a Cocopah who became something of a celebrity among early tourists to the Mexican border town. Whether there were curio stores in Mexicali then is uncertain, but clearly the locals themselves were a kind of attraction.

Calle Melgar was not part of Rockwood's original 1902 plat (see fig. 9.1) but was created in 1920 by the municipal government of Mexicali. The need to have a street at the border crossing above the railroad corridor resulted in the appropriation of several properties on block 4 of the original plat and the laying of a street perpendicular to the

American Tourists and "Old Borrego" a 100 years old Indian on the bank of the River, Mexicali, Mexico.

FIGURE 11.31 Women posing with "Old Borrego," a Cocopah Indian who was a local celebrity. Early tourists to Mexicali were passengers on excursions through the Imperial Valley via the Southern Pacific Railway, identified on the verso of this print postcard. Published by M. Rieder, no. 7973, Los Angeles, CA, 1900s.

international boundary and connecting south to Avenida Ramón Corral, later Avenida Reforma.[30] As a result, Calle Melgar emerged as a short street of only two blocks.

Curio stores first appeared on the initial stretch of Calle Melgar below the border crossing. Figure 11.32 is a 1920s street view of this crossing before the arched metal border sign was erected (see chap. 10). Proximate to the international boundary on the east side of the street (right side of image), wedged between the Climax Café and the Compañía Bancaría, is a curio store. This is one of the only postcard views of a curio shop in Mexicali during the Prohibition era. It is likely that curio stores did not appear again in any number until after the repeal of Prohibition in 1933 and the latter years of the Great Depression.[31]

From the Arreola Collection, postcards showing Calle Melgar curio stores, which were almost exclusively on the second block of the street between Avendia Madero and Avenida Reforma, begin to appear in the 1940s. Figure 11.33 is a Frashers Foto postcard of Calle Melgar looking north to the border crossing. On the left of the image is the tower sign for the former A. B. W. Club (the Owl) on the corner of Avenida Madero and Calle Melgar. On the right side of the street is a distinctive neon sign for El Charro, an early vendor of *curiosidades* or curios. In another photo postcard of Calle Melgar from the 1940s, a view looking south to Avenida Reforma and across the street from figure 11.33 is a curio store with a neon sign signaling Curios Artes Mexicanas (fig. 11.34). The portico section of the block across the street also shows (with magnification) another curio store.

FIGURE 11.32 Early curio store on Calle Melgar near the border crossing. Iris Studio, 1920s.

FIGURE 11.33 El Charro Curiosidades on Calle Melgar below Avenida Madero, 1940s. The metal-arched border sign is visible in the distance at the international boundary. Frashers Foto, no. F-7568, Pomona, CA, 1940s.

FIGURE 11.34 Curios Artes Mexicanas on Calle Melgar looking south near its intersection with Avenida Reforma. México Fotográfico 77, 1940s.

FIGURE 11.35 Replica horse, a fixture on Mexicali's tourist street, on which visitors could be photographed mounted and sporting a sombrero labeled "Viva Mexico." Frashers Foto, no. F-7567, Pomona, CA, 1940s. Carol Hann Collection.

An added feature of Mexicali's tourist street during the 1940s was the staged horse—a replica of a real animal complete with saddle and bridle—positioned on the sidewalk of Calle Melgar, where visitors could be photographed mounted on the horse wearing a sombrero (fig. 11.35). This was Mexicali's answer to Tijuana's burro carts so common along its Avenida Revolución during the same period (chap. 6).

In 1944 Calle Melgar was paved, and into the 1950s the section of the street between Avenida Madero and Avendia Reforma, according to one resident, became "un centro elegante nocturne" (an elegant center of nightlife) with bars and cafés.[32] During the day, however, Calle Melgar was a tourist shopping street, and curio stores expanded. Figure 11.36 is a 1950s photo postcard snapped from near the same position as seen in figure 11.33 a decade earlier. In the more recent view, the street is active with cars parked on both curbs, and curio stores are visible on each side. Figure 11.37 is another 1950s view looking south to Avenida Reforma along Calle Melgar. On the left merchants can be seen standing in front of Chez Vouz, La Casa de Usted, a gift and curio store.

The shops themselves, however, were rarely captured in postcards, which was an unusual condition because curio stores were very popular with postcard photographers in other Mexican border towns. An exception was Artes Mexicanas at its previous location on Avenida Madero around the corner from the Prado Bar yet proximate to Calle

FIGURE 11.36 Calle Melgar looking north during the 1950s. The street was an active gathering place for visitors to Mexicali only blocks from the crossing, and curio stores were part of the daytime attraction. México Fotográfico 59, 1950s.

FIGURE 11.37 Curio store Chez Vouz La Casa de Usted on Calle Melgar looking south to Avenida Reforma, 1950s. México Fotográfico 127, 1950s.

FIGURE 11.38 Artes Mexicanas. A curio store on Avenida Madero around the corner from Calle Melgar and close to the crossing. Tinted photo postcard, México Fotográfico 24, 1950s. Carol Hann Collection.

FIGURE 11.39 Interior view of Tecolote Curios in Mexicali, a rare glimpse inside a curio store that reveals the range of tourist products available. Photo postcard, 1950s. André Williams Collection.

FIGURE 11.40 Calle Melgar looking south from Avenida Madero to the block where the street ends at its intersection with Avenida Reforma circa 1960. Campos Curios and Anita's Curios are visible at left. Chrome postcard, 1960s.

Melgar (fig. 11.38). Equally rare in Mexicali were postcards that showed the interior of curio stores (fig. 11.39).

By the 1960s Calle Melgar was still recognized as a daytime shopping street where Campos Curios and Anita's Curios were new additions to the street (fig. 11.40). Other curio stores in the vicinity during this period included Mitla Curios on the corner of Calle Melgar and Avenida Reforma and Laura Curios around the corner on Avenida Reforma, which advertised leather goods, perfumes, and jewelry.

PART IV

Other Baja Border Towns

Far enough from Tijuana to be off the main tourist route, the somnolent . . . settlement of Tecate more closely resembles a mainland Mexico pueblo *(town) than does any other locality in northern Baja California.*

—Wayne Bernhardson[1]

Go a few miles west of Yuma on Interstate 8 and you'll see a sign that reads: Old Mexico. Highway 186 will take you to a little-known port of entry at Andrade/ Algodones, B. C.

—Rick Cahill[2]

TWELVE

Tecate and Algodones

In the 1986 book *La Frontera: The United States Border with Mexico*, the first and in many ways still the best of dozens of border travelogues that followed it, author Alan Weisman used 190 pages to describe the towns of the border, both Mexican and American, accompanied by an array of incredible photographic images by photographer Jay Dusard. In all of the elegance of that volume, Weisman does not mention the small Baja California border town of Algodones. But he did have this to say about Tecate: "spa and brewery on the Mexico side; store and customs house in the United States."[1] On the other hand, in 1964 Mexican President Gustavo Díaz Ordaz called Tecate "La ventana mas limpia de México" (the cleanest window of Mexico).[2] This reference was a declaration of Tecate being free of any cabaret stain, an association neither Tijuana nor Mexicali could deny. Decades later, a writer for the *San Diego Union-Tribune* would call Tecate "the border's great exception," a reference, perhaps, to Carey McWilliams's onetime claim for California.[3] And, as geographer–travel writer Wayne Bernhardson noted in an epigraph to part 4, Tecate is more like an interior Mexico *pueblo* than a border town. Algodones, a hamlet compared to the small town of Tecate, has been absent from most standard guidebooks of Baja California.[4] That neglect has changed in the last few decades as Algodones has become what some call a "medical mecca" border town, a reference to the enormous popularity of discount prescription drug sales and now dental and other medical services available in the tiny town.[5]

This chapter probes the place identity of these Baja California border towns using historic postcards and maps to assign stature to small places that have been largely forgotten in previous accounts. Like all border towns, Tecate and Algodones have a historical geographical past that can be uncovered through an assessment of their townscapes and particular visual representations as presented in the popular postcard.

TECATE

The urban plan of Tecate emerged out of the late nineteenth-century colonization scheme for the Tecate Valley (see chap. 1). The routing of the San Diego and Arizona Railway was the impetus for town settlement at the site circa 1914. By 1919 land was being subdivided for about a dozen families into lots occupied by tents, adobe and frame houses, out buildings, and corrals located along Avenida Hidalgo (then called Libertad) above the railroad alignment.[6] Later development spread west across the grid of streets (fig. 12.1). The population of the town counted in 1900 and 1910 had been less than 150 (table 1.1). In 1921 the United States relocated a customs house from Campo to Tecate, California, on the north side of the international boundary. In the same year, Tecate, Baja California, became a municipal seat, and the town population hovered near five hundred. The Mexican government purchased land from Ramón Salazar to extend Tecate, Baja California, north to the border. The crossing at this time was a simple wooden *garita* on the Mexican side of the line with the U.S. customs house and a general store on the American side (fig. 12.2).

During the 1920s agriculture expanded in the Tecate Valley, where wheat and wine grapes were planted, and the town of Tecate became a service center for outlying dispersed populations. This period witnessed the initial rooting of Tecate's industrial base when a flour mill was established. Local capitalist Alberto Aldrete opened a malt mill to

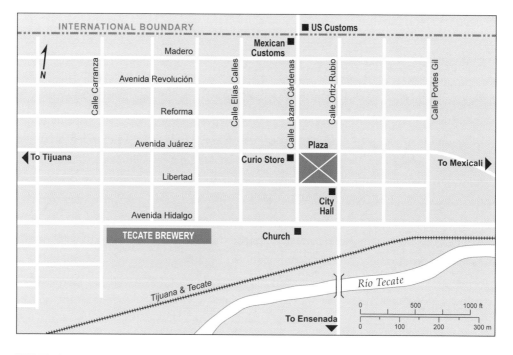

FIGURE 12.1 Tecate town map with street grid, 1950s. After Automobile Club of Southern California, *Baja California Norte* (guide), 59. Cartography by Barbara Trapido-Lurie.

process local barley as well as grain imported from the Ensenada district. He also opened a pressing plant to extract oil from copra, shipped from the South Pacific to San Diego and then by train to Tecate; the oil was shipped back to the states and used in soap manufacture and stock feed.[7]

Public facilities for the small town were improved during the 1920s and into the next several decades. The previously open dirt plaza was planted with trees and a *kiosco* (bandstand) was built. The site became known as Parque Hidalgo in honor of Mexico's hero from the wars of independence from Spain. The park matured into an oasis-like town center that would, by the 1940s, be identified as the town's main plaza (fig. 12.3). A municipal palace was erected off the plaza, and a parish church was built on Avenida Hidalgo at its intersection with Calle Lázaro Cárdenas (see fig. 12.1).[8]

In the 1940s almost all of Tecate's commercial development was on Avenida Hidalgo, two blocks south of the plaza. Services were modest and included a hotel, bar, café, and hardware store (fig. 12.4). The residential landscape in the center of town comprised single-story, box-like houses with flat roofs in a mix of popular architectural styles. Some had walled or fenced front yards (fig. 12.5).

In 1944 the single most significant development in Tecate was the founding of the brewery. During the Prohibition era Tecate had a distillery—Donlevy Whiskey—but the factory was shut down in 1932. Aldrete, who previously had founded the malt factory in

FIGURE 12.2 *Garita*, or boundary crossing guardhouse, looking north to the border from Tecate, Baja California. On the Tecate, California, side of the boundary was the U.S. customs house and a general store. Photo postcard, 1920s.

FIGURE 12.3 Tecate's main plaza, 1940s. México Fotográfico 2, 1940s.

FIGURE 12.4 Tecate commercial development on Avenida Hidalgo, then the town's main street. Photo postcard, 1940s.

FIGURE 12.5 Tecate residential street. México Fotográfico 1, 1940s.

the 1920s, then the major employer in Tecate, opened the brewery to meet the post–World War II demand for beer. Cervecería Tecate, built near the railroad track and off the main street Avenida Hidalgo (figs. 12.1, 12.6), was a fixture in the small town. In the 1950s it was purchased by the Monterrey, Mexico, brewing giant Cervecería Cuauhtémoc. The Tecate brewery was the exclusive producer of Tecate Beer, although it also manufactured Carta Blanca, a major Cevercería Cuauhtémoc brand. Barley production was already established in the area, and water was locally sourced. Hops were imported from the United States and Germany.[9]

The Cervecería Tecate brought enormous prosperity to the Baja border town. With the increase in work opportunities related to the brewing industry, the population of Tecate more than doubled between 1940 and 1950 to nearly 3,700 (table 1.1). Between 1946 and 1951 hundreds of businesses were opened in the small town.[10] The late 1940s railroad connection between Baja and Sonora via Mexicali improved travel and trade along the highway linking the northern border to Tijuana, and cross-border commerce improved with new customs houses built on the Mexican and American sides of the boundary. Into the 1950s the brewery remained the most significant economic engine of Tecate (fig. 12.7).

The post–World War II boom brought further changes to Tecate. The previous main street—Avenida Hidalgo—yielded to a new thoroughfare with the construction of Mexico Highway 2. Two panoramic photo postcards show the shift and consequent expansion of the town. Figure 12.8 is a 1940s view looking west from a hill east of town near where

FIGURE 12.6 Cervecería Tecate, the signature industrial development of the town, was founded in 1944. The factory was under construction when this photo postcard was made, 1940s.

FIGURE 12.7 Brewery and the railroad station in Tecate, 1950s. México Fotogáfico 16, 1950s.

FIGURE 12.8 1940s panoramic photo postcard looking west over Tecate with the main street, Avenida Hidalgo, at lower left extending west across the vista. México Fotográfico 4, 1940s.

FIGURE 12.9 1950s panoramic photo postcard looking west over Tecate with Avenida Juárez, the new main street of the border town, at lower left extending across the vista. Tecate's townscape expanded west and north toward the border during this decade. México Fotográfico 14, 1950s.

a previous 1920s view (see fig. 1.7) was photographed. Avenida Hidalgo is at the lower left of the 1940s view with the Cervecería Tecate and the railroad alignment on the west end of town. Figure 12.9 is a 1950s panoramic photo postcard also looking west. The main roadway is now Avenida Juárez that coincides with Mexico Highway 2 through town, two blocks north of Avenida Hidalgo (see fig. 12.1). Avenida Juárez emerged as Tecate's new main street, and commercial businesses opened along this corridor because this was the principal highway connecting Mexicali to Tijuana (fig. 12.10).

FIGURE 12.10 Avenida Juárez, Tecate's new main street in the 1950s. This roadway became part of Mexico Highway 2, the border road that linked Mexicali to Tijuana, passing through Tecate. The mountain in the background left of center is Tecate Peak, also known as Cuchumá, sacred landmark to the Indigenous Kumeyaay people, and located just north of the international boundary in the United States. México Fotográfico 15, 1950s.

The growth of Tecate during the 1950s to a population of nearly seven thousand complicated the small-town ideal that had long defined Tecate for its residents. When curio store business owners decided that they might profit from the new highway traffic, the town at first resisted but then relented to allow just a handful of shops (fig. 12.11). Tecate had previously permitted the Rancho La Puerta, a European-style health spa, to locate on an extensive tract of land west of town. Founded in 1940 by Edmond Bordeaux Szekley, the spa was a kind of early commune, which during the 1950s evolved into a full-fledged resort accommodating about one hundred guests, mostly American.[11] The center of the complex was the Essene School and Grape Valley Lodge, which included a large outdoor swimming pool. Advertisements declared relaxation and renewed health and vigor through organic foods, sun, and water therapy (fig. 12.12).

Tecate Roadside Vignette

In spite of Tecate's reputation as the cleanest window into Mexico, the declaration made in the 1960s by President Gustavo Díaz Ordaz, there was a time during Prohibition when

FIGURE 12.11 Rosita Curios, one of a handful of gift shops allowed in Tecate during the 1950s near the new highway through town. México Fotográfico 2, 1950s.

FIGURE 12.12 Rancho La Puerta, founded in 1940, a European-style health spa on hundreds of acres of land west of Tecate, Baja California. It was one of the border town's only tourist developments. Photo postcard, 1950s. Carol Hann Collection.

FIGURE 12.13 Wheels and meals on the highway through Tecate, 1920s.

FIGURE 12.14 Cantinas and cabarets operated by the Santana brothers on the road through Tecate during the Prohibition era.

FIGURE 12.15 Hotel Santana, cantina, and cabaret on the Tecate highway, 1920s.

FIGURE 12.16 Cantina in Tecate advertising 15 cent beer. Miguel González's Lower California Commercial Company owned the Cervecería Mexicali in Mexicali and various Prohibition businesses in Tijuana as well as this cantina.

Tecate was a kind of roadside cantina town. The route that paralleled the border between Mexicali and Tijuana had been a crude road used since the early twentieth century (see fig. 1.18 and chap. 1). During the reign of Esteban Cantú as governor of the northern district of Baja California, a road development scheme emerged to improve highways that could bind Baja towns in the north and south. By 1919 the Tecate Valley was principally a transport corridor crossing the Peninsular Range of northern Baja. Some of the earliest commercial services in Tecate during the 1920s were roadside attractions that offered alcoholic beverages.[12] This vignette (figs. 12.13–12.16) exhibits a handful of photographic postcards by an unknown photographer that showed this concentration of highway cantinas.

ALGODONES

The smallest of the Baja California border towns, Algodones, was carved out of a part of the Andrade land grant in northeastern Baja California (see fig. 1.10 and chap. 1). The property was a long tract of land along and including parts of the Colorado River from the international boundary south, a landscape that was shown as unoccupied when mapped by the international boundary survey in 1889 (fig. 12.17). The parcel of land was named Rancho Los Algodones and mapped by William Denton in 1873. Several colonization schemes were launched by Andrade to populate Rancho Los Algodones, and several family groups were settled in the area by 1900. Decades of legal entanglements followed claims made by various potential owners of the parcel. Andrade prevailed and ultimately sold the tract to various landed interests in the late nineteenth century. Andrade's name survives in its attachment to a small settlement north of the international boundary opposite Algodones.[13]

In the late 1900s the Mexican government under Porfirio Díaz established a customs house at the international boundary where the Colorado River crossed Rancho Los Algodones (fig. 12.18). Less than one hundred people constituting some of the early colonization families resided in the area at this time (table 1.1). The customs house gained notoriety during the Mexican Revolution in 1911 when rebels who were engaged in the battle with federal troops in Mexicali ventured east to burn the *aduana*.[14]

Beyond the customs house, which began to concentrate activity at the border location, the Inter-California Railroad reached Los Algodones in 1909 and brought further notice to the site (see figs. 1.13, 1.15, and chap. 1). Algodones was being subdivided into properties, and the town was legally declared in 1918 (fig. 12.19). The origin of the name is peculiar because most sources suggest that it derives from *algodón*, the Spanish word for cotton, a cultivated crop that became especially associated with irrigated agriculture in the Colorado River Delta in the early twentieth century. However, the name Algodones predates any commercial planting of cotton in the area. One source suggests that the

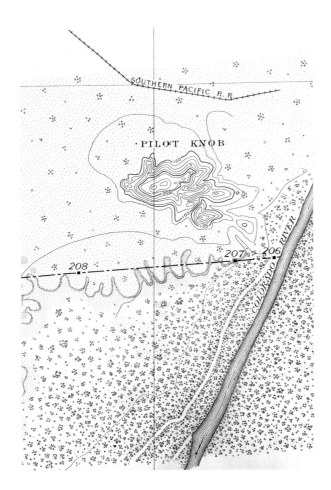

FIGURE 12.17 Map detail from 1889 showing two boundary monuments—206 and 207—that would be near the future location of the town of Algodones. The Rancho Los Algodones land grant would be carved out of the larger Andrade tract south of the international boundary and parallel to the Colorado River. International Boundary Commission, *Boundary Between the United States and Mexico*, Map no. 4.

name stems from a Yuman tribe that previously occupied the delta. It might also derive from a Spanish expression for the cotton bolls that come from the cottonwood tree, a common riparian poplar that was once pervasive along the waterways of the Colorado and its many fragmented channels in the delta region during the late nineteenth and early twentieth centuries.[15]

Los Algodones developed a municipal presence with the construction of a city hall and associated town services. A school had been built in the 1910s and was remodeled in the 1920s. Rail traffic created sufficient cross-border commerce, and the hamlet became a service center for the dispersed agricultural population nearby. In the decade of the 1920s, Algodones grew from close to two hundred to over five hundred residents (table 1.1).

FIGURE 12.18 *Aduana* (customs house) at Algodones in 1909. The wattle-and-daub structure was built near the Colorado River next to the international boundary to service traffic into and out of the Rancho Los Algodones settlements. Author's collection.

FIGURE 12.19 Town of Algodones, 1900s. The town was a cluster of buildings carved out of the Rancho Los Algodones and declared a legal settlement in 1918. Cyanotype photo postcard, 1900s.

A 1947 town map of the *fundo legal*, or municipal town limits, showed that Algodones was partitioned into some seventy town blocks wedged between the Álamo Canal and the international boundary. The Inter-California railroad alignment cut across the street grid (fig. 12.20). East–west calles starting in the northeast corner were numbered 1, 2, 3, et cetera, and north–south streets were labeled Avenidas starting with International and progressing A, B, C, and so forth. The map shows that Algodones had a large city park in its residential zone and a depot and customs house close to the crossing where commercial services were probably concentrated.

The Canal del Álamo (see fig. 12.20) was constructed circa 1900 to divert water from the Colorado River along a fourteen-mile channel to the head of the Álamo River to facilitate irrigated agriculture across the border in the Imperial Valley. The canal was necessary because diversions on the U.S. side of the boundary at the time could not negotiate the Algodones Dunes, which blocked access to water from the Colorado River (see fig. 1.5). In the 1940s a major infrastructure project, the Morelos Dam diversion on the Colorado River, was constructed in accordance with the 1945 Mexican Water Treaty to irrigate farmland in the Mexicali Valley district and brought greater focus to Algodones.[16] The population of the border town nearly doubled to one thousand during the 1940s (table 1.1).

The proximity of Algodones to U.S. Route 80, the famous ocean-to-ocean highway, made the small Baja California border town accessible to cross-country travelers in the 1940s. A large billboard strategically positioned on this route directed motorists

FIGURE 12.20 Los Algodones town limits, 1947. *X*, border crossing; *M*, Monument 207; *A*, customs house; *D*, depot; *RR*, Inter-California Railway; *1*, San Diego Café, 1920s; *2*, A. B. W. Club, 1920s. After Méndez Sáinz, *Arquitectura nacionalista*, 41.

FIGURE 12.21 Algodones' proximity to U.S. Route 80 enabled a roadside billboard to direct cross-country travelers to the Baja border town in Old Mexico just two miles south of the highway. Photograph, 1940s. Carol Hann Collection.

FIGURE 12.22 Mariano Café, a restaurant, bar, and curio store all in one, Algodones. Photo postcard, 1940s.

to Algodones in Old Mexico, only two miles south from the highway (fig. 12.21). One Algodones entrepreneur, Mariano Ma, operated a successful restaurant, bar, and curio store that appealed to visitors who found themselves in the small town during the booming 1940s (fig. 12.22). Mariano's retail establishment continued to attract customers into the 1950s, and Ma devised exotic real photo postcards to promote his business (see fig. 2.9).

Algodones Cabaret

In January 1915, on the heels of prohibition in Arizona, a report in the *Calexico Chronicle* announced, "Paris has her Versailles, El Paso her Juarez, Detroit her Windsor, Calexico her Mexicali, and now comes Yuma with Algodones." The international border crossing at what became known as Algodones began to attract opportunists looking to benefit from cabaret activity following early state restrictions on alcohol consumption initiated in Arizona. The San Diego and El Tecolotito buildings were two of the first at the site circa 1905–1906. The new cabaret operators were from Yuma, Arizona, and following the necessary concessions from the Mexican government, they intended to run a jitney service across the Colorado River to the town of Andrade, California, so customers could cross the line to Algodones. The transport service was set to operate with the cost of the fare enabling a coupon for an equal amount of drink in the town's joy palaces. It was reported that there would be plenty of women to draw the boys from Yuma. Thus, Algodones became a cabaret town even before passage of the Volstead Act and five years before Prohibition came to be enforced in January 1920.[17]

The San Diego Café was the first cabaret visitors would encounter on entering Algodones (fig. 12.23). It was nearest the crossing gate on a sandy diagonal road parallel to the railroad between Calles 1 and Calle 2 (see fig. 12.20). The San Diego, along with the

FIGURE 12.23 San Diego Café, one of the oldest cabarets in Algodones, was positioned closest to the crossing gate from Andrade, California, while El Tecolotito, or A. B. W. Club, was one block beyond. Photo postcard proof, 1920s. Author's collection.

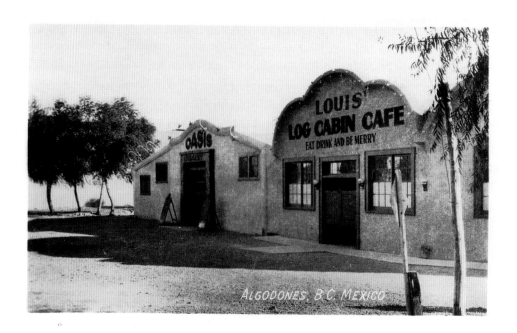

FIGURES 12.24 *a*, Louis' Log Cabin, and *b*, Oasis were popular Algodones cabarets during the Prohibition era where patrons were encouraged to "Eat, Drink, and Be Merry." Photo postcards, 1920s.

Tecolotito (Little Owl), also known as the A. B. W. Club and Casino and operated by financial partners of the Owl in Mexicali, were the oldest cabarets in Algodones. The Tecolotito was positioned at the corner of Calle 2 and Avenida A, only a block in from the San Diego Café[18] (see fig. 12.20).

During the peak years of Prohibition there might have been a half dozen separate cabarets in Algodones. Besides the San Diego and El Tecolotito were the Oasis and Louis' Log Cabin Café, two cabarets within walking distance of the international boundary (fig. 12.24*a*). The Log Cabin opened a boxing arena behind the café in 1929.[19] The Oasis was a popular cabaret that featured live music (fig. 12.24*b*).

The 1930s proved challenging for cabarets in Algodones. Having survived the 1925 call to close prostitution operations, a Mexican federal edict that affected all of the Baja California border, the Great Depression brought reduced attendance and, in 1933, the repeal of Prohibition in the U.S.[20] In 1932 three separate fire incidents nearly destroyed the cabaret operations of Algodones. In January of that year, the Big Four and Algodones Club burned to the ground. The flames also threatened but spared the nearby A. B. W. Club and the San Diego Café. That April, the Oasis and Log Cabin Café burned down with losses estimated at twenty thousand and twenty-five thousand dollars, respectively. Finally, in December, the A. B. C. Bar, Green Front Saloon, and O.K. Saloon and Restaurant were destroyed by a conflagration near the boundary line.[21] Fires, as previously seen in Tijuana and Mexicali, were a hazard of cabaret operations especially when structures were wood and subject to easy ignition. Nevertheless, arson was known to have been committed in several instances to offset financial losses and, when possible, collect fire insurance.

Cabarets continued to operate in Algodones in the 1950s with new businesses, such as Club Rey de Algodón, that catered to American visitors who crossed into Algodones to savor some of the magic of an earlier era.[22]

PART V

Looking Back to See Forward

Mataix wrote pieces commissioned by a number of newspapers . . . from short stories to some magnificent travel columns about places he'd never visited. I remember one titled "The Mysteries of Byzantium" that at the time I considered a masterpiece, and which Mataix invented from beginning to end with no more documentation than a set of old postcards of Istanbul.

—Carlos Ruiz Zafón[1]

I can say that I possess all of Old Paris.

—Eugène Atget[2]

━ THIRTEEN ━

The Baja Border Past Through Postcards

The past, it has been said, is a foreign country. That metaphor implies not only that the past is exotic but, more commonly, little understood. We all have a past, but until recently, with the popularity of ancestral history, most have had little appreciation of those distant connections. As geographers know well, places, like people, also have a past. In most cases the past of a place is not broadly understood, although for several decades now Americans have probed the pasts of their hometowns through preservation movements and popular local histories stimulated by a flood of small books published by a single company.[1]

Postcards from the Baja California Border, like its three predecessor volumes, engages the relationship between image—the popular postcard view—and place—the Mexican border town. The exercise is a kind of historical geography because its larger concern is to see and understand how these border places were represented by popular postcard imagery in the first half of the twentieth century, a time frame that corresponds to the adolescent place personalities of the towns. This way of seeing and understanding is not intended as analysis; rather, it is presented as synthesis. It leans more toward the concept that "geography, like history and unlike the sciences, is not the study of any particular kind of thing, but a particular way of studying almost anything."[2] Geography in this regard is a point of view, a way of looking at things.

In this volume as in the three volumes of similar approach for other Mexican border regions, the particular point of view has been historical geographic and the method of looking has been an exploration of places as landscapes. The landscape concept is not unique to geography, but cultural geographers notably have made the idea central to their studies. Implicit in this approach is that landscape is not a naive surface. It is, instead, a socially and historically constructed terrain, a palimpsest that embeds cultural preference in built forms.[3] Accepting that premise, *Postcards from the Baja California*

Border is a cultural geography as well as a historical geography because it uses postcard views of Mexican border towns to expand understanding of how the built landscape or townscape is revealed in that imagery and what can be learned from this form of cultural representation.

This concluding chapter revisits some of the major themes examined in this work and shares an interpretation of those findings as they relate to postcards and the historical and cultural geography of Baja's border towns.

POSTCARD AS TIME AND PLACE MARKER

As Gloria Fraser Giffords noted in her essay that accompanied a special issue of *Arte México*, postcards of Mexico are more than nostalgic remnants of vacation travels. In retrospect the postcard harbors "unsuspected historical and social dimensions."[4] For this reason and more, chapter 2 introduces the reader to the legacy and anatomy of postcard types and their associated eras.

The photograph from which most picture postcards are derived is a media form utilized historically by geographers to interpret places. Geographers and others have contemplated how photographs such as a postcard are a form of spectating, a kind of framing view that can mediate vision.[5] Historic photographic postcards may testify to unedited views of place, but of course composition of view remained the purview of the photographer. A visual snapshot of place, the picture postcard, although based on a photograph, was often converted to a print format for commercial sale. In that process it was graphically altered to add color and eliminate or add elements to a scene.

For the Baja border towns, views became standardized to a certain degree in the use of similar postcard imagery popular among all the Mexican border towns. Street views, buildings, landmarks, the border crossing, interior scenes, and sporting events were the fundamental visual nomenclature—a set of perspectives common to almost all postcard photography. These types of views were how the world was captured in the first half of the twentieth century. They survive to the present, an accepted vocabulary of urban and town place representation.

What this means for the Baja border towns is that each town might experience similar generalized postcard views, yet because each town was a different place with its own geographic personality, nuance was possible. In Tijuana, for example, Avenida Olvera, which became Main Street, then Avenida A, and finally Avenida Revolución, was the most popular postcard view of that border town. Revolución was home first to curio stores and subsequently to cabarets, then more curio stores, and then restaurants, an evolutionary transformation that is made clear by charting the changes evident in five decades of postcard representation of that infamous strip. Similarly, but with variation,

Mexicali was early shown to be a set of cabarets popularly rendered in night postcard views to advance the idea of a "Great White Way" during the Prohibition era.

On the other hand, postcards by their very nature as commercial products and through their repetition over time of landmark, street, and building views enable a serial vision of place that is extraordinary. There are no known media formats that were intended to be historical markers through time, although clearly photographs of past places can be resurrected by contemporary researchers to compare change.[6] Postcard photographers and publishers circulated their views of the same landmarks and scenes over and over and over again, thereby inadvertently allowing views of a place in one era to be compared easily with those of succeeding periods. This quality may be unique to postcard imagery. That condition potentially affords the historical geographic researcher an unrivaled insight into changes of places through time should the researcher consult a postcard archive with sufficient image density to reconstruct views. Chapter 6 showed how postcard views through time for Avenida Revolución enable a first step in this process. Beyond a single street, all content chapters in this work—whether Tijuana, Mexicali, or Tecate and Algodones—make possible this type of time-place comparison because the Arreola Collection is sufficiently deep to permit multiple views of the same landscapes.

BAJA BORDER TOWN LANDSCAPES

When the author and fellow geographer James Curtis first began to study the Mexican border towns, the initial motivation was to understand the contemporary cities with only a preliminary appreciation of the historic dimensions of each town.[7] There were, then, a modest number of important studies about the border, but chiefly the scholarship was being conducted by American researchers.[8] Some three decades hence, the volume of published research about the Mexico-U.S. border can fill a small library, and, significantly, Mexican scholars are now the driving force behind these studies.

A particular emphasis in this border-postcard project has been to focus a geographical lens on the border-town past, especially the visual dimension that seemed to have largely escaped much serious scholarship. This is not to say that the visual dimension has been completely ignored, because some historical surveys directed attention to imagery about border towns by particular photographers. Increasingly, more work that is place based is now emerging in this arena.[9]

The important question at this point is what has been learned about Baja California border-town landscapes through this geographic postcard investigation. Three categories of findings can be outlined.

First, the historical geographic study of Baja border towns through postcards has enabled a clearer understanding of landscape sequencing for particular locations within and surrounding the towns. This is demonstrated, for example, in the changing arrangement of border crossings at Tijuana and Mexicali. Careful inspection of postcards and historic maps make visible how boundary crossing points changed with circumstances from river flooding to railroad routing decisions. Further, postcards illustrate how the landscape of crossings evolved from simple checkpoints to multilane automobile passageways with greater control and physical presence over time. Landscape sequencing is also enhanced by the study of postcards that illustrate the changing locations of businesses and activities in Mexicali and Tijuana. The multiple locations of cabarets such as the Owl in Mexicali, the Red Mill and Caesar's restaurant in Tijuana, and bullrings in each town are made legible through the comparisons of postcard views with historic maps. In Tecate, postcards enable a visual sequencing of the earliest commercial street, Avenida Hidalgo, in comparison with the more recent business corridor, Avenida Juárez.

A second finding from the study of postcards of the Baja border towns is the identification of landscape discontinuities. This is the presence or absence of a land use that stands against the conventional form, or morphology, of a Mexican border town as presented in generalizations about towns from previous study. Perhaps the most significant example of this discontinuity is the presence or absence of a town plaza, arguably one of the most fundamental landscape expressions of any Mexican town, not just border towns.[10] Because plaza spaces were typically shown in postcard views, a collection of plaza views for a town enables an understanding of the location of the plaza in time as well as space. In Mexicali, a plaza (called *parque*, or park) was established in the first decade of the town's founding, yet the location of the space was unconventional in that it was not central to the street grid of the town. Instead, it was peripheral and proximate to the boundary line. Further, the space was not a proportional rectangle but an oblong rectangle that extended over several town blocks. In Tijuana, despite the call for plazas in the original town plan, a central community space was not laid out for almost three decades. Even then, it was peripheral to the center of town. At Tecate, a traditional plaza was fixed early and has persisted over time, whereas at Algodones, a plaza park was not part of the town plan for decades after the earliest settlement.

The reason for this particularly striking landscape discontinuity is not easily explained. Foremost, none of the Baja California border towns has a colonial pedigree. Therefore, the traditional plaza that was dictated by legal ordinance under Spain was never required. In the case of Mexicali and Tijuana, one is tempted to rationalize that the plaza position and shape may have been a consequence of an American influence in the early town structure. In Mexicali, the plaza park was positioned on the international boundary because the first town plan, drafted by an American, included plaza space proximate to the line. In the case of Tijuana, the early community evolved to serve outsiders, and Avenida Olvera/Main Street was clearly the center of activity. It was only later that residential districts evolved independently of that singular spine. Tecate more closely mirrors the conventional tradition. Nevertheless, even there the position of the plaza was determined in part by its proximity to the railroad alignment—an American inspired routing—that was the reason for founding the town.

A second landscape discontinuity is the difference in curio streets and curio activity in the two largest Baja border towns, Tijuana and Mexicali. By convention, Mexican border towns exhibit curio streets proximate to the major border-crossing point and often several blocks deep along the main street extending from that crossing.[11] Avenida Revolución in Tijuana closely resembles the model for border towns, although the drag is distant from the crossing because of the Tijuana River. Curio stores were an early land use and tourist draw in Tijuana from the late nineteenth century that then exploded in popularity in the post-Prohibition and post–World War II eras. Mexicali, by comparison, was never much of a curio store border town despite the presence of a handful of stores along Calle Melgar, particularly in the post–World War II period. As discussed in chapter 11, Mexicali's comparatively small-scale curio store development was probably a consequence of the town's distance from large population centers in Southern California that might have contributed a steady stream of visitor shoppers. Neither Tecate nor Algodones have ever been centers of curio trade. In fact Tecate intentionally distanced itself, initially, from the tourist economy in an attempt to keep outsiders away and to preserve the traditional small-town ambience.

The popularity of certain places shown in postcards resulted in many more overlooked spaces in these towns. This reveals a third discontinuity. Residential areas of Mexicali were sometimes captured in postcards. Pueblo Nuevo, however, on the border town's west side and a large working-class district, was almost completely avoided. Nevertheless, Mexicali middle-class and elite residential neighborhoods became popular subjects for real photo postcard imagery in the post–World War II era. This contrasts sharply with Tijuana during the period of study, where postcards rarely revealed residential landscapes at all—whether affluent or poor. Perhaps this is not surprising since the postcard was chiefly a form of advertisement; showing the everyday was less important to what photographers thought tourists wanted. In any event the near absence of residential district representation in Tijuana is counter to what has been shown for other Mexican border towns such as Ciudad Juárez and Nogales, where neighborhoods regularly appeared in postcards.[12] Admitting this bias is an important condition of using postcards for geographic and historic research.

A third category of findings about Baja border-town landscapes as revealed in postcards is persistence. This means that certain landscapes and spaces show a strong presence throughout the study period of one half century and provide a means to see the persistence of a land use over time. In Mexicali, the Chinese ethnic quarter, La Chinesca, piqued the curiosity of postcard photographers and publishers from the earliest days of the town. That attraction continued into the 1950s. The perception of this distinctive quarter evolved from that of a restrictive zone for cabaret to one of a tourist district that brought visitors seeking the exotic allure of the foreign, if even for just a meal. The Chinese imprint on the city survives into the present as one of the highlights of Mexicali among all Mexican border towns. In Tijuana, the Mexicali Beer Hall, known locally as La Ballena (The Whale), persisted as a landmark along Avenida Revolución from the 1920s through the 1960s to its demise in the 1970s. More than any single Tijuana establishment, Mexicali Beer Hall remained an institution to generations of visitors and locals alike. Its popularity in postcards was surpassed only by Agua Caliente, which it predated and lived well beyond.

Finally, the Baja California border towns exhibited a persistent association and connection to their counterpart American region of Southern California. This was especially the case with the larger towns: Tijuana tied to Los Angeles and San Diego and Mexicali with its linkages to both San Francisco and Los Angeles. This association is borne out by the evidence of key American investors in the respective towns, California visitors to the towns, and the regional economic interests that cemented relationships across the international divide. This finding mirrors what has been learned through the larger border-town postcard project. The border towns of the Río Bravo showed striking connections to Texas places, and the Sonora border towns displayed a similar strong linkage to Phoenix and southern Arizona towns. While the Chihuahua border towns also demonstrated a regional connection to West Texas and California, the success of El Paso as a transcontinental railroad pivot point ensured that its Mexican neighbor Juárez would experience a greater national exposure than perhaps any Mexican border town. That popularity was reinforced with the crossroads nature of automobile travel along the southern corridor. This finding is significant to a deeper understanding of the plurality of the Mexican borderlands. While the tendency in popular writing has been to cast all Mexican border towns as the same, it is necessary to appreciate that important regionalisms were created at the beginnings and later evolutions of these places.

BAJA BORDER-TOWN POSTCARD THEMES

Beyond the postcard as time and place marker and a looking-glass window to viewing historical geographic landscapes is the simple allure of the postcard as a graphic format that accentuates place. While it might be argued that postcards expose many dimensions of the Mexican border towns, the promotion of particular landmarks and spaces shown in postcards of the Baja border are especially revealing. Four themes in particular emphasize this reflection.

First, postcards elevate the graphic representation of adult entertainment space or cabaret. While this can be said about postcards in other Mexican border towns, on the

Baja border, California's attention to celebrity and entertainment generated a tempting appeal toward Tijuana and Mexicali. Table gaming, racetrack gambling, jai alai contests, prizefights, and bullfights all contributed to a visitor allure because many of these activities were prohibited in early twentieth-century California. Postcard photographers and publishers were ready and able to visually capture and represent these spaces and activities. Further, postcards became the visual fix that exploited joy palaces and the excesses of Prohibition-era celebration. Business names such as Tivoli, Alhambra Café, Aloha Café, Ben-Hur Café, Mona Lisa Nite Club, El Gato Negro (The Black Cat), Blue Fox, Bambi Club, and Midnight Follies were meant to suggest the exotic if not the nefarious. Particular club names featured in postcards such as the Climax in Mexicali or the Red Mill/Molino Rojo/Moulin Rouge in Tijuana were intentional associations of sexual innuendo and risqué floorshow entertainments.

A second theme accentuated in postcards of Baja border towns was trendy architectural design. In the first half of the twentieth century, Southern California was a fountain of innovative aesthetics, and this spilled over into Tijuana and Mexicali. Mission Revival, Spanish Revival, art deco, and Streamline Moderne were avant-garde styles exhibited in postcards highlighting popular commercial and public buildings and even some residences. Architectural novelty became standard practice in Baja border towns from the whimsical art deco façade of the San Francisco Café (later the Villa Colonial curio arcade) to the Moorish-themed exterior of the Jai Alai Palace, both located on Avenida Revolución and still standing to this day in Tijuana. In Mexicali buildings such as the Palacio del Gobierno, Escuela Cuauhtémoc, and the Owl Café (El Tecolote), all of which survive to the present, experimented with exterior concrete construction in the early decades of the twentieth century. Perhaps the crème de la crème of architectural showcases of the entire Mexican border was the Agua Caliente Resort, where Moorish and Spanish Revival design flowered with exotic splendor. One visual legacy of those remarkable buildings razed in the 1930s is the hundreds of colorful print postcards that captured their romance.

A third postcard theme particular to the Baja border was the postcard as souvenir. Again, whereas any Mexican border-town postcard might be a souvenir, in Tijuana the postcard as personalized memento was burned into the popular consciousness of the era by the infamous burro cart snapshot, exclusively a photo postcard. No single Mexican border town approached the intensity of this photographic activity, although several towns did accommodate staged horse or burro carts where such postcard souvenirs could be made. In Tijuana this became a local industry that both sustained entrepreneurship and enhanced the tourist experience. Thousands of these postcard representations survive to this day in private and some public collections. In fact, only Tijuana has a museum that features the history of this activity. That burro cart photographers are still part of the tourist scene on Avenida Revolución is testimony to the staying power of this visual format.

A fourth postcard theme from the universe of Baja border-town images is the disaster representation. While river floods were regular occurrences in Rio Grande border towns, on the Baja border seismic events were the paramount natural disasters affecting chiefly Mexicali. Postcards sometimes captured those events in the same manner that postcards showed flooding in river towns or destroyed buildings in towns that witnessed revolutionary battles. More common, however, was human-induced disaster in the form of fire. Early wooden construction and careless or sometimes intentional ignition brought repeated catastrophe to sections of Tijuana and Mexicali. Shifting proprietorship in Baja border towns meant frequent owner turnover of entertainment businesses. Investment losses sometimes led to desperate actions. The frequency of fires suggests that arson may have been at play in some or many of the conflagrations. Once again, the postcard was a means to document and sensationalize those events.

ADIÓS

Postcards are one material artifact of the tourist experience, and they help us to see multiple aspects of the Baja California border.

> Postcards provide the world's most complete visual inventory. Few things, people or places have not at some time or other ended up as the subject, or an unwitting or unintentional component, of a postcard.[13]

Through postcards, we come to understand how Tijuana and Mexicali were not equivalent border places despite the seeming commonalities frequently attributed to them as border towns. Postcards similarly enable an appreciation of Tecate and Algodones, small towns of the Baja California border, as places with their own identities and stories.

The popular postcard is a valuable instrument in sifting out geographical as well as historical and cultural qualities of the Mexican American borderland. As a pictorial device, the postcard encourages an appreciation of place personality. Seeing the Baja California border towns through this format promotes time travel that is unique among visual media. It is a journey worthy of our continued attention and focus.

NOTES

INTRODUCTION

1. Cole, "Places We Go Aren't Passive," 17.

2. Arreola, *Postcards from the Río Bravo Border*; *Postcards from the Sonora Border*; *Postcards from the Chihuahua Border*.

3. Vanderwood, "Writing History with Picture Postcards."

4. Vanderwood and Samponaro, *Border Fury*; Samponaro and Vanderwood, *War Scare on the Rio Grande*.

5. John A. Jakle, *Postcards of the Night*; Morris, *Taming the Land*; Jakle and Sculle, *Picturing Illinois*; Arreola, "La cerca y las garitas de Ambos Nogales"; Arreola and Burkhart, "Photographic Postcards and Visual Urban Landscape"; DeBres and Sowers, "Emergence of Standardized, Idealized, and Placeless Landscapes"; Hurt and Payne, "Postcard Imagery and Geographical Imagination."

PART I

1. *Where North Meets South*, 48.

2. "Mexican Postcards: Diverse Echoes," 66.

CHAPTER 1

1. Kniffen, *Natural Landscape of the Colorado Delta*, gives a comprehensive overview of the environments of the delta.

2. Paula Rebert, *La Gran Línea*, offers the most comprehensive assessment of the mapping exercises that created the boundary. Originally, the United States desired the borderline to fall below the mouth of the Colorado River at the Gulf of California, but Mexico protested and pressed for a more northerly location to the line so a potential Mexican port might be

founded on the Gulf to offset the American insistence on possessing San Diego Bay. Ironically, a Mexican port of any consequence never developed on the Gulf of California.

3. Proffitt, *Tijuana*, 17; David Piñera and Gabriel Rivera, *Tijuana in History*, 55–61.

4. Speth, "Tecate, Baja California," (thesis) reproduces Bandini's 1833 Mapa de la Cañada de Tecate land grant, 51, and discusses in detail the various ranch and agricultural colonization efforts of the late nineteenth century, 46–79. See also Ramírez López, "Tecate," 315–18.

5. Santiago Guerrero, "Profile of the Origins of Tecate's Population," 13; Gómez Cavazos, "La ruta de *company towns* en la península de Baja California," 122–23.

6. Meade, *El distrito norte de Baja California*, 158–59; Arreola and Curtis, *The Mexican Border Cities*, 21.

7. The famous 1905–1906 flood of the region was the fault of the California Development Company, which was intent on diverting water from the Colorado River to the Imperial Valley for irrigation. Water could not be diverted directly from the river to the Imperial Valley then because the Algodones Dunes (called the Sand Hills at the time and shown in fig. 1.5) blocked the easy construction of a canal. Instead, water was diverted to the Álamo Canal, which had been dredged in the late nineteenth century to transfer water across the upper part of the delta in Baja California toward Mexicali and across the boundary into the Imperial Valley. This was the lowest elevation path to the U.S. side of the border, and once the Álamo Canal overflowed, water entered the Río Nuevo / New River drainage that flows north into the Imperial Valley west of Mexicali, flooding the entire district. See Ward, *Border Oasis*, 4–7.

8. Ward, *Border Oasis*, 5; Rojas and Courtade, *Paso de los Algodones*, 126.

9. Kirchner, *Baja California Railways*, 63.

10. Kirchner, 72–91.

11. *Corona Daily Independent*, "Through Trains Mexico City to L. A. Inaugurated."

12. Kirchner, *Baja California Railways*, 92–110; Castilla, "El ferrocarril San Diego–Arizona."

13. Kirchner, *Baja California Railways*, 116–29. For documentation on the depot at Tecate, see *Catálogo nacional, monumentos históricos inmuebles: Baja California, municipio de Tecate*, 3:551–52.

14. Piñera and Rivera, *Tijuana in History*, 133.

15. For number of tourists to Tijuana in 1902–1903, see Proffitt, *Tijuana*, table 8.1, p. 204.

16. Vanderwood, *Satan's Playground*, 240.

17. The following paragraphs about the Baja rebellion depend, in part, on information presented in Owens, "Mexican Revolution and the Role Played by Tijuana," and Richard Griswold del Castillo, "The Discredited Revolution."

18. Griswold del Castillo, "The Discredited Revolution," 2.

19. Proffitt, *Tijuana*, table 7.1, p. 150.

20. Weeks and Ham-Chande, *Demographic Dynamics*, fig. 2.1, p. 37.

21. Arreola and Curtis, *The Mexican Border Cities*, fig. 2.3, p. 29.

22. Arreola and Curtis, fig. 2.2, p. 27.

23. Ganster and Lorey, *U. S.-Mexican Border Today*, 93, 132.

CHAPTER 2

1. Previous postcard volumes that explore Mexican towns along the Río Bravo, the Sonora, and Chihuahua borders have each explained postcard formats and appropriate postcard publication histories in their respective regions. See Arreola, *Postcards from the Río Bravo Border*, 41–63; *Postcards from the Sonora Border*, 24–42; *Postcards from the Chihuahua Border*, 27–52. Websites that discuss the history of postcards can be found at "About Postcards: A Reference for Postcard Collectors"; Smithsonian Institution Archives, "Postcard History"; and "150 Years of Postcards." Glossaries of postcard terms are online in Petrulis, "Glossary." A recent story about the use of postcards to study New York City gives some idea of how collectors assemble view cards to understand a place in the past; see Gill, "Tracing Lost New York Through Postcards."

2. Phillips, *The Postcard Century*; Hurt and Payne, "Postcard Imagery and Geographical Imagination."

3. Bogdan and Weseloh, *Real Photo Postcard Guide*, 223.

4. Werther and Mott, *Linen Postcards*.

5. Arreola, *Postcards from the Río Bravo Border*, 47–48; *Postcards from the Sonora Border*, 27–30; *Postcards from the Chihuahua Border*, 38–39.

6. Bogdan and Weseloh, *Real Photo Postcard Guide*, 56–91; Pablo Guadiana Lozano, "Fotógrafos extranjeros en Tijuana."

7. Photographic archive research was conducted at the Research Library of the San Diego History Center in Balboa Park. Biographical information about Averret and Sensor was located in the typescript "Photographers of New Town and Gaslamp Quarter San Diego, California," along with the photographic files for Tijuana housed in the research collection. The Averret photograph used to make the Tijuana bandstand photo postcard is catalog no. 6947–6, and the photographs used to make the print multiview postcard of the Moulin Rouge are catalog nos. 6761, 6761–1, 6761–2, and 6761–3. Sensor photographs used to make the Avenida "A" print postcard, the Hotel Comercial postcards, and the Jai Alai Palace photo postcard are, respectively, catalog nos. 8–33, 34–14, and 34–8.

8. Josué Beltrán Cortez, *Como deben mirarnos*, 73–77, 98–104.

9. Information about Magruder can be found in Guadiana Lozano, "El uso de la tarjeta postal" (thesis), 62–68; Guadiana Lozano, "Fotógrafos extranjeros en Tijuana."

10. Guadiana Lozano, "Colección André Williams." The André Williams Collection is featured in Acuña Borbolla et al, *Tijuana*.

11. Rafael Castillo's biographical information was researched and provided to the author by William Manger. I am indebted to Professor Manger for his assistance with these details. Here are the source materials consulted: *Calexico Chronicle*, "News of City and Valley," "Rafael

Castillo Photographer"; Ellison, "In the Sea of Pearls," 165–75; Edith González Cruz, *Motivaciones y actors de la revolución Mexicana*; *Los Angeles City Directory, 1916*, and *1917*; National Archives and Records Administration, *Manifests of Alien Arrivals at Calexico*; "R. ayuntamiento de la municipalidad de Mexicali B. C."

12. Samponaro and Vanderwood, *War Scare on the Rio Grande*; Vanderwood and Samponaro, *Border Fury*.

13. Information presented for La Compañía México Fotográfico is summarized from Arreola, *Postcards from the Río Bravo Border*, 55–56. See also Uribe Eguiluz, "La compañía México."

14. Arreola, *Postcards from the Chihuahua Border*, 42–48.

15. The two most useful postcard club websites are the Metropolitan Postcard Club of New York City and the San Francisco Bay Area Post Card Club (see websites in bibliography). The Metropolitan Postcard Club online site includes a lengthy inventory of postcard photographers, publishers, printers, and manufacturers compiled and updated by Alan Petrulis. The San Francisco club archives its newsletters online; these documents sometimes have substantial essays about postcard publishers. See, for example, the following references that elaborate biographical and business information about San Francisco native Edward H. Mitchell, who published postcards of Tijuana in the early twentieth century: Baer, "Edward H. Mitchell, Himself" (website) and Stark, "Edward H. Mitchell" (website).

16. *Maxwell's Los Angeles City Directory and Gazetteer of Southern California, 1896*; U. S. Department of Commerce, Bureau of the Census, *Thirteenth Census of the United States*; *Sixteenth Census of the United States*; Petrulis, "Postcard Publishers, Printers, and Distributors of Note" (website).

17. Curt Teich Postcard Archives Collection, "Curt Teich Company Geographic Index" (website).

18. Petrulis, "Postcard Publishers, Printers, and Distributors of Note" (website).

19. The story of Curt Teich is perhaps best told in Meikle, *Postcard America*, 2–68, quotation on 37.

20. Jakle, *Postcards of the Night*, 28.

21. Hamilton-Smith, "Curt Teich Postcard Archives"; Curt Teich Postcard Archives Collection (website).

22. The code sequence for fig. 2.29, for example, shows A, which designates 1930s, preceded by 5, which is the year in the 1930s, and followed by an H, which signified C. T. Art-Colortone style, or full-color linen, followed by a production number. Curt Teich Postcard Archives Collection, "Guide to Dating Curt Teich Postcards" (website).

23. Arreola, *Postcards from the Sonora Border*, 233–34, n. 39; Arreola, *Postcards from the Chihuahua Border*, 48. For a historical discussion of the evolution of the "photochrome process," see Petrulis, "Glossary" (website).

24. Petrulis, "Postcard Publishers, Printers, and Distributors of Note" (website); Roberts, *Wish You Were Here*, 10, 83; "Retouching the Life and Times of America's Postcard King" (website).

25. Roberts, *Wish You Were Here*, 14–48; "Bob Roberts on Mike Roberts."

26. Caddick, "Mike Roberts."

27. Caddick, "Mike Roberts"; Roberts, "Bob Roberts on Mike Roberts."

28. Uribe Eguiluz, "Una aproximación a la compañía México fotográfico" (thesis) 84–87.

29. The general discussion that follows closely parallels the rationale about postcard selection and dating used in previous projects. See Arreola, *Postcards from the Río Bravo Border*, 56–63; *Postcards from the Sonora Border*, 41–42; *Postcards from the Chihuahua Border*, 51–52.

PART II

1. "Across the Borders of History: Tijuana and San Diego Exchange Futures," 44.

CHAPTER 3

1. On place naming see, Marinacci and Marinacci, *California's Spanish Place Names*. Early Tijuana place names are cited in Padilla Corona, "The Rancho Tía Juana (Tijuana) Grant," 30, who suggests the word is a corruption of a local Kumayeey Native word, and Piñera and Rivera, *Tijuana in History*, 43–44, who note that the word may have originally attached to a Native group of southern Baja and was transported north by Spanish missionaries. "The Souvenir of Tijuana de Zaragoza, Baja California, Mexico" postcard folder was published by Western Publishing and Novelty Company, Los Angeles, 1920s, and it is in the author's collection.

2. This section draws on the following sources to establish locations and dates for early Tijuana. Padilla Corona, *Inicios urbanos del norte de Baja California*; "The Rancho Tía Juana (Tijuana) Grant"; Zúñiga Méndez, *Zona centro de Tijuana*; Piñera Ramirez and Ortiz Figueroa, *Historia de Tijuana, 1889–1989*; and Piñera and Rivera, *Tijuana in History*.

3. Herzog, *Where North Meets South*, 91–99. See also Padilla Corona, "Mapa del pueblo Zaragoza del rancho de Tijuana."

4. Piñera Ramírez, Espinosa Meléndez, Sánchez Vega, "Las vicissitudes de la catedral de Tijuana."

5. Padilla Corona, *Inicios urbanos del norte de Baja California*, 129–36, 196–99.

6. Padilla Corona, *El Callejón Z*, 47–50, discusses the *tranvía* tram that ferried tourists to the Tijuana Fair and includes several photographs of the transport system.

7. Alvarado, *Semblanza de Tijuana*, 313; Herzog, *Where North Meets South*, 97.

8. Tijuana's first electrical system is referenced in Alvarado, *Semblanza de Tijuana*, 314.

9. Piñera and Rivera, *Tijuana in History*, 164.

10. Rafla González, Alvarez de la Torre, and Ortega Villa, "Expansion fisica y desarrollo urbano de Tijuana, 1900–1984."

CHAPTER 4

1. Frederick Simpich (1878–1950) was an assistant editor at the National Geographic Society, and over the course of thirty-five years he was said to have published more articles

in *National Geographic*—over eighty—than anyone up to that time or since. See Simpich, "Along Our Side of the Mexican Border," and "Baja California Wakes Up."

2. *San Diego Union and Daily Bee*, "Picturesque Tijuana Lures Sightseers."

3. Piñera and Rivera, *Tijuana in History*, quotation on 101.

4. Proffitt, *Tijuana*, table 8.1, p. 204; Price, *Tijuana*, 56–57.

5. Proffitt, *Tijuana*, 186.

6. Alvarado, *Semblanza de Tijuana*, 74.

7. Arreola, *Postcards from the Chihuahua Border*, 60–61.

8. Wilhoit, "'Reuben the Guide' and His Historic Haunts" (website); Arrizón, *Tijuana*, 1:19.

9. Alvarado, *Semblanza de Tijuana*, 36–38; Piñera and Rivera, *Tijuana in History*, 107–10.

10. Samaniego, *El gremio de choferes y la línea internacional*.

11. Arreola and Curtis, *The Mexican Border Cities*, 97–99; *Oakland Tribune*, "Tijuana Passports No Longer Issued at Mexico Border."

12. Price, *Tijuana*, 56–57.

13. *Santa Ana Daily Register*, "Sleepy Tijuana Awakens, Finds Streets Thronged"; *Oxnard Press-Courier*, "Tijuana Is Wide Open Town."

14. Benitez, "Social History of the Mexico-United States Border" (dissertation), 76.

15. Hughes, "'La Mojonera' and the Making of California's U. S.-Mexico Boundary Line," 140–42.

16. Blanco, *Memoria de la sección mexicana de la comisión internacional de límites entre*; Dear, "Bajalta California," 91.

17. Metz, *Border: The U.S.–Mexico Line*, 113; Padilla Corona, *El Callejón Z*, 43.

18. Grant, "Sojourn in Baja California," 128.

19. Price, *Tijuana*, 49–50; Piñera and Rivera, *Tijuana in History*, 134–35; Proffitt, *Tijuana*, 188, which includes the reference to tequila and the posing woman.

20. Pablo Filemón Guadiana Lozano, "El uso de la tarjeta postal" (thesis), 52–61; "That 'Something Different' Can be found at Tijuana," advertisement, *Coronado Eagle and Journal*, 1915.

21. Padilla Corona, *El Callejón Z*, 50, includes a photograph showing the *tranvia* or mule car rails down the middle of the street leading to the Tijuana Fair.

22. Potts, *Souvenir*, 2, quotation from flyleaf.

23. *Corona Daily Independent*, "Tijuana Peddlers Must 'Spruce Up.'"

24. Contreras García, *Al rescate de los sitios historicos de la vieja Tijuana*, 30–31; Nishikawa Aceves, "De la internacionalción de Tijuana," 86–89.

25. In 2014 the donkey cart tradition in Tijuana spawned a museum on Avenida Revolución called "Tijuanidad." Owner Roberto Lango says of the donkey, "Ésta es el alma de mi ciudad" (This is the spirit of my city). See Lango, "Tijuanidad" (website). See also, Lango Triana, "La evolución del burrocebra" (website). In February 2020 there were three donkey cart photographers operating on Avenida Revolución.

26. On the history of Mexican street photography, see Patricia Massé Zendejas, *Simulacro y elegancia en tarjetas de visita*. Corroboration of staged Tijuana postcard views in Southern California is found in Arrizón, *Tijuana*, 2:384.

CHAPTER 5

1. Excerpt from Stephen Chambers's story in the *New York Times*, June 6, 1920, cited in Paul J. Vanderwood, *Satan's Playground: Mobsters and Movie Stars at America's Greatest Gaming Resort*, 111.

2. José Salazar Ylarregui, *Datos de los trabajos astronómicos y topográficos dispuestos en forma de diario*. This map is reproduced in Dear, "Bajalta California," 88, and redrafted in Padilla Corona, *Inicios urbanos del norte de Baja California*, 137. The latter source reproduces two additional historic maps of the era that show the road; see pages 143–44.

3. Padilla Corona, *Inicios urbanos del norte de Baja California*, 104–10.

4. Several of these early buildings at the original crossing are visible in an 1887 photograph published in Padilla Corona, *El Callejón Z*, 31.

5. A hypothetical map showing the overlay of the original crossing onto a map of Orozco's 1889 "Plan of Pueblo Zaragoza" is published in Padilla Corona, *El Callejón Z*, 34.

6. Taylor Hansen, "El ferrocarril urbano entre San Diego y Tijuana," 11–12. Photographs showing the rails into Tijuana and the *tranvía* with passengers are published in Padilla Corona, *El Callejón Z*, 49–50.

7. Arrizón, *Tijuana*, 1:172–73, 2:453–54; Padilla Corona, *El Callejón Z*, 57.

CHAPTER 6

1. Rodriguez, "Across the Borders of History," 42.

2. See, for example, Miller, *Writing on the Edge*, which includes eighty-three writings about the border without a single reference made to Avenida Revolución. An edited volume devoted to a chiefly contemporary cultural interpretation of the street is Castillo Udiarte, García Cortez, and Morales Lira, *La revolución también es una calle*.

3. Postcard representations of Avenida Guerrero in Nuevo Laredo, Avenida Obregón in Nogales, and Avenida Juárez in Ciudad Juárez are examples of comparable popular border-town streets. See, Arreola, *Postcards from the Río Bravo Border*; *Postcards from the Sonora Border*; and *Postcards from the Chihuahua Border*.

4. Piñera and Rivera, *Tijuana in History*, 111–12.

5. Grandoschek, "Seeing Mexico."

6. Price, *Tijuana*, 89–90.

7. Zúñiga Méndez, *Zona centro de Tijuana*, quotation on 146. Author translation: "The image of Avenida Revolución is constructed through histories that date back to the origin of the city, to the Black Legend and the Dry Law. . . . The imprints include the curio stores that

sell craft products from all corners of the country, margarita cocktails, Caesar's salad, and Zebra-striped burros."

8. Herzog, *From Aztec to High Tech*, 206, quotation on 208.

9. Burkhart, "Visualizing Commercial Landscape Change" (thesis). The André Williams Collection is one of the largest private collections of Tijuana postcards and ephemera; see Acuña Borbolla et al., *Tijuana*.

10. Burkhart constructed velocities of change in the following manner. First, he counted the total number of buildings appearing in a postcard scene. With this recorded, he determined the number of buildings appearing for the first time and the number of buildings that, even if reconfigured, persisted from the last view. This was repeated for all postcards for a block. The calculation of change for each block was then expressed as a percentage change where 0 corresponds to no change and 100 corresponds to complete change on a block of the street.

11. Guadiana Lozano, "El uso de la tarjeta postal" (thesis), 32–41; Piñera and Rivera, *Tijuana in History*, 107–8. See also Torres Covarrubias, "Reflexiones desde el mostrador las 'Curios Shop' y la Calle Revolución," 78–79.

12. Guadiana Lozano, "El uso de la tarjeta postal" (thesis), 41–45.

13. *Calexico Chronicle*, "Flames Wipe Out Block in Tijuana;" Guadiana Lozano, "El uso de la tarjeta postal" (thesis), 49.

14. Burian, *Architecture and Cities of Northern Mexico*, 242–44; *Catálogo nacional, monumentos históricos inmuebles*, 4:629–30.

15. Piñera Ramirez and Ortiz Figueroa, *Historia de Tijuana, 1889–1989*, 1:106–7.

16. Piñera and Rivera, *Tijuana in History*, 190.

17. Burian, *Architecture of Cities of Northern Mexico*, 242–43; *Catálogo nacional, monumentos históricos inmuebles*, 4:627–28.

18. See Barbara Rubin, "Aesthetic Ideology and Urban Design," 339–61. See also Burian, *Architecture and Cities of Northern Mexico*, 245–46.

CHAPTER 7

1. Demaris, *Poso del Mundo*, 3–4, quotation on 4.

2. Félix Berumen, *Tijuana la horrible*, 93–106.

3. Rodriguez, "Across the Borders of History," 42.

4. Wood, *The Borderlands*, 217.

5. Piñera Ramirez and Ortiz Figueroa, *Historia de Tijuana, 1889–1989*, 1:99.

6. *Berkeley Daily Gazette*, "Tijuana: Built by the Eighteenth Amendment."

7. Thomas, *The Wanderer in Tijuana*, 3.

8. Price, *Tijuana*, 12.

9. Piñera and Rivera, *Tijuana in History*, 142–45; Gobierno del Distrito Norte de Baja California [Abelardo L. Rodríguez], *Memoria administrativa, 1924–1927*.

10. Rachel St. John, "Selling the Border," 113–42.

11. Aurelio de Vivanco, *Baja California al día/Lower California Up to Date*, cited in Piñera and Rivera, *Tijuana in History*, 141–42, quotation on 141.

12. Piñera and Rivera, *Tijuana in History*, 142.

13. Cited in Girven, "Hollywood's Heterotopia," 93.

14. Girven, "Hollywood's Heterotopia," 109–16; Vanderwood, *Satan's Playground*, 222–37.

15. See Guadiana Lozano, "El uso de la tarjeta postal" (thesis), gráfica 3, p. 144, and gráfica 4, p. 145. This project studied 444 postcards from three collections—André Williams (private), Andreas Brown (San Diego History Center), and John and Jane Adams (San Diego State University)—but does not give precise numbers for the postcards mailed from Tijuana, only percentages. It is not known what percent of the total number of cards studied were actually mailed.

16. Guadiana Lozano, "El uso de la tarjeta postal" (thesis), 48.

17. Piñera Ramirez and Ortiz Figueroa, *Historia de Tijuana, 1889–1989*, 1:99.

18. Piñera and Rivera, *Tijuana in History*, 140; Cummings, *Baja Handbook* (guidebook), 172.

19. Zumoff, "Tijuana the American Town," 35–48, quotation on 40.

20. *Calexico Chronicle*, "Flames Wipe Out Block in Tijuana"; "Local Men to Rebuild in Tijuana."

21. Piñera and Rivera, *Tijuana in History*, 188–91; Arreola and Curtis, *The Mexican Border Cities*, 102–3. Border-crossing numbers are found in Proffitt, *Tijuana*, table 8.2, p. 206.

22. Piñera and Rivera, *Tijuana in History*, 190, list restaurants on Constitución as well as several Chinese eateries that were popular with tourists in the post–World War II era.

23. Leaf and Ochs, "Tijuana, Mexico—September 22, 1949: A night exterior view of the Aloha Cantina restaurant in Tijuana, Mexico." Archives/Getty Images (photograph).

24. Mariani, *Dictionary of American Food and Drink*, xxii–xxiii; Freedman, *Ten Restaurants That Changed America*, xxix–xlvi.

25. Popular restaurants in post–World War II Tijuana are given in Piñera and Rivera, *Tijuana in History*, 190, and, Ganster, *Tijuana 1964*, 6–7.

26. In Ciudad Juárez, the Álcazar Restaurant Bar, also known as the House of Porron, was a fashionable and popular Spanish restaurant. See Arreola, *Postcards from the Chihuahua Border*, 207–8.

27. Price, *Tijuana*, 60.

28. Jordan, *El otro Mexico*, 100–101. Author's translation "Tijuana is . . . a dark street where a cabaret follows a bar . . . from the bar to a hotel and then another cabaret and another bar. . . . This is the Tourist way and of Tijuana the only memory is this street."

29. The Zona Norte in Tijuana is described in Arreola and Curtis, *The Mexican Border Cities*, 104–5, quotations on 105. The Zona Norte district was also called "Chihuahuita" (Little Chihuahua) by Southern Californians who had experience with Tijuana. See Alvarez, "*Los Re-Mexicanizados*," 15–23.

30. For references to U.S. military personnel in Tijuana after World War II, see Piñera and Rivera, *Tijuana in History*, 188; Price, *Tijuana*, 59, 92–93; Proffitt, *Tijuana*, 194. For a map showing the proximity of U.S. military installations to Mexican border towns, see Arreola and Curtis, *The Mexican Border Cities*, figure 2.2, p. 27.

31. Price, *Tijuana*, 93, quotation on 59.

32. Price, *Tijuana*, 57; Taylor, "Wild Frontier Moves South," 219.

33. Curtis and Arreola, "Zonas de Tolerancia on the Northern Mexican Border," 333–46.

34. The Tijuana Bibles were probably not produced in Tijuana, and they clearly were not Bibles. Rather, a Tijuana Bible was a small booklet that rendered in drawing and limited text the explicit sexual adventures of American comic-strip characters, celebrities, and folk heroes. They apparently first appeared in the late 1920s and remained popular through the Depression years before losing appeal in the post–World War II period. Their connection with Tijuana seems only an association of the Mexican border town with a sin city reputation. See Adelman, *Tijuana Bibles*.

CHAPTER 8

1. Lynch, *Image of the City*, 78–83.

2. Clay, *Close-Up*, 23–24.

3. Piñera and Rivera, *Tijuana in History*, 104–7, 134; Proffitt, *Tijuana*, 201. A separate bullring was built circa 1915 as part of Antonio Elosúa's Tijuana Fair; see Vanderwood, *Satan's Playground*, 86–87.

4. See Arrizón, *Tijuana*, 2:382, which shows the bullring in 1935.

5. A massive, all-concrete bullring at Playas de Tijuana, a seaside location, was built in 1960; see Piñera and Rivera, *Tijuana in History*, 286. Modeled after the plaza de toros in Ciudad Juárez, the Plaza Monumental was said to be the second largest bullfighting arena in the world. It stands today as Tijuana's only bullring. The Arreola Collection includes six chrome postcards that show this ring.

6. The 1938 bullring is lamented and its dismantling shown in Arrizón, *Tijuana*, 2:723. Next door to the 1938 bullring, although not captured by postcard photographers, was a *palenque*, or cockfighting arena; see Arrizón, *Tijuana*, 2:552.

7. Vanderwood, *Satan's Playground*, 88–92, 96–97; Price, *Tijuana*, 50. Photographs of the destruction of the racetrack from the 1916 flood are shown in Arrizón, *Tijuana*, 1:102–3.

8. David J. Beltran, *The Agua Caliente Story*, 9–34; *Santa Ana Daily Register*, "New System of Starting Horse Races Invented;" Proffitt, *Tijuana*, 192.

9. Vanderwood, *Satan's Playground*, 80–84, 101; Price, *Tijuana*, 51.

10. Ridgley, "Tijuana 1920"; Price, *Tijuana*, 54–55.

11. Standard histories of Tijuana fail to assign an exact date for the Mexicali Beer Hall, but most assume sometime in the 1920s. See Acevedo Cárdenas, Piñera, and Ortiz, "Semblanza

de Tijuana 1915–30," 98. Burian, *Architecture and Cities of Northern Mexico*, 242, gives 1922 as date of construction.

12. Pablo Filemón Guadiana Lozano, "El uso de tarjeta postal" (thesis), 48.

13. Piñera and Rivera, *Tijuana in History*, 142. The precise length of the Mexicali Beer Hall bar is disputed by various sources, some saying less than and others certain it was more than two hundred feet.

14. Broadside, author's collection. The Mexicali Beer Hall known as La Ballena is lamented as one of Tijuana's nocturnal landmarks in Zúñiga Méndez, *Zona centro de Tijuana*, 235–45.

15. Vanderwood, *Satan's Playground*, 138; Lindsay, "Foreign Club, Tijuana" (website).

16. Lindsay, "Foreign Club, Tijuana" (website); Vanderwood, *Satan's Playground*, 39.

17. Vanderwood, *Satan's Playground*, 39.

18. Alejandro F. Lugo Jr., "El casino de Agua Caliente," 114–17; Piñera and Rivera, *Tijuana in History*, 146–56; Vanderwood, *Satan's Playground*, 119, 141. See Gerhard and Gurlick, *Lower California Guidebook*, "Tijuana map," for location of Agua Caliente in Tijuana. José Ramón García provides abundant detail about Wirt Bowman and other border barons and their involvement with Tijuana in his *Rousing Tales from the Line City*, 41–133.

19. Padilla Corona, *Agua Caliente*; Newcomb, *Spanish-Colonial Architecture*.

20. *Catálogo nacional, monumentos históricos inmuebles*, 4:605–13; Piñera and Rivera, *Tijuana in History*, 146–56; Beltran, *The Agua Caliente Story*, 35–42; Vanderwood, *Satan's Playground*, 37–50, 140–51; Burian, *Architecture and Cities of Northern Mexico*, 243–45.

21. Vanderwood, *Satan's Playground*, 304–14.

22. Schantz, "Behind the Noir Border," 130–60; Gómez Estrada, *Gobierno y casinos*.

23. Dean Curtis, "Caesar's, Tijuana, Mexico" (website); Mark S. Lindsay, "Caesar's Salad" (website); *Catálogo nacional, monumentos históricos inmuebles*, 4:633–34.

24. The origin of the Caesar Salad is contested, and according to Dean Curtis, can be summarized in several separate stories. (1) Cardini's daughter Rosa claims in a story in *Better Homes and Gardens* in 1960 that Caesar invented the salad on July 4, 1924, mixing a coddled egg, garlic croutons, Parmesan or Romano cheese, lemon juice, garlic, mustard, Worcestershire sauce, whole pepper, pear vinegar, and olive oil (no anchovies), and the dressing served on whole Romaine lettuce leaves. (2) In 1968 Caesar's brother Alessandro claimed he invented the salad in 1926 in Mexico City and named it after his brother. Alessandro's granddaughter Carla Cardini suggests that Alessandro actually invented the salad in Tijuana, naming it the Aviator's Salad because he made it for a group of airmen from San Diego. (3) A 1988 story in the *Los Angeles Times* reports that in 1918 an Italian named Beatriz Santini created the salad in Austria, and her son, Livio Santini, who worked for Caesar Cardini in Tijuana in 1925, made his mother's salad and it became popular with Caesar's customers. See Curtis, "Caesar's, Tijuana, Mexico" (website), and Vanderwood, *Satan's Playground*, 109. Curtis also notes that the Caesar Salad became especially popular nationwide in the United States in

1949 after it was touted as a favorite at Chasen's, Romanoff's, Hansen's Scandia, and Perino's in Los Angeles.

25. National Jai-Alai Association, "History of Jai-Alai" (website).

26. *Catálogo nacional, monumentos históricos inmuebles*, 4:635–36; Alvarado, *Semblanza Tijuana*, 95–99; Piñera and Rivera, *Tijuana in History*, 283. Burian, *Architecture and Cities of Northern Mexico*, 283, assigns Eugene Hoffman as architect.

27. Arrizón, *Tijuana*, 2:550–51.

28. Alvarado, *Semblanza Tijuana*, 250. The statue has since been removed from the parking lot and repositioned near the main entrance on Avenida Revolución.

29. Jesse Hardman, "Jai Alai at Low Tide," 36–47 (website).

PART III

1. "Mexicali is said to have been born . . . in 1902. . . . Its name derived from Calexico, from the anagram MEX-ico CALI-fornia. . . . Therefore, the cities of Mexicali, the Mexican side, and Calexico, the North American, are rightly TWIN SISTERS." *Compendio histórico-biográfico de Mexicali*, 55–56.

CHAPTER 9

1. Aguirre Bernal, *Compendio histórico-biográfico de Mexicali*, 55–56. While Mexicali is not a true anagram for Calexico, the repositioning of letters in place names on political boundaries is a recognized practice in the United States. See, for example, Calneva and Calvada on the California-Nevada borderline cited in Stewart, *Names on the Land*, 364.

2. Rockwood, *Born of the Desert*, 24–25. Tracey Henderson gives credit to L. M. Holt, director of the Imperial Land Company, for naming the twin towns of Calexico and Mexicali; see Henderson, *Imperial Valley*, 272. That attribution, however, is contested by two Spanish-language sources that claim Guillermo Andrade may have initiated the town names; see Andrade Verdugo, *Monumento 220 A*, 1–2, and José Rogelio Álvarez, *Diccionario enciclopédico de Baja California*, 361. For a summary of the many interests and actors engaged in the development of desert lands in the Imperial and Mexicali Valleys, see Hendricks, "Developing San Diego Desert Empire," 1–11. The origin stories about Mexicali are recounted in Meade, *Origen de Mexicali*, 119–21; Robles Cairo, *La architectura de Mexicali*, 27–31; Padilla Corona, *Inicios urbanos del norte de Baja California*, 153–59; and Antonio Padilla Corona and David Piñera Ramírez, "El surgimiento de Mexicali," 183–86.

3. Lorenia Ruiz Muñoz, "Un pueblo sin orden y sin ley Mexicali 1901–1908," 4. Testimonials by early residents in Mexicali are presented in Estrada Barrera, *Pioneros de Mexicali* (no page numbers). These important accounts speak to the shacks erected by settlers, "aquí vá el canalito que servía de linea . . . todo esto era puro cachanillal" (here along the canal that was the boundary line . . . all was constructed of reeds) and "cuándo llegamos al río, que era aquí

en Mexicali, ya había carpas, levantadas junto a los mesquites" (when we arrived at the river, here in Mexicali, there were tents built next to mesquite bushes).

4. Herrera Moreno, "Antecedentes urbanos de Mexicali," 60–61; Robles Cairo, *La architectura de Mexicali*, 33, 41; Padilla Corona, *Inicios urbanos del norte de Baja California*, fig. 47, showing properties on lots along Avenida Ramón Corral. *Imperial Valley Press*, "New River's Work," gives a contemporary account of the devastation. For examples of house styles in pre-inundation Mexicali, see Berumen, *La conquista del agua y del imaginario*, 94–101.

5. Bernal Rodríguez, "Mexicali," 25; Aguirre Bernal, *Compendio histórico-biográfico de Mexicali*, 63; Robles Cairo, *La architectura de Mexicali*, 45–53.

6. Aguirre Bernal, *Compendio histórico-biográfico de Mexicali*, 82–85; Robles Cairo, *La architectura de Mexicali*, fig. 8, p. 32.

7. Eugene Keith Chamberlain, "Mexican Colonization Versus American Interests in Lower California," 43–55; Aguirre Bernal, *Compendio histórico-biográfico de Mexicali*, 67–68; Dorothy Pierson Kerig, *El Valle de Mexicali y la Colorado River Land Company 1902–1946*; Pablo Herrera Carrillo, *Reconquista y colonización del Valle de Mexicali*.

8. Blanco Fenochio and Dillingham, *La plaza Mexicana*, 3–13; Robles Cairo, *La architectura de Mexicali*, 62–63; María Isabel Verdugo Fimbres, *Crónicas sobre Mexicali*, 93–102.

9. Robles Cairo, *La architectura de Mexicali*, 50–53. See Sanborn Map Company, *Mexicali Baja California December, 1921*, sheet 3, and *Mexicali Baja California May, 1925*, sheet 3.

10. *Catálogo nacional, monumentos históricos inmuebles*, 2:429–30; González González and Robles Cairo, "20 elementos," 98; Herrera Moreno, "Antecedentes urbanos de Mexicali," 61; Burian, *The Architecture and Cities of Northern Mexico*, 251.

11. Robles Cairo, *La architectura de Mexicali*, 58–59; Aguirre Bernal, *Compendio histórico-biográfico de Mexicali*, 96, quotation on 89. For a deeper appreciation of the influence of Esteban Cantú on Baja California and Mexicali, see Clair Kenamore, "The Principality of Cantu," and Calvillo Velasco, "Indicios para descifrar la trayectoria política de Esteban Cantú." The Cuartel is documented in Sanborn Map Company, *Mexicali Baja California Mexico December, 1921*, sheet 6.

12. The second bullring was built next to Mexicali's main church, Nuestra Señora de Guadalupe, on Calle Morelos, but it proved incompatible with the religious land use next door and was relocated in 1919 to the southeast edge of town near the railroad corridor (Avenida López Mateos); see Robles Cairo, *La architectura de Mexicali*, 57, 71, and fig. 53.

13. Robles Cairo, *La architectura de Mexicali*, 78–79 refers to the 1920s addition as an extension of the Primera Sección; Aguirre Bernal, *Compendio histórico-biográfico de Mexicali*, 239–40, refers to the 1920s addition as the Segunda Sección, as does Pedro F. Pérez y Ramírez, "Panorama de Mexicali 1915–1930," 402.

14. Herrera Moreno, "Antecedentes urbanos de Mexicali," 61; Aguirre Bernal, *Compendio histórico-biográfico de Mexicali*, 222. For discussion of the Teatro México, Mexicali's first

movie theater, built in 1915 and burned down several years later, see Robles Cairo, *La architectura de Mexicali*, 72–74.

15. The layout of the Hotel Imperial along with surrounding land uses can be seen in Sanborn Map Company, *Mexicali Baja California Mexico December, 1921*, sheet 2.

16. Aguirre Bernal, *Compendio histórico-biográfico de Mexicali*, 293, 304; Gobierno del Distrito Norte de Baja California, *Memoria administrativa, 1924–1927*, 136–37; *Van Nuys News*, "Louis S. Granger Takes Interesting Mexico Trip."

17. Antonio Gastélum Gamez, *Mi viejo Mexicali remembranzas*, 159–62; Aguirre Bernal, *Compendio histórico-biográfico de Mexicali*, 257; Verdugo Fimbres, *Crónicas sobre Mexicali*, 125–39.

18. *Calexico Chronicle*, "Midnight Crowd in Mexicali Panic-Stricken."

19. Robles Cairo, *La architectura de Mexicali*, 81–82.

20. Felipe Güicho Gutiérrez, *Y nació Pueblo Nuevo*, 19; Robles Cairo, *La architectura de Mexicali*, 82–83; Verdugo Fimbres, *Crónicas sobre Mexicali*, 141–49.

21. Gastélum Gamez, *Mi viejo Mexicali remembranzas*, 152–54. This street and the location of the restaurant are documented in Sanborn Map Company, *Mexicali Baja California Mexico December, 1921*, sheet, 3.

22. For La Maderería, see Gastélum Gamez, *Mi viejo Mexicali remembranzas*, 226; for La Nacional, see González González and Robles Cairo, "20 elementos," 111–12. La Nacional is listed in *Catálogo nacional, monumentos históricos inmuebles*, 2:397–98, and the date given for its first construction is 1940.

23. Robles Cairo, *La architectura de Mexicali*, 119, 125; Gastélum Gamez, *Mi viejo Mexicali remembranzas*, 102–03; González González and Robles Cairo, "20 elementos," 100–101; Burian, *Architecture and Cities of Northern Mexico*, 251.

24. Robles Cairo, *La architectura de Mexicali*, 72, describes the sequence of Mexicali bullring locations. The Arreola Collection includes only one other photo postcard of the interior of the Plaza de Toros Mexicali. Years later, a fifth bullring at a new location was built in Mexicali, the Plaza de Toros Calafia.

25. Dwellings and residential spaces in Mexican border cities are discussed in Arreola and Curtis, *The Mexican Border Cities*, 153–82, and Herzog, *From Aztec to High Tech*, 43–90.

26. Lucero Velasco, "Los paisajes del viejo Mexicali," 86–87; Herrera Moreno, "Antecedentes urbanos de Mexicali," 61–62. For examples of Arts and Crafts and Spanish Revival housing in 1920s Mexicali, see Gobierno del Distrito Norte de Baja California, *Memoria administrativa, 1924–1927*, 33–35.

27. Herzog, *From Aztec to High Tech*, 105–21.

CHAPTER 10

1. Arreola, *Postcards from the Sonora Border*, 83–86, 108–12.

2. Calexico, a place name traced to Guillermo Andrade in 1889, was probably platted at close to the same time as Mexicali. See, Andrade Verdugo, *Monumento 220 A*, 46–47, and

especially the map on page 50, which shows the two towns on the same plat map published by General Real Estate in Calexico.

3. U.S. Department of State, *Proceedings of the International Boundary Commission United States and Mexico*.

4. The German lithograph print postcard is reproduced in Carlos Manuel Reyes Moreno, "Mexicali al inicio de la revolución mexicana," 2–4. Another version of this postcard, a four-fold black-and-white print made from the original panoramic photograph, exists in the Carol Hann Collection.

5. *Calexico Chronicle*, "Meeting of Governors of Two Californias" and *Imperial Valley Press*, "Governor at Border Sees Head Lower California." I thank Carol Hann of El Centro, California, for locating these stories and thereby enabling me to identify the photographic postcard.

6. For the changing positions of the customs house in Mexicali, see Aguirre Bernal, *Compendio histórico-biográfico de Mexicali*, 57–58, 391–93; Robles Cairo, *La architectura de Mexicali*, 41; for 1921, see Sanborn Map Company, *Mexicali Baja California Mexico December, 1921*, sheet, 2; and for 1952 street location, see figure 9.15. A historic print postcard of the first customs house can be viewed in the John and Jane Adams Postcard Collection, Special Collections and University Archives, San Diego State University. A historic image of the second customs house in 1920 is reproduced in Lucero Velasco, "Los paisajes del viejo Mexicali," 66–67, and Andrade Verdugo, *Monumento 220 A*, 27.

7. Simpich, "Baja California Wakes Up," 256; *Coronado Eagle and Journal*, "Gateway to Friendship."

8. *Catálogo nacional, monumentos históricos inmuebles*, 2:423–24. See also González González and Robles Cairo, "20 elementos," 116, which declares the Hotel del Norte was inaugurated in 1951.

9. Kostof, *The City Shaped*, 249–55. The name *boulevard* owes its origin to a Paris bastion, the Grand Boulevard; Arreola, *Postcards from the Chihuahua Border*, 239–40.

10. González González and Robles Cairo, "20 elementos," 102; Burian, *Architecture and Cities of Northern Mexico*, 251; *Catálogo nacional, monumentos históricos inmuebles*, 2:405–07.

11. Gastélum Gamez, *Mi viejo Mexicali remembranzas*, 319–20; *Catálogo nacional, monumentos históricos inmuebles*, 2:409–10. Mexicali had no interest in celebrating Obregón, a Sonoran, and the statue was said to have been placed at the request of Abelardo Rodríguez; see Valdéz, *Monumentos y gajos para la historia de Mexicali*, 41. In any event the tradition of statues and monuments in public spaces across Mexico is a long-standing practice; see Escobedo and Gori, *Mexican Monuments*.

12. Gastélum Gamez, *Mi viejo Mexicali remembranzas*, 316–21. El León de Oro (the Golden Lion) advertised itself by a postcard showing the exterior of the establishment located at Calle México and Avenida Teniente Guerrero (Avenida Reforma). On the verso of the card the caption reads "The Golden Lion Café, operated by the Padilla Brothers, serves the best of

Mexican and American dishes and caters to the best trade with a complete line of the finest wines, liquors and the best brands of beer." Print postcard in the Arreola Collection, published by M. Kashower Company, no. 32959, Los Angeles, CA, 1920s. The Golden Lion Café attracted top Hollywood celebrities when they visited Mexicali; see Schantz, "All Night at the Owl," 137.

13. For descriptions of railroads in Mexican border cities, see Arreola and Curtis, *The Mexican Border Cities*, 183–201. For the railroad in Piedras Negras, see Arreola, *Postcards from the Río Bravo Border*. For railroad locations in Agua Prieta, Naco, and Nogales, see Arreola, *Postcards from the Sonora Border*. For the railroad in Ciudad Juárez, see Arreola, *Postcards from the Chihuahua Border*.

14. Noriega Verdugo, "Desarrollo industrial 1915–2000," 118–20; Aguirre Bernal, *Compendio histórico-biográfico de Mexicali*, 283–84.

15. Robles Cairo, *La architectura de Mexicali*, 65–66.

16. *Santa Ana Daily Register*, "Mexicali Plans to Make Its Own Beer"; Gastélum Gamez, *Mi viejo Mexicali remembranzas*, 219–20.

17. Robles Cairo, *La architectura de Mexicali*, 47–49.

18. A motorized *tranvía* operated in the border town of Matamoros in the early twentieth century; see Arreola, *Postcards from the Río Bravo Border*, figs. 3.17, 3.18, p. 81.

19. Aguirre Bernal, *Compendio histórico-biográfico de Mexicali*, 356–57; Estrada Barrera, *El Río*, 119.

CHAPTER 11

1. *Bakersfield Californian*, "Methodists Want Tijuana Barred"; *Santa Ana Daily Register*, "Drinkers' Oasis on Border Doomed"; quotation from Shortell, "Thirsty Hordes from States Cross Line," 1.

2. *Imperial Valley Press*, "Ask President Diaz to Clean Mexicali," and *Imperial Valley Press*, "The Nuisance at Mexicali," cited in Ruiz Muñoz, *Un pequeño Montecarlo en el desierto Mexicali 1901–1913*, 72, 75.

3. Schantz, "From *Mexicali Rose* to the Tijuana Brass" (dissertation), 456.

4. Schantz, "All Night at the Owl," 116.

5. Quotation from *Los Angeles Times*, "Mexican Monte Carlo Shut Up," cited in Schantz, "All Night at the Owl," 93.

6. Price, *Tijuana*, 51; Vanderwood, *Satan's Playground*, 82–83. The Owl was said to have been the most lucrative tax source for Mexicali in the years Cantú was the district governor; see Schantz, "All Night at the Owl," 99–101.

7. California Institute of Technology, Southern California Earthquake Data Center, "Imperial Valley Earthquake, June 22, 1915" (website).

8. *Calexico Chronicle*, "Mexicali Move Made Tonight."

9. For the prostitution enterprise operated out of the Owl, see Schantz, "All Night at the Owl," 116.

10. Vanderwood, *Satan's Playground*, 83. Jack Tenney's connection to Mexicali and the story behind the song *Mexicali Rose* that was created at the Hotel Imperial Cabaret are summarized in *Calexico Chronicle*, "Mexicali Rose Composer Honored History of Composition Told."

11. *Calexico Chronicle*, "All-Colored Revue at Owl Declared Great Attraction." The dance floor of the Owl is shown in a historic photograph reproduced in Gabriel Trujillo Muñoz, *Mexicali centenario*, and the many cabarets, including the Owl, in Mexicali are discussed on page 82.

12. *Calexico Chronicle*, "Famous Gambling Hall and Bar Complete Loss." See also Vanderwood, *Satan's Playground*, 116.

13. *Calexico Chronicle*, "Contract to Be Let This Week for Re-Building Owl Resort in Mexicali."

14. *Calexico Chronicle*, "Rumor That A. B. W. Club May Close," and "A. B. W. Club in Mexicali Has Been Closed."

15. "Grand Opening of Cabaret and Café at the Owl. A. B. W. Club, Mexicali, Mexico," advertisement in the *Calexico Chronicle*, December 24, 1932; *Palm Springs Desert Sun*, "Owl Club Gambling Closes Up at Mexicali."

16. A print postcard in the Arreola Collection advertised offtrack betting and foreign booking. "Caliente Turf Club Night Club, Mexicali, B. California, Mexico," published by the National Postcard Company, Arlington, TX, 1950s. Schantz, "From *Mexicali Rose* to the Tijuana Brass" (dissertation), 527, 533, cites interviews with Mexicali residents who participated in offtrack betting.

17. Aikman, "Hell Along the Border."

18. Curtis, "Mexicali's Chinatown," 336. See also Hu-DeHart, "Los chinos del norte de México, 1875–1930."

19. Chang, "Outsider Crossings" (dissertation), 45.

20. The numbers of Chinese cited here are from Curtis, "Mexicali's Chinatown," 338. The number of Chinese in the Mexicali Valley may well have exceeded the total population of the town of Mexicali during this period, reaching about twenty thousand by the 1920s; see Chang, "Outsider Crossings," 75. See also Gobierno del Distrito Norte de Baja California, *Memoria administrativa, 1924–1927*, 229, which states there were five thousand Chinese in the *municipio* of Mexicali in 1927.

21. Gobierno del Distrito Norte de Baja California, *Memoria administrativa*, 135, lists 1,464 in Primera Sección, 1,230 in Segunda Sección, and 780 in Tercera Sección (Pueblo Nuevo). See figure 10.16 for approximate boundaries of the sections of Mexicali.

22. Curtis, "Mexicali's Chinatown," 344–46.

23. Chang, "Outsider Crossings," 73.

24. Velázquez Morales, *Los inmigrantes chinos en Baja California, 1920–1937*.

25. *Calexico Chronicle*, "$2,000,000 Fire Sweeps Mexicali."

26. *Calexico Chronicle*, "Mexicali Has Big Fire Loss in Chinatown," and *Calexico Chronicle*, "Damage in Fire Mounts to Near 20 Million Pesos."

27. Chang, "Outsider Crossings," 131; Arreola and Curtis, *The Mexican Border Cities*, 21.

28. Bernhardson, *Baja California* (travel guide), 177, 181; Warren, Yu, and Ruiz y Costello, "La Chinesca," 72–74.

29. For discussions about curio shopping streets in other Mexican border towns, see Arreola, *Postcards from the Río Bravo Border*, 171–77; *Postcards from the Sonora Border*, 154–64; and *Postcards from the Chihuahua Border*, 154–67.

30. Aguirre Bernal, *Compendio histórico-biográfico de Mexicali*, 188–89.

31. *Calexico Chronicle*, "Mexicali Is Mecca for Tourist Crop."

32. Antonio Gastélum Gamez, *Mi viejo Mexicali remembranzas*, 47.

PART IV

1. *Baja California*, 124.

2. *Border Towns of the Southwest*, 67.

CHAPTER 12

1. Weisman and Dusard, *La Frontera*, 171.

2. The Díaz Ordaz quotation is from Price, "Tecate," 35.

3. Rowe, "Tecate, the Border's Great Exception." Carey McWilliams titled his 1949 classic book, explaining the phenomenon of the Golden State, *California: The Great Exception*.

4. Bernhardson, *Baja California* (travel guide), 124. Neither Bernhardson's *Baja California*, nor Cummings's *Baja Handbook* (guidebook) mention Algodones. Cahill's *Border Towns of the Southwest* gives it a passing reference on page 67.

5. Oberle and Arreola, "Mexican Medical Border Towns," 35.

6. Plat map of Tecate, 1919, Pavon, *Terreno Perteneciente al Municipo de Tecate*. Speth, "Tecate, Baja California" (thesis), 80, 95–96; Ramírez López, "Semblanza de Tecate," 477; Meade, *Tecate*, 36, reproduces several historic maps for Tecate.

7. Santiago Guerrero, *La gente al pie de Cuchumá*, 261; Irigoyen, *Carretera peninsular de la Baja California*, 1:191–92; Ramírez López, "Semblanza de Tecate," 479; Meade, *Tecate*, 106–7.

8. Santiago Guerrero, "Profile of the Origins of Tecate's Population," 15; Speth, "Tecate, Baja California" (thesis), 98.

9. Price, "Tecate," 44–45; Speth, "Tecate, Baja California" (thesis), 101, 108–9.

10. Santiago Guerrero, *La gente al pie de Cuchumá*, 472–77, lists these businesses and their owners.

11. Speth, "Tecate, Baja California," 105; Price, "Tecate," 45.

12. *Calexico Chronicle*, "New Road to be Scenic Route"; Gobierno del Distrito Norte de Baja California, *Memoria administrativa, 1924–1927*, 156–57; Speth, "Tecate, Baja California"

(thesis), 87–88; Santiago Guerrero, *La gente al pie de Cuchumá*, 257–61; Santana Sandoval, "Testimonios de antiguos residentes de Tecate"; Ramírez López, "Semblanza de Tecate," 480.

13. Hendricks, *Guillermo Andrade y el desarrollo del delta mexicano del Río Colorado*, 81–87, 268–69; Celso Aguirre Bernal, *Compendo histórico-biográfico de Mexicali*, 20–24.

14. *Imperial Valley Press*, "Algodones Custom House"; "Algodones Raided by Insurrectos."

15. On the possibility of a Yuman tribal origin for Algodones, see Francisco Dueñas M, *Territorio norte de la Baja California (Temas históricos)*, 174. Webster, "Reconnaissance of the Flora and Vegetation of *La Frontera*," 23–24, discusses cottonwood trees (*Populus fremontii*) as common to the desert oasis and riparian woodland habitats of the Sonoran Floristic Province of the Colorado River Delta. Cottonwoods were much more densely concentrated along waterways of the delta before the clearing of native vegetation for cropland and the invasion of salt cedar (*Tamarix ramosissima*).

16. Ward, *Border Oasis*, 31–37.

17. Quotation from *Calexico Chronicle*, "Yuma Will Have Young Mexicali." See also Rojas and Courtade, *Paso de los Algodones*, 126–27; *Catálogo nacional, monumentos históricos inmuebles*, 2:483–86; *Los Angeles Herald*, "Monte Carlo in Mexico Across Arizona Line."

18. For cabaret locations, see map in *Catálogo nacional, monumentos históricos inmuebles*, 2:479.

19. *Calexico Chronicle*, "Algodones to Open New Arena."

20. *Calexico Chronicle*, "Orders Issued Today to Close Red Light Houses."

21. *Calexico Chronicle*, "Fire Sweeps Two Cantinas in Algodones"; "Algodones Is Scene of Fire"; "Algodones Has Its Third Serious Fire."

22. Rojas and Courtade, *Paso de los Algodones*, 129.

PART V

1. *The Labyrinth of the Spirits*, p. 349.

2. In Nossiter, "Atget's Paris, 100 Years Later."

CHAPTER 13

1. The expression the past is a foreign country is attributed to historical geographer David Lowenthal and his book *The Past Is a Foreign Country*. Arcadia Publishing (website) founded in 1993 is an American publisher of local and regional history of the United States in pictorial format.

2. Meinig, *A Life of Learning*, 18.

3. Meinig, *Interpretation of Ordinary Landscapes*; Wylie, *Landscape*; Jakle, *The Visual Elements of Landscape*.

4. Giffords, "Mexican Postcards," 66–68, quotation on 66.

5. Jakle, "Camera and Geographical Inquiry."

6. Vale and Vale, *U.S. 40 Today*; Wyckoff, *Riding Shotgun with Norman Wallace*. A recent discovery of a 1930s photographic archive of every building on every block in New York City made for tax assessment purposes is an example of a collection of materials that offers potential for an urban rephotography study. See Barron, "Every Building on Every Block" (website).

7. Arreola and Curtis, *The Mexican Border Cities*.

8. Three pioneering works were Ross, *Views Across the Border*; House, *Frontier on the Rio Grande*; and Martínez, *Troublesome Border*.

9. See especially the many works of Miguel Ángel Berumen, such as *La conquista de agua y del imaginario*. A second edition of Ganster, *Tijuana 1964*, includes a valuable concluding essay that compares the Tijuana of 1964 with the same city in 2014; see 63–71.

10. Arreola and Curtis, *The Mexican Border Cities*, 133–43.

11. Arreola and Curtis, *The Mexican Border Cities*, 79–96, and fig. 3.9, p. 69.

12. See, Arreola, *Postcards from the Sonora Border*, 136–43; *Postcards from the Chihuahua Border*, 216–42.

13. Phillips, *The Postcard Century*, 17.

BIBLIOGRAPHY

ARCHIVES AND COLLECTIONS

Andreas Brown Collection, San Diego History Center, San Diego, CA.

André Williams Collection, Tijuana, Baja California.

Archivo Histórico de Mexicali, Mexicali, Baja California.

Archivo Histórico de Tijuana, Tijuana, Baja California.

Arreola Collection, Placitas, NM.

Biblioteca Regional, Museo Comunitario de Tecate, Tecate, Baja California.

Border Collection, San Diego State University, Imperial Valley Campus Library, Calexico, CA.

California Digital Newspaper Collection, Center for Bibliographical Studies and Research, University of California, Riverside, CA.

Carol Hann Collection, El Centro, CA.

Center for Southwest Research and Special Collections Library, University of New Mexico, Albuquerque, NM.

Curt Teich Postcard Archives Collection, Newberry Library, Chicago, IL.

Frashers Foto Collection, Pomona Public Library, Pomona, CA.

Geography and Map Division, Library of Congress, Washington, DC.

Instituto de Investigaciones Históricas, Universidad Autónoma de Baja California, Tijuana, Baja California.

John and Jane Adams Postcard Collection, Special Collections and University Archives, San Diego State University Library, San Diego, CA.

Museo de Historia de Tijuana, Tijuana, Baja California.

Research Library, San Diego History Center, San Diego, CA.

Sanborn Fire Insurance Atlas Collection, California State University, Northridge, CA.

Special Collections and Archives Library, University of California, San Diego, CA.

Special Collections Library, San Diego Public Library, San Diego, CA.

NEWSPAPERS

Bakersfield Californian

Berkeley Daily Gazette

Calexico Chronicle

Corona Daily Independent

Coronado Eagle and Journal

Imperial Valley Press

Los Angeles Herald

Los Angeles Times

New York Times

Oakland Tribune

Oxnard Press-Courier

Palm Springs Desert Sun

San Diego Union and Daily Bee

Santa Ana Daily Register

Van Nuys News

WEBSITES

About Postcards: A Reference for Postcard Collectors. https://aboutcards.blogspot.com/2007 /01/bamforth-co-postcard-publisher.html.

Acervo fotográfico, taller de historia de Tecate. https://tallerdehistoriadetecate.org/proyectos -permanentes/.

Arcadia Publishing. https://www.arcadiapublishing.com/.

Baer, Lewis. "Edward H. Mitchell, Himself." http://www.thepostcard.com/walt/pub/ehm/chklst /mitbio2.htm.

Barron, James. "Every Building on Every Block: A Time Capsule of 1930s New York." *New York Times*, December 28, 2018. https://www.nytimes.com/interactive/2018/12/28/nyregion /nyc-property-tax-photos.html.

California Institute of Technology, Southern California Earthquake Data Center. "Imperial Valley Earthquake, June 22, 1915." https://scedc.caltech.edu/significant/imperial1915.html.

Curtis, Dean. "Caesar's, Tijuana, Mexico." Le Continental, December 16, 2016. http://deanjab .com/2016/12/caesars-tijuana-mexico/.

Curt Teich Postcard Archives Collection. https://www.newberry.org/curt-teich-postcard -archives-collection.

——. "Guide to Dating Curt Teich Postcards." https://www.newberry.org/sites/default/files /researchguide-attachments/Teich_Postcard_Dating_Guide_2016.pdf.

——. "Curt Teich Company Geographic Index." https://www.newberry.org/curt-teich-post card-archives-collection.

Detroit Publishing Company. Library of Congress, Prints and Photographs Online Catalog. http://www.loc.gov/pictures/collection/det/background.html.

Frasher Foto Postcard Collection. Calisphere, University of California. https://calisphere.org /collections/7781/?q=&facet_decade=1940s&rq=Mexicali.

Gill, John Freeman. "Tracing Lost New York Through Postcards." *New York Times*, December 6, 2019. https://www.nytimes.com/2019/12/06/realestate/lost-new-york-through-post cards.html?smid=nytcore-ios-share.

Hardman, Jesse. "Jai Alai at Low Tide." *Racquet Magazine* 5:36–47. Listening Post Collective, December 29, 2017. http://jessehardman.com/jai-alai-at-low-tide/.

Lango, Roberto. "Tijuanidad." https://www.tijuanidad.com.

Lango Triana, Roberto David. "La evolución del burrocebra." Congreso de patrimonio histórico y cultural de Baja California, May 2, 2017. https://congresodepatrimonio.wordpress.com /2017/05/02/la-evolucion-del-burrocebra-de-objeto-turistico-olvidado-a-recurso-turistico -historico-educativo-y-cultural/.

Lindsay, Mark S. "Caesar's Salad: The Myth of Giacomo Junia." Classic San Diego: Tasty Bites from the History of America's Finest City, 2015–2020, January 24, 2021. https://classicsan diego.com/2021/01/caesars-salad-the-myth-of-giacomo-junia/.

Lindsay, Mark S. "Foreign Club, Tijuana." Classic San Diego: Tasty Bites from the History of America's Finest City, 2015–2020. https://classicsandiego.com/restaurants/foreignclub -tijuana/.

Metropolitan Postcard Club of New York. http://metropolitanpostcardclub.com/.

National Jai-Alai Association. "History of Jai-Alai." http://www.tampabayjaialai.com/history _of_jai-alai/index.php.

"150 Years of Postcards, History of Postcards." https://150yearsofpostcards.com/history.

Petrulis, Alan. "Glossary." Metropostcard.com. http://www.metropostcard.com/glossaryp.html.

Petrulis, Alan. "Postcard Publishers, Printers, and Distributors of Note." Metropostcard.com. http://www.metropostcard.com/metropcpublishers.html.

"Retouching the Life and Times of America's Postcard King." The Image Flow Photography Center, Mill Valley, CA. https://theimageflow.com/photography-blog/fine-art-photography -retouching-americas-postcard-king/.

San Francisco Bay Area Post Card Club. http://www.postcard.org/.

Smithsonian Institution Archives. "Postcard History." https://siarchives.si.edu/history/exhibits /postcard/postcard-history.

Stark, Sam. "Edward H. Mitchell, His Life and Times: Postcard Publisher, 1867–1932." http:// www.thepostcard.com/walt/pub/ehm/chklst/ehmlife.pdf.

Wilhoit, Sandee. "'Reuben the Guide' and His Historic Haunts." *San Diego Downtown News*, October 6, 2017. https://sandiegodowntownnews.com/reuben-the-guide-and-his-historic -haunts/.

GOVERNMENT DOCUMENTS

Blanco, Jacobo. *Memoria de la sección mexicana de la comisión internacional de límites entre México y los Estados Unidos que restableció los monumentos de El Paso al Pacífico.* New York: [International Boundary Commission, United States and Mexico], 1901.

Catálogo nacional, monumentos históricos inmuebles: Baja California. 4 vols. Mexico City: Secretaría de Educación Pública, Instituto Nacional de Antropología e Historia, Programa Cultural de las Fronteras, 1986.

Emory, William H. *Report on the United States and Mexican Boundary Survey, Made Under the Direction of the Secretary of the Interior.* 3 vols. Austin: Texas State Historical Association, 1987. First published 1857–1859 by C. Wendell.

Estados Unidos Mexicanos, censo general de habitantes de 1921, Baja California, Distritos Norte y Sur. Mexico City: Departamento de la Estadística Nacional, 1926.

Estados Unidos Mexicanos, division territorial, Territorio de la Baja California, censo de 1910. Mexico City: Dirreción General de Estadística, 1913.

Estados Unidos Mexicanos, quinto censo de poblacion de 1930, Baja California (Distrito Norte). Mexico City: Dirreción General de Estadística, 1932.

Estados Unidos Mexicanos, VIII censo general de poblacion 1960, Estado de Baja California. Mexico City: Dirreción General de Estadística, 1963.

Estados Unidos Mexicanos, septimo censo general de poblacion 1950, Baja California Territorio Norte. Mexico City: Dirreción General de Estadística, 1952.

Gobierno del Distrito Norte de Baja California [Abelardo L. Rodríguez]. *Memoria administrativa, 1924–1927.* [Mexicali]: n.p., 1928.

International Boundary Commission. *Boundary Between the United States and Mexico, as Surveyed and Marked by the International Boundary Commission Under the Convention of July 29th, 1882: Revised February 18th, 1889.* Washington, DC: Government Printing Office, 1899.

National Archives and Records Administration. *Manifests of Alien Arrivals at Calexico, California, March 1907–December 1952.* NAI 2843448, record group no. 85, microfilm roll no. 01.

Prechtel-Kluskens, Claire, comp. *Nonstatistical Manifests and Statistical Index Cards of Aliens Arriving at El Paso, Texas, 1905–1927.* Washington, DC: National Archives and Records Administration, 2005.

U.S. Department of Commerce, Bureau of the Census. *Thirteenth Census of the United States, 1910: Population.* Washington, DC: Government Printing Office, 1910.

———. *Sixteenth Census of the United States, 1940—Population.* Washington, DC: Government Printing Office, 1940.

U.S. Department of State. *Proceedings of the International Boundary Commission United States and Mexico Relating to the Placing of an Additional Monument to More Perfectly Mark the International Boundary Line Through the Towns of Caléxico, California, and*

Mexicali, Baja California, and the Restoration of International Monument No. 221, Near Those Towns. Washington, DC, 1909.

U.S. Selective Service System. *World War I Selective Service System Draft Registration Cards, 1917–1918*. Registrar's Report 42-1-65-A. San Antonio, TX: National Archives and Records Administration, 1917.

MAPS, DIRECTORIES, GUIDES, PHOTOGRAPHS

Aerial view of Tijuana in 1924. National Archives 18-AA-176–31. Washington, DC: National Archives, 1924.

Automobile Association of America. *Mexico by Motor Including Central America*. Washington, DC: Automobile Association of America, 1957.

Automobile Club of Southern California. *Baja California Norte*. Los Angeles, 1972.

Baja California (map). *National Geographic Magazine*, August 1942.

Baja California-Norte (map). 1:1,000,000 scale. American Geographical Society of New York, 1928.

Bernhardson, Wayne. *Baja California*. 4th ed. Hawthorn, Australia: Lonely Planet, 1998.

Bunnell, S. U. [Bird's-eye view of Mexicali and Calexico]. May 10, 1911. Library of Congress, Prints and Photographs Division, Washington, DC.

Cahill, Rick. *Border Towns of the Southwest: Shopping, Dining, Fun and Adventure from Tijuana to Juarez*. Boulder, CO: Pruett, 1987.

Compañia del Ferrocarril Inter-California (map). 1926.

Cummings, Joe. *Baja Handbook: Mexico's Western Peninsula, Including Cabo San Lucas*. 2nd ed. Chico, CA: Moon, 1994.

Denton, William. *Plano del terreno nombrado los Algodones*, 1873. In *Guillermo Andrade y el desarrollo del delta mexicano del Río Colorado 1874–1905*, by William O. Hendricks. Mexicali: Universidad Autónoma de Baja California, 1996.

Echeverría, Serapio. *Plano de los Terrenos del S. D. Guillermo Andrade en los Estados de Sonora y Baja California*. Mexico City, 1888.

Fernández, Juan de D. *Plano de la población de Tijuana, 1925*. Tijuana, Baja California, 1925. Special Collections and Archives Library, University of California, San Diego.

Gates, A. C. *Aerial Shot of Calexico and Mexicali After 1927 Earthquake*. Los Angeles Times Photographic Archive, Department of Special Collections, Charles E. Young Research Library, University of California, Los Angeles. https://dl.library.ucla.edu/islandora/object/edu.ucla.library.specialCollections.latimes:534.

Gerhard, Peter, and Howard E. Gulick. *Lower California Guidebook: A Descriptive Traveller's Guide*. 3rd. ed., rev. and enl. Glendale, CA: Arthur H. Clark, 1964.

Hart, J. *Colorado Desert, Sonora Mesa, and Delta of the Rio Colorado*. Colorado River Irrigation Company, 1893.

Leaf, Earl, and Michael Ochs. "Tijuana, Mexico—September 22, 1949: A Night Exterior View of the Aloha Cantina Restaurant in Tijuana, Mexico." Archives/Getty Images. https://www.gettyimages.com/detail/news-photo/an-night-exterior-view-of-the-aloha-cantina-restaurant-in-news-photo/589962807.

Los Angeles City Directory, 1916. Los Angeles: Los Angeles Directory Company.

Los Angeles City Directory, 1917. Los Angeles: Los Angeles Directory Company.

Map of Mexico and Baja California. Chicago: H. M. Gousha, 1961.

Maxwell's Los Angeles City Directory and Gazetteer of Southern California, 1896. Los Angeles: Los Angeles Directory Company.

Orozco, Ricardo. *Plano topográfico de Tijuana con la division del predio en porciones de igual valor*, 1889. Special Collections Library, San Diego Public Library.

———. *Pueblo Zaragoza*, 1889. Tijuana: Archivo del Centro de Investigaciones Históricas UNAM-UABC.

Pavon, Luis. *Terreno perteneciente al municipo de Tecate*, 1923. Special Collections and Archives Library, University of California, San Diego.

Plano catastral de la población de Tijuana, Municipalidad de Zaragoza, Distrito Nte. Baja California, 1929. In Francisco Manuel Acuña Borbolla, Mario Ortiz Villacorta Lacave, Federico Valdés Martínez, et al., *Tijuana: Identidades y nostalgias: La colección de André Williams.* Tijuana: XVIII Ayuntamiento de Tijuana, 2007.

Renié Map Service, Union Oil Company of California. *Baja California Road Map.* Los Angeles: Renié Map Service, 1951.

Rockwood, Charles R. *Mapa de la Ciudad Mexicali en la Baja California, Mex.*, 1902. In Alfonso Herrera Moreno, "Antecedentes urbanos de Mexicali," *El Río: Revista de historia regional de Mexicali y su valle* 9, no. 32 (April–June 2016): 59–62.

Sanborn Map Company. *Mexicali Baja California Mexico December, 1921.* New York: Sanborn Map Company, 1921.

Sanborn Map Company. *Mexicali Baja California Mexico May, 1925.* New York: Sanborn Map Company, 1925.

Sanborn Map Company. *Tijuana Baja California Mexico November, 1924.* San Diego, CA: V. Wankowski, 1924.

BOOKS

Acuña Borbolla, Francisco Manuel, Mario Ortiz Villacorta Lacave, Federico Valdés Martínez, et al. *Tijuana: Identidades y nostalgias: La colección de André Williams.* Tijuana: XVII Ayuntamiento de Tijuana, 2007.

Adelman, Bob. *Tijuana Bibles: Art and Wit in America's Forbidden Funnies, 1930s–1950s.* New York: Simon and Schuster, 1997.

Aguirre Bernal, Celso. *Compendio histórico-biográfico de Mexicali*, 8th ed. Mexico City: Anaya, 1994.

———. *Compendio histórico-biográfico de Mexicali, 1539–1966.* Mexicali: n.p., 1968.

Alvarado, Adilú. *Semblanza de Tijuana: Cronología histórica de esta noble ciudad.* Tijuana: ICLSA, 2009.

Andrade Verdugo, Gilberto. *Monumento 220 A: Punto de partida del trazo y levantamiento del primer plano de la Cd. de Mexicali B. C.* Mexicali: published by the author, 1996.

Arreola, Daniel D. *Postcards from the Chihuahua Border: Revisiting a Pictorial Past, 1900s–1950s.* Tucson: University of Arizona Press, 2019.

———. *Postcards from the Río Bravo Border: Picturing the Place, Placing the Picture, 1900s–1950s.* Austin: University of Texas Press, 2013.

———. *Postcards from the Sonora Border: Visualizing Place Through a Popular Lens, 1900s–1950s.* Tucson: University of Arizona Press, 2017.

Arreola, Daniel D., and James R. Curtis. *The Mexican Border Cities: Landscape Anatomy and Place Personality.* Tucson: University of Arizona Press, 1993.

Arrizón, Arturo. *Tijuana, 130 años de imágenes (1889–2019).* 2 vols. Tijuana: ILCSA, 2019.

Beltrán Cortez, Josué. *Como deben mirarnos: La fotografía como tecnología de la reconstitución discursive del yo; Los tijuanenses y su leyenda blanca.* La Paz: Gobierno del Estado de Baja California Sur, Instituto Sudcaliforniano de Cultura, and Archivo Histórico Pablo L. Martínez, 2015.

Beltran, David J. *The Agua Caliente Story: Remembering Mexico's Legendary Racetrack.* Lexington, KY: Eclipse Press, 2004.

Berumen, Miguel Ángel. *La conquista de agua y del imaginario: Mexicali y Valle Imperial, 1901–1916.* Ciudad Juárez: Imagen y Palabra, 2013.

Blanco Fenochio, Anthinea, and Reed Dillingham. *La plaza mexicana: Escenario de la vida pública y espacio simbólico de la ciudad.* Mexico City: Universidad Nacional Autónoma de México, 2002.

Bogdan, Robert, and Todd Weseloh. *Real Photo Postcard Guide: The People's Photography.* Syracuse, NY: Syracuse University Press, 2006.

Burian, Edward R. *The Architecture and Cities of Northern Mexico from Independence to the Present.* Austin: University of Texas Press, 2015.

Castillo Udiarte, Roberto, Alfonso García Cortez, and Ricardo Morales Lira, eds. *La revolución también es una calle: Vida cotidiana y prácticas culturales en Tijuana.* Tijuana: XV Ayuntamiento de Tijuana and Universidad Iberoamericana Noroeste, 1996.

Clay, Grady. *Close-Up: How to Read the American City.* Chicago: University of Chicago Press, 1973.

Contreras García, Juana Irene. *Al rescate de los sitios históricos de la vieja Tijuana.* Tijuana: FORTISA, 1991.

Delpar, Helen. *The Enormous Vogue of Things Mexican: Cultural Relations Between the United States and Mexico, 1920–1935.* Tuscaloosa: University of Alabama Press, 1992.

Demaris, Ovid. *Poso del mundo: Inside the Mexican-American Border, from Tijuana to Matamoros.* Boston: Little, Brown, 1970.

Dueñas M, Francisco. *Territorio norte de la Baja California (Temas históricos) 1932–1953.* Mexicali: Instituto de Investigaciones Históricas de Baja California, 1991.

Escobedo, Helen, and Paolo Gori, eds. *Mexican Monuments: Strange Encounters.* New York: Abbeville Press, 1989.

Estrada Barrera, Enrique. *El Río: Cronologia de Mexicali.* Mexicali: published by the author, 1978.

———. *Pioneros de Mexicali.* Mexicali: published by the author, 1973.

Félix Berumen, Humberto. *Tijuana la horrible: Entre la historia y el mito.* Tijuana: El Colegio de la Frontera Norte, 2003.

Flandrau, Charles Macomb. *Viva Mexico!* Urbana: University of Illinois Press, 1964. First published 1908 by D. Appleton (New York).

Freedman, Paul. *Ten Restaurants That Changed America.* New York and London: Liveright, 2016.

Ganster, Paul, ed. *Tijuana 1964: Una visión fotográfica e histórica / A Photographic and Historic View.* San Diego, CA: San Diego State University Press, Institute for Regional Studies of the Californias, 2000.

Ganster, Paul, and David E. Lorey. *The U.S.-Mexican Border Today: Conflict and Cooperation in Historical Perspective.* 3rd ed. Lanham, MD: Roman and Littlefield, 2016.

García, José Ramón. *Rousing Tales from the Line City.* [Nogales, AZ]: Privately published, 2016.

Gastélum Gamez, Antonio. *Mi viejo Mexicali remembranzas.* Mexicali: Miguel Angel López, 1991.

Gómez Estrada, José Alfredo. *Gobierno y casinos: El origen de la riqueza de Abelardo L. Rodríguez.* Mexicali: Universidad Autónoma de Baja California and Instituto Mora, 2002.

González Cruz, Edith. *Motivaciones y actors de la revolución mexicana en Baja California Sur.* Baja California Sur: Gobierno del Estado de Baja California Sur, 2011.

Güicho Gutiérrez, Felipe. *Y nació Pueblo Nuevo.* Mexicali: Instituto Nacional para la Educación de los Adultos, XVI Ayuntamiento de Mexicali, Instituto de Cultura de Baja California, 1999.

Gutiérrez Ruvalcaba, Ignacio. *Una mirada estadunidense sobre México: William Henry Jackson empresa fotográfica.* Mexico City: Testimonios del Archivo, 2012.

Henderson, Tracey. *Imperial Valley.* San Diego, CA: Neyenesch, 1968.

Hendricks, William Oral. *Guillermo Andrade y el desarrollo del delta mexicano del Río Colorado, 1874–1905.* Mexicali: Universidad Autónoma de Baja California, 1996.

Herrera Carrillo, Pablo. *Reconquista y colonización del Valle de Mexicali: Y otros escritos paraleros.* Mexicali: XVII Ayuntamiento de Mexicali, Instituto de Cultural de Baja California, Universidad Autónoma de Baja California, 2002.

Herzog, Lawrence A. *From Aztec to High Tech: Architecture and Landscape Across the Mexico-United States Border.* Baltimore: Johns Hopkins University Press, 1999.

———. *Where North Meets South: Cities, Space, and Politics on the U. S.-Mexico Border.* Austin: University of Texas Press, 1990.

House, John W. *Frontier on the Rio Grande: A Political Geography of Development and Social Deprivation.* Oxford Research Studies in Geography. Oxford: Clarendon Press, 1982.

Irigoyen, Ulisis. *Carretera peninsular de la Baja California.* 2 vols. México: Editorial América, 1943.

Jakle, John A. *Postcards of the Night: Views of American Cities.* Santa Fe: Museum of New Mexico Press, 2003.

———. *The Visual Elements of Landscape.* Amherst, MA: University of Massachusetts Press, 1987.

Jakle, John A., and Keith A. Sculle. *Picturing Illinois: Twentieth-Century Postcard Art from Chicago to Cairo.* Urbana: University of Illinois Press, 2012.

Jordan, Fernando. *El otro Mexico: Biografía de Baja California.* México, D. F.: Biografías Gandesa, 1951.

Kerig, Dorothy Pierson. *El Valle de Mexicali y la Colorado River Land Company 1902–1946.* Mexicali: Universidad Autónoma de Baja California, XVI Ayuntamiento de Mexicali, 2001.

Kirchner, John A. *Baja California Railways.* San Marino, CA: Golden West Books, 1988.

Kniffen, Fred B. *The Natural Landscape of the Colorado Delta.* University of California Publications in Geography 5. Berkeley: University of California Press, 1932.

Kostoff, Spiro. *The City Shaped: Urban Patterns and Meanings Through History.* Boston: Bulfinch Press, 1991.

Lowenthal, David. *The Past Is a Foreign Country.* Cambridge: Cambridge University Press, 1985.

Lynch, Kevin. *The Image of the City.* Cambridge, MA and London: The M.I.T. Press, 1960.

Mariani, John F. *The Dictionary of American Food and Drink.* New Haven and New York: Tichnor and Fields, 1983.

Marinacci, Barbara and Rudy Marinacci. *California's Spanish Place Names: What They Mean and the History They Reveal.* Santa Monica, CA: Angel City Press, 2005.

Martínez, Oscar J. *Troublesome Border.* Revised edition. Tucson: University of Arizona Press, 2006. First published 1988.

Martínez Zepeda, Jorge, and Lourdes Romero Navarrete. *Mexicali: Una historia.* 2 vols. Mexicali: Instituto de Investigaciones Históricas, Universidad Autónoma de Baja California, 1991.

Massé Zendejas, Patricia. *Simulacro y elegancia en tarjetas de visita: Fotografías de Cruces y Campa.* Mexico City: Instituto Nacional de Antropología e Historia, Colección Alquimia, 1998.

McCrossen, Alexis, ed. *Land of Necessity: Consumer Culture in the United States–Mexico Borderlands.* Durham, NC: Duke University Press, 2009.

Meade, Adalberto Walther. *El Distrito norte de Baja California.* Mexicali: Universidad Autónoma de Baja California, 1986.

———. *Origen de Mexicali*. Mexicali: Universidad Autónoma de Baja California, 1991.

———. *Tecate: Cuarto municipio*. Mexicali: Universidad Autónoma de Baja California, 1985.

Meikle, Jeffrey L. *Postcard America: Curt Teich and the Imaging of a Nation, 1931–1950*. Austin: University of Texas Press, 2015.

Meinig, D. W., ed. *The Interpretation of Ordinary Landscapes: Geographical Essays*. New York: Oxford University Press, 1979.

———. *A Life of Learning: Charles Homer Haskins Lecture for 1992*. ACLS Occasional Paper 19. New York: American Council of Learned Societies, 1992.

———. *The Shaping of America*. Vol. 3, *Transcontinental America, 1850–1915*. New Haven, CT: Yale University Press, 1998.

———. *Southwest: Three Peoples in Geographical Change, 1600–1970*. New York: Oxford University Press, 1971.

Méndez Sáinz, Eloy. *Arquitectura nacionalista: El proyecto de la revolución mexicana en el noreste (1915–1962)*. Mexico City: Plaza y Valdés, 2004.

Metz, Leon C. *Border: The U.S.–Mexico Line*. El Paso, TX: Mangan Books, 1989.

Miller, Tom, edited. *Writing on the Edge: A Borderlands Reader*. Tucson: University of Arizona Press, 2003.

Morris, John Miller. *Taming the Land: The Lost Postcard Photographs of the Texas High Plains*. College Station: Texas A&M University Press, 2009.

Newcomb, Rexford. *Spanish-Colonial Architecture in the United States*. New York: J. J. Augustin, 1937.

Padilla Corona, Antonio. *Agua Caliente: Oasis en el tiempo; Entrevista a Wayne D. McAllister diseñador del centro turístco de Agua Caliente*. Tijuana: Instituto Municipal de Arte y Cultura, 2006.

———. *El Callejón Z: Huella del pasado, patrimonio urbano de presente*. Tijuana: CONACULTA, UABC, ICBC, XIX Ayuntamiento de Tijuana, Consejo Ciudadano Municipal de Tijuana, 2010.

———. *Inicios urbanos del norte de Baja California: Influencias e ideas, 1821–1906*. Mexicali: Universidad Autónoma de Baja California, 1998.

Phillips, Tom. *The Postcard Century: 2000 Cards and Their Messages*. New York: Thames and Hudson, 2000.

Piñera, David, and Gabriel Rivera. *Tijuana in History: Just Crossing the Border*. Tijuana: Centro Cultural Tijuana, 2013.

Piñera Ramirez, David, and Jesús Ortiz Figueroa. *Historia de Tijuana, 1889–1989*. 2 vols. Tijuana: Universidad Autónoma de Baja California, 1989.

Potts, Rolf. *Souvenir*. New York: Bloomsbury Academic, 2018.

Price, John A. *Tijuana: Urbanization in a Border Culture*. Notre Dame: University of Notre Dame Press, 1973.

Proffitt, T. D., III. *Tijuana: The History of a Mexican Metropolis.* San Diego, CA: San Diego State University Press, 1994.

Rebert, Paula. *La Gran Línea: Mapping the United States-Mexico Boundary, 1849–1857.* Austin: University of Texas Press, 2001.

Roberts, Bob. *Wish You Were Here: Mike Roberts, the Life and Times of America's Postcard King.* Menlo Park, CA: Ancash Press, 2015.

Robles Cairo, Cuauhtémoc. *La architectura de Mexicali (Orígenes).* Mexicali: Universidad Autónoma de Baja California, 2006.

Rockwood, Charles R. *Born of the Desert.* Calexico: Calexico Chronicle, 1930. First published 1913.

Rogelio Álvarez, José. *Dicctionario enciclopédico de Baja California.* Mexico City: Compañía Editora de Enciclopedias de México, 1989.

Rojas, Manuel, and Enrique Courtade. *Paso de los Algodones.* Mexicali: Instituto de Cultura de Baja California, 2010.

Romero, Robert Chao. *The Chinese in Mexico, 1882–1940.* Tucson: University of Arizona Press, 2010.

Ross, Stanley R., ed. *Views Across the Border: The United States and Mexico.* Albuquerque: University of New Mexico Press and Weatherhead Foundation, 1978.

Ruiz Muñoz, Lorenia. *Uno pequeño Montecarlo en el desierto Mexicali 1901–1913.* La Paz: Instituto Sudcaliforniano de Cultural, Archivo Histórico Pablo L. Martínez, 2017.

Ruiz Zafón, Carlos. *The Labyrinth of the Spirits.* Translated by Lucia Graves. New York: Harper Perennial, 2019.

Samaniego, Marco Antonio. *El gremio de choferes y la línea internacional, 1920–1933.* Tijuana: Entrelíneas, 1991.

Samponaro, Frank N., and Paul J. Vanderwood. *War Scare on the Rio Grande: Robert Runyon's Photographs of the Border Conflict, 1913–1916.* Austin: Texas State Historical Association. 1992.

Santiago Guerrero, L. Bibiana. *La gente al pie de Cuchumá: Memoria histórica de Tecate.* Mexicali: Instituto Históricas, Universidad Autónoma de Baja California, and Fundación La Puerta, 2005.

Stewart, George R. *Names on the Land: A Historical Account of Place-Naming in the United States.* New York: Random House, 1945.

Thomas, Edward C. *The Wanderer in Tijuana.* Coppell, TX: Press of Ill Repute and Viva Mexico!, 2020. First published 1922 by Wanderer (Los Angeles).

Trujillo Muñoz, Gabriel. *Mexicali centenario: Una historia comunitaria, 1902–2003.* Mexicali: Universidad Autónoma de Baja California, 2002.

Valdéz, Daniel. *Monumentos y gajos para la historia de Mexicali.* [Mexicali]: privately published by the author, 1978.

Vale, Thomas R., and Geraldine R. Vale. *U.S. 40 Today: Thirty Years of Landscape Change in America*. Madison: University of Wisconsin Press, 1983.

Vanderwood, Paul J. *Satan's Playground: Mobsters and Movie Stars at America's Greatest Gaming Resort*. Durham, NC: Duke University Press, 2010.

Vanderwood, Paul J., and Frank N. Samponaro. *Border Fury: A Picture Postcard Record of Mexico's Revolution and U.S. War Preparedness, 1910–1917*. Albuquerque: University of New Mexico Press, 1988.

Velázquez Morales, Catalina. *Los inmigrantes chinos en Baja California, 1920–1937*. Mexicali: Universidad Autónoma de Baja California and XVIII Ayuntamiento de Mexicali, 2007.

Verdugo Fimbres, María Isabel. *Crónicas sobre Mexicali*. Mexicali: Instituto de Cultura de Baja California and Secretaría de Cultura, 2017.

Ward, Evan R. *Border Oasis: Water and the Political Ecology of the Colorado River Delta, 1940–1975*. Tucson: University of Arizona Press, 2003.

Weeks, John R., and Roberto Ham-Chande. *Demographic Dynamics of the U. S.-Mexico Border*. El Paso: Texas Western Press, 1992.

Welles, Orson. *Touch of Evil*. Edited by Terry Comito. New Brunswick, NJ: Rutgers University Press, 1995.

Werther, Mark, and Lorenzo Mott. *Linen Postcards: Images of the American Dream*. Wayne, PA: Sentinel, 2002.

Wiseman, Alan, and Jay Dusard. *La Frontera: The United States Border with Mexico*. San Diego, CA: Harcourt Brace Jovanovich, 1986.

Wood, Andrew G., ed. *The Borderlands: An Encyclopedia of Culture and Politics on the U.S.-Mexico Divide*. Westport, CT: Greenwood Press, 2008.

Wyckoff, William. *Riding Shotgun with Norman Wallace: Rephotographing the Arizona Landscape*. Albuquerque: University of New Mexico Press, 2020.

Wylie, John. *Landscape*. London: Routledge, 2007.

Zúñiga Méndez, Christian Moisés. *Zona centro de Tijuana: Paisaje e imaginario urbano*. Mexicali: Universidad Autónoma de Baja California, 2016.

DISSERTATIONS AND THESES

Benitez, Juan Manuel. "A Social History of the Mexico-United States Border: How Tourism, Demographic Shifts and Economic Integration Shaped the Image and Identity of Tijuana, Baja California, since World War II." PhD diss., University of California, Los Angeles, 2005.

Burkhart, Nick. "Visualizing Commercial Landscape Change on Tijuana's Avenida Revolución." Bachelor's thesis, Barrett Honors College, Arizona State University, 2010.

Chang, Jason Oliver. "Outsider Crossings: History, Culture, and Geography of Mexicali's Chinese Community." PhD diss., University of California, Berkeley, 2010.

Guadiana Lozano, Pablo Filemón. "El uso de la tarjeta postal: Actividades turísticas y sociales en Tijuana de 1901 a 1935." Master's thesis, Universidad Autónoma de Baja California, 2014.

Schantz, Eric Michael. "From the *Mexicali Rose* to the Tijuana Brass: Vice Tours of the United States-Mexico Border, 1910–1965." PhD diss., University of California, Los Angeles, 2001.

Speth, Terry M. "Tecate, Baja California: Evolution of Townscape of a Mexican Border Community." Master's thesis, California State College, Los Angeles, 1969.

Uribe Eguiluz, Mayra N. "Una aproximación a la compañía México fotográfico y la promoción del turismo finales de los años veinte." Master's thesis, Universidad Nacional Autónoma de México, Mexico City, 2011.

ARTICLES, BOOK CHAPTERS, NEWS STORIES, TYPESCRIPTS

Acevedo Cárdenas, Conrado, David Piñera, and Jesús Ortiz. "Semblanza de Tijuana 1915–30." In *Historia de Tijuana, 1889–1989*, edited by David Piñera Ramirez and Jesús Ortiz Figueroa, 1:93–105. Tijuana: Universidad Autónoma de Baja California, 1989.

Aikman, Duncan. "Hell Along the Border." *American Mercury* 5 (May 1925): 17–23.

Alvarez, Robert. "*Los Re-Mexicanizados: Mexicanidad*, Changing Identity and Long-Term Affiliation on the U. S-Mexico Border." *Journal of the West* 40, no. 2 (Spring 2001): 15–23.

Arellano Vázquez, Lucila. "Historia de la gráfica editorial en Mexicali a través de las tarjetas postales durante los primeros 27 años de su fundación." *H+D Hábitat Más Diseño* 2, no. 4 (2010): 76–86.

Arreola, Daniel D. "La cerca y las garitas de Ambos Nogales: A Postcard Landscape Exploration." *Journal of the Southwest* 43, no. 4 (Winter 2001): 505–41.

Arreola, Daniel D., and Nick Burkhart, "Photographic Postcards and Visual Urban Landscape." *Urban Geography* 31, no. 7 (2010): 885–904.

Bakersfield Californian. "Methodists Want Tijuana Barred." September 24, 1920.

Berkeley Daily Gazette. "Tijuana: Built by the Eighteenth Amendment." October 30, 1925.

Bernal Rodríguez, Francisco A. "Mexicali: 100 años de agua y vida." In *Mexicali, 100 años: Arquitectura y urbanismo en el desierto del Colorado*, edited by Héctor Manuel Lucero Velasco, 17–32. Mexico City: Grupo Patria Cultural, 2002.

Caddick, Jim. "Mike Roberts—Photographer Turned Publisher." *San Francisco Bay Area Post Card Club* 25, no. 3 (March 2010): 6–9.

Calexico Chronicle. "A. B. W. Club in Mexicali Has Been Closed." August 31, 1931.

——. "Algodones Has Its Third Serious Fire." December 6, 1932.

——. "Algodones Is Scene of Fire." April 27, 1932.

——. "Algodones to Open New Arena." October 12, 1929.

——. "All-Colored Revue at Owl Declared Great Attraction." February 22, 1934.

——. "Contract to Be Let This Week for Re-Building Owl Resort in Mexicali." June 11, 1923.

——. "Damage in Fire Mounts to Near 20 Million Pesos." September 27, 1945.

——. "Famous Gambling Hall and Bar Complete Loss: Fire Due to Incendiarism, Charge." June 28, 1922.

——. "Fire Sweeps Two Cantinas in Algodones." January 30, 1932.

——. "Flames Wipe Out Block in Tijuana." September 22, 1925.

——. "Local Men to Rebuild in Tijuana." September 23, 1925.

——. "Meeting of Governors of Two Californias Is Held on Line at Noon." June 11, 1918.

——. "Mexicali Has Big Fire Loss in Chinatown." June 29, 1931.

——. "Mexicali Is Mecca for Tourist Crop." May 21, 1931.

——. "Mexicali Move Made Tonight." May 31, 1916.

——. "Mexicali Rose Composer Honored History of Composition Told." May 2, 1968.

——. "Midnight Crowd in Mexicali Panic-Stricken as Buildings Are Tossed by First Temblor." January 3, 1927.

——. "New Road to be Scenic Route: Promises to be Tourist Mecca; Tecate Highway Work Rushed." April 28, 1916.

——. "News of City and Valley." September 12, 1922.

——. "Orders Issued Today to Close Red Light Houses Throughout Northern District." March 27, 1925.

——. "Rafael Castillo Photographer." July 20, 1931.

——. "Rumor That A. B. W. Club May Close." February 7, 1931.

——. "To Clean Front Street of Mexicali: Order Enclosure in New Plan." April 16, 1916.

——. "$2,000,000 Fire Sweeps Mexicali." May 23, 1923.

——. "Yuma Will Have Young Mexicali, Algodones Threatens Much in Way of Diversion, Yuma Is Half Way Delighted." January 28, 1915.

Calvillo Velasco, Max. "Indicios para descifrar la trayectoria política de Esteban Cantú." *Historia Mexicana* 59, no. 3 (January–March 2010): 981–1040.

Castilla, María Eugenia. "El ferrocarril San Diego–Arizona y el ferrocarril Tijuana-Tecate: Un corredor herencia cultural binacional." *Frontera Norte* 16, no. 32 (July–December 2004): 118–23.

Chamberlain, Eugene Keith. "Mexican Colonization Versus American Interests in Lower California." *Pacific Historical Review* 20 (1951): 43–55.

Cole, Teju. "The Places We Go Aren't Passive: They Act on Us, Inviting Us to Photograph Them in Certain Ways." *New York Times Magazine* (July 1, 2018): 14–17.

Corona Daily Independent. "Through Trains Mexico City to L. A. Inaugurated." April 9, 1948.

——. "Tijuana Peddlers Must 'Spruce Up.'" June 19, 1931.

Coronado Eagle and Journal. "Gateway to Friendship." February 13, 1941.

Cruz Piñero, Rodolfo, and Elmyra Ybáñez Zepeda. "Demographic Dynamics of Tecate." In *Tecate, Baja California: Realities and Challenges in a Mexican Border Community*, edited by Paul Ganster, Felipe Cuamea Velázquez, and José Luis Castro Ruiz, 16–23. San Diego, CA: San Diego State University Press, 2002.

Curtis, James R. "Mexicali's Chinatown." *Geographical Review* 85, no. 3 (July 1995): 335–48.

Curtis, James R., and Daniel D. Arreola. "Zonas de Tolerancia on the Northern Mexican Border." *Geographical Review* 81, no. 3 (July 1991): 333–46.

Dear, Michael. "Bajalta California: The Border That Divides Brings Us Together." *Boom: A Journal of California* 4, no. 1 (Spring 2014): 86–97.

DeBres, Karen, and Jacob Sowers. "The Emergence of Standardized, Idealized, and Placeless Landscapes in Midwestern Main Street Postcards." *Professional Geographer* 61 (2009): 216–30.

Ellison, O. C. "In the Sea of Pearls: The Gulf of California and Its Buried Treasures—An Unknown Land of Promise." *Sunset* (December 1905): 165–75.

Giffords, Gloria Fraser. "Mexican Postcards: Diverse Echoes." *Artes de México* 48 (1999): 66–68.

Girven, Tim. "Hollywood's Heterotopia: US Cinema, the Mexican Border and the Making of Tijuana." *Travesia* 3 (1/2): 93–133.

Gómez Cavazos, Enrique Esteban. "La ruta de *company towns* en la península de Baja California: Trazados urbanos y patrimonio industrial, siglos xix y xx." *Boletín de monumentos históricos* 41 (September–December 2017): 112–50.

González González, Ana Margarita, and Cuauhtémoc Robles Cairo. "20 elementos." In *Mexicali, 100 años: Arquitectura y urbanism en el desierto del Colorado*, edited by Héctor Manuel Lucero Velasco, 98–119. Mexico City: Grupo Patria Cultural, 2002.

Grandoschek, William J. "Seeing Mexico." *Bakersfield Californian*, November 15, 1938.

Grant, U. S., IV. "A Sojourn in Baja California, 1915." *Southern California Quarterly* 45, no. 2 (June 1963): 123–68.

Griswold del Castillo, Richard. "The Discredited Revolution: The Magonista Capture of Tijuana in 1911." *Journal of San Diego History* 26, no. 4 (Fall 1980): 1–8.

Guadiana Lozano, Pablo. "Colección André Williams, tarjetas postales desde la frontera de Tijuana." 6° Congreso Mexicano de Tarjetas Postales, Tijuana, México, 2013.

———. "Fotógrafos extranjeros en Tijuana (1874–1942)." In *Tijuana Senderos en el Tiempo*, edited by Mario Ortiz Villacorte Lacave and Fco. Manuel Acuña Borbolla, 30–38. Tijuana: XVIII Ayuntamiento de Tijuana, 2006.

Hamilton-Smith, Katherine. "The Curt Teich Postcard Archives: Dedicated to the Postcard as a Document Type." *Popular Culture in Libraries* 3, no. 2 (1996): 5–16.

Hendricks, William O. "Developing San Diego Desert Empire." *Journal of San Diego History* 17, no. 3 (1971): 1–11.

Herrera Moreno, Alfonso. "Antecedentes urbanos de Mexicali." *El río: Revista de historia regional de Mexicali y su valle* 9, no. 32 (April–June 2016): 59–62.

Hu-DeHart, Evelyn. "Los chinos del norte de México, 1875–1930: La formación de una pequeña burguesía regional." In *China en las Californias: Colección divulgación*, 11–44. Tijuana: Consejo Nacional para la Cultural y las Artes, Centro Cultural Tijuana, 2002.

Hughes, Charles W. "'La Mojonera' and the Making of California's U. S.-Mexico Boundary Line." *Journal of San Diego History* 53, no. 3 (2007): 126–47.

Hurt, Douglas, and Adam Payne, "Postcard Imagery and Geographical Imagination Along the Lincoln Highway." *Material Culture* 51 (2019): 1–20.

Imperial Valley Press. "Algodones Custom House." April 16, 1910.

——. "Algodones Raided by Insurrectos." February 25, 1911.

——. "Governor at Border Sees Head Lower California." June 11, 1918.

——. "New River's Work." July 7, 1906.

Jakle, John A. "The Camera and Geographical Inquiry." In *Geography and Technology*, edited by Stanley D. Brunn, Susan L. Cutter, and James W. Harrington, 221–42. Boston: Kluwer Academic, 2004.

Jerome, Helen. "Mexico, the Pit! Hell-Dives on Border." *Oakland Tribune*, May 30, 1920.

Kenamore, Clair. "The Principality of Cantu." *Bookman* 46 (September 1917–February 1918): 23–28.

Los Angeles Herald. "Monte Carlo in Mexico Across Arizona Line." February 5, 1915.

Lucero Velasco, Héctor Manuel. "Los paisajes del viejo Mexicali." In *Mexicali, 100 años: Arquitectura y urbanism en el desierto del Colorado*, edited Héctor Manuel Lucero Velasco, 56–97. Mexico City: Grupo Patria Cultural, 2002.

Lugo, Alejandro F., Jr. "El casino de Agua Caliente." In *Historia de Tijuana, 1889–1989*, edited by David Piñera Ramirez and Jesús Ortiz Figueroa, 1:114–17. Tijuana: Universidad Autónoma de Baja California, 1989.

Méndez Sáinz, Eloy. "De Tijuana a Matamoros: Imágenes y forma urbana." *Revista de El Colegio de Sonora* 4, no. 6 (1993): 45–61.

Nishikawa Aceves, Kiyoko. "De la internacionalción de Tijuana." In *La revolución también es una calle: Vida cotidiana y prácticas culturales en Tijuana*, edited by Roberto Castillo Udiarte, Alfonso García Cortez, and Ricardo Morales Lira, 85–90. Tijuana: XV Ayuntamiento de Tijuana y Universidad Iberoamericana Noreste-Tijuana, 1996.

Noriega Verdugo, Sergio. "Desarrollo industrial 1915–2000." In *Monografía de Mexicali y su valle 1903–2003*, edited by Jaime Rafael Díaz Ochoa, Margarita Mercado Medina, and Óscar Sánchez Ramírez, 115–50. Mexicali: XVII Ayuntamiento de Mexicali, Dirección Municipal de Cultural, Sociedad Mexicana de Geografía y Estadística, 2004.

Nossiter, Adam. "Atget's Paris, 100 Years Later." *New York Times.* May 27, 2020.

Oakland Tribune. "Tijuana Passports No Longer Issued at Mexico Border." October 10, 1920.

Oberle, Alex P., and Daniel D. Arreola. "Mexican Medical Border Towns: A Case Study of Algodones, Baja California." *Journal of Borderland Studies* 19, no. 2 (Fall 2004): 27–44.

Owens, Bob. "The Mexican Revolution and the Role Played by Tijuana." *San Diego Reader*, February 25, 1988.

Oxnard Press-Courier. "Tijuana Is Wide Open Town." February 27, 1945.

Padilla Corona, Antonio. "Mapa del pueblo Zaragoza del rancho de Tijuana: Utopia o realidad?" *Meyibó* 3, no. 7/8 (1988): 23–37.

——. "The Rancho Tía Juana (Tijuana) Grant." *Journal of San Diego History* 50, no. 1 (March 2004): 30–41.

Padilla Corona, Antonio, and David Piñera Ramírez. "El surgimiento de Mexicali." In *Mexicali: Una historia*, edited by Jorge Martínez Zepeda and Lourdes Romero Navarrete, 1:149–99. Mexicali: Instituto de Investigaciones Históricas, Universidad Autónoma de Baja California, 1991.

Palm Springs Desert Sun. "Owl Club Gambling Closes Up at Mexicali." January 4, 1935.

Pérez y Ramírez, Pedro F. "Panorama de Mexicali 1915–1930." In *Panorama histórico de Baja California*, edited by David Piñera Ramírez, 396–418. Tijuana: Centro de Investigaciones Históricas UNAM-UABC, 1983.

Piñera Ramírez, David, Pedro Espinosa Meléndez, and Pahola Sánchez Vega. "Las vicisitudes de la catedral de Tijuana: Sus orígenes como pequeño templo de madera." *Letras históricas* (2019): 1–39.

Price, John A. "Tecate: An Industrial City on the Mexican Border." *Urban Anthropology* 2, no. 1 (Spring 1973): 35–47.

Rafla González, Arturo, Guillermo Alvarez de la Torre, and Guadalupe Ortega Villa, "Expansion fisica y desarrollo urbano de Tijuana, 1900–1984." In *Historia de Tijuana, 1889–1989*, edited by David Piñera Ramirez and Jesús Ortiz Figueroa, 2:327–34. Tijuana: Universidad Autónoma de Baja California, 1989.

Ramírez López, Jorge. "Semblanza de Tecate." In *Panorama histórico de Baja California*, edited by David Piñera Ramírez, 477–81. Tijuana: Centro de Investigaciones Históricas UNAM-UABC, 1983.

———. "Tecate." In *Panorama histórico de Baja California*, edited by David Piñera Ramírez, 315–21. Tijuana: Centro de Investigaciones Históricas UNAM-UABC, 1983.

"R. ayuntamiento de la municipalidad de Mexicali B. C." *Periodico oficial organo del gobierno del Distrito Norte de la Baja California*, May 10, 1918, 3.

Reyes Moreno, Carlos Manuel. "Mexicali al inicio de la revolución mexicana." *El río: Revista de la Sociedad de Historia "Centenario de Mexicali"* 3, no. 8 (April–June 2010): 2–4.

Ridgley, Roberta. "Tijuana 1920: Prohibition Pops the Cork; The Man Who Built Tijuana, Part IV." *San Diego and Point Magazine*, May 1967, 78–81, 114–18.

Roberts, Bob. "Bob Roberts on Mike Roberts, His Pop." *San Francisco Bay Area Post Card Club* 11 (November-December 2015): 10.

Rodriguez, Richard. "Across the Borders of History: Tijuana and San Diego Exchange Futures." *Harper's Magazine* (March 1987): 42–53.

Rowe, Peter. "Tecate, the Border's Great Exception." *San Diego Union-Tribune*, June 24, 2016.

Rubin, Barbara. "Aesthetic Ideology and Urban Design." *Annals of the Association of American Geographers* 69 (1979): 339–61.

Ruiz Muñoz, Lorenia. "Un pueblo sin orden y sin ley Mexicali 1901–1908." *El río: Revista de historia regional de Mexicali y su valle* 9, no. 32 (April–June 2016): 4–10.

San Diego Union and Daily Bee. "Picturesque Tijuana Lures Sightseers." January 20, 1920.

Santana Sandoval, María. "Testimonios de antiguos residentes de Tecate." In *Panorama histórico de Baja California*, edited by David Piñera Ramírez, 482–83. Tijuana: Centro de Investigaciones Históricas UNAM-UABC, 1983.

Santa Ana Daily Register. "Drinkers' Oasis on Border Doomed." August 20, 1920.

——. "Mexicali Plans to Make Its Own Beer." September 27, 1922.

——. "New System of Starting Horse Races Invented." November 16, 1927.

——. "Sleepy Tijuana Awakens, Finds Streets Thronged." May 8, 1937.

Santiago Guerrero, Leticia Bibiana. "Profile of the Origins of Tecate's Population." In *Tecate, Baja California: Realities and Challenges in a Mexican Border Community*, edited by Paul Ganster, Felipe Cuamea Velázquez, and José Luis Castro Ruiz, 3–15. San Diego, CA: San Diego State University Press, 2002.

Schantz, Eric M. "Behind the Noir Border: Tourism, the Vice Racket, and Power Relations in Baja California's Border Zone, 1938–65." In *Holiday in Mexico: Critical Reflections on Tourism and Tourist Encounters*, edited by Dina Berger and Andrew G. Woods, 130–60. Durham, NC: Duke University Press, 2010.

Schantz, Eric Michael. "All Night at the Owl: The Social and Political Relations of Mexicali's Red Light District, 1909–1925." In *On the Border: Society and Culture Between the United States and Mexico*, edited by Andrew Grant Wood, 91–143. Lanham, MD: SR Books, 2004.

Shortell, Alfonso J. "Thirsty Hordes from States Cross Line to Revel in Cantu Land." *Bakersfield Californian*, March 29, 1920.

Simpich, Frederick. "Along Our Side of the Mexican Border." *National Geographic Magazine* 38, no. 1 (July 1920): 61–80.

——. "Baja California Wakes Up." *National Geographic Magazine* 82, no. 2 (August 1942): 253–75.

St. John, Rachel. "Selling the Border: Trading Land, Attracting Tourists, and Marketing American Consumption on the Baja California Border, 1900–1934." In *Land of Necessity: Consumer Culture in the United States–Mexico Borderlands*, edited by Alexis McCrossen, 113–42. Durham, NC: Duke University Press, 2009.

Taylor, Lawrence D. "The Wild Frontier Moves South: U.S. Entrepreneurs and the Growth of Tijuana's Vice Industry, 1908–1935." *Journal of San Diego History* 48, no. 3 (September 2002): 204–29.

Taylor Hansen, Lawrence Douglas. "El ferrocarril urbano entre San Diego y Tijuana, 1916–1918." *Journal of Transborder Studies-Research and Practice* (Summer 2014): 1–20.

Torres Covarrubias, Karla. "Reflexiones desde el mostrador las 'Curios Shop' y la calle Revolución." In *La revolución también es una calle: Vida cotidiana y prácticas culturales en Tijuana*, edited by Roberto Castillo Udiarte, Alfonso García Cortez, and Ricardo Morales Lira, 77–82. Tijuana: XV Ayuntamiento de Tijuana y Universidad Iberoamericana Noreste-Tijuana, 1996.

Turok, Marta. "Mark Turok y la postal de los 50." *Artes de México* 48 (1999): 30–31.

Uribe Eguiluz, Mayra N. "La compañía México fotográfico en la política de turismo nacional de los años veinte." *Alquimia* 42 (May–August 2011): 21–29.

Vanderwood, Paul J. "Writing History with Picture Postcards: Revolution in Tijuana." *Journal of San Diego History* 34, no. 1 (March 1988): 38–63.

Van Nuys News. "Louis S. Granger Takes Interesting Mexico Trip." December 25, 1925.

Warren, Scott, Yu Wan, and Donna Ruiz y Costello. "La Chinesca: The Chinese Landscape of the Mexico-U. S. Borderlands." *Yearbook of the Association of Pacific Coast Geographers* 77 (2015): 62–79.

Webster, Grady L. "Reconnaissance of the Flora and Vegetation of *La Frontera.*" In *Changing Plant Life of La Frontera: Observations on Vegetation in the U.S./Mexico Borderlands,* edited by Grady L. Webster and Conrad J. Bahre, 6–38. Albuquerque: University of New Mexico Press, 2001.

Zumoff, J. A. "Tijuana the American Town: Images of the Corrupt City in Hammett's 'The Golden Horseshoe.'" *Clues* 26, no. 4 (2008): 35–48.

INTERVIEWS, PERSONAL COMMUNICATIONS

Hann, Carol. Personal communication with author, El Centro, California, multiple instances in January-March, 2020.

Manger, William. Personal communication with author, Natchitoches, Louisiana, August 29, 2019.

Williams, André. Interview, Tijuana, Baja California, February 26, 2020.

INDEX

ABOUT THE AUTHOR

Daniel D. Arreola is a cultural and historical geographer who specializes in the study of the Mexican American borderlands. A native Southern Californian, he earned a bachelor's degree and a PhD in geography from the University of California, Los Angeles. He is an emeritus professor in the School of Geographical Sciences and Urban Planning at Arizona State University, where he was a member of the faculty for twenty-six years. His most recent book is *Postcards from the Chihuahua Border: Revisiting a Pictorial Past, 1900s–1950s.* He resides in Placitas, New Mexico.